GLOBAL WARMING AND THE WORLD TRADING SYSTEM

GLOBAL WARMING AND THE WORLD TRADING SYSTEM

GARY CLYDE HUFBAUER
STEVE CHARNOVITZ
JISUN KIM

PETERSON INSTITUTE FOR INTERNATIONAL ECONOMICS
WASHINGTON, DC
MARCH 2009

Gary Clyde Hufbauer has been the Reginald Jones Senior Fellow at the Peterson Institute for International Economics since 1992. He was formerly the Maurice Greenberg Chair and Director of Studies at the Council on Foreign Relations (1996–98), Marcus Wallenberg Professor of International Finance Diplomacy at Georgetown University (1985–92), senior fellow at the Institute (1981–85 and 1992–96), deputy director of the International Law Institute at Georgetown University (1979–81), deputy assistant secretary for international trade and investment policy of the US Treasury (1977–79), and director of the international tax staff at the Treasury (1974–76). His publications include *Maghreb Regional and Global Integration: A Dream to Be Fulfilled* (2008), *Economic Sanctions Reconsidered*, 3d ed. (2007), *US Taxation of Foreign Income* (2007), *China Trade Disputes: Rising Tide, Rising Stakes* (2006), and *NAFTA Revisited: Achievements and Challenges* (2005).

Steve Charnovitz is an associate professor of law at the George Washington University Law School. Before joining the faculty, he practiced law at WilmerHale in Washington. Earlier he was the director of the Global Environment & Trade Study at Yale University and policy director of the (US) Competitiveness Policy Council. He serves on the Board of Editors of the *American Journal of International Law* and on the editorial boards of the *Journal of International Economic Law*, *World Trade Review*, and *Journal of Environment & Development*. He contributed a chapter on labor and environmental issues to *Restarting Fast Track* (1998).

Jisun Kim is a research assistant at the Peterson Institute for International Economics. Her areas of research at the Institute include international trade, international tax, and climate change issues. She holds a US CPA certificate and previously worked as a tax consultant at PricewaterhouseCoopers in Seoul, Korea. She received her MA degree in international relations, focusing on global markets and Asia, from the Maxwell School of Syracuse University. She has coauthored several papers with Gary Clyde Hufbauer and assisted with *US Taxation of Foreign Income* (2007) and *Economic Sanctions Reconsidered*, 3d ed. (2007).

PETER G. PETERSON INSTITUTE FOR INTERNATIONAL ECONOMICS
1750 Massachusetts Avenue, NW
Washington, DC 20036-1903
(202) 328-9000   FAX: (202) 659-3225
www.petersoninstitute.org

C. Fred Bergsten, *Director*
Edward Tureen, *Director of Publications, Marketing, and Web Development*

Typesetting by Susann Luetjen
Printing by Kirby Lithographic Company, Inc
Cover photo: © Michalis Palis—Fotolia.com
Jisun Kim photo by Jeremey Tripp

Printed in the United States of America

11   10   09   5   4   3   2   1

Library of Congress Cataloging-in-Publication Data

Hufbauer, Gary Clyde.
  Global warming and the world trading system / Gary Clyde Hufbauer, Steve Charnovitz, Jisun Kim.
    p. cm.
  Includes bibliographical references and index.
  1. International trade. 2. Global warming. I. Charnovitz, Steve. II. Kim, Jisun. III. Title.
  HF1379.H86 2009
  363.738'747—dc22

                           2009004929

Contents

Preface

The ongoing global negotiations on global warming are likely to produce the greatest changes in international institutional architecture since the end of the Second World War. The new climate change regime is in turn likely to have profound effects on the world trading system and its institutions. Hence the relationship between the prospective rules on greenhouse gases and international trade will be of enormous importance to both the global environment and the world economy. This study analyzes those linkages and proposes a course of action that would maximize the success of the attack on global warming while minimizing the risk to world trade.

Before the financial crisis hit the world economy in 2008, optimism prevailed that US emission controls would soon be enacted. Congressional debate on the design of climate change measures was vigorous as experts and the public alike reconsidered their attitudes toward global warming. The severe global downturn, however, has slowed momentum toward climate action both in the United States and internationally. Domestically, it seems unlikely that the United States will enact its own emissions control legislation before 2010. Internationally, it seems likely that countries will agree on broad principles at the Copenhagen conference, scheduled for December 2009, but hard decisions could be delayed another year or more.

A stumbling block for the United States in enacting mandatory emission targets is the apprehension that heavy costs will lead to "leakage" of production and jobs to foreign firms located in countries that do not equivalently limit carbon emissions, such as China and India. Not surprisingly, the severe economic downturn has intensified fears of losing competitiveness. To address these "leakage" concerns, US legislators have drafted special provisions in their greenhouse gas control bills such as free allocation of allowances, exemptions from the new controls, and border adjustments. Other countries have done the same in binding legislation (the European Union) or draft proposals (e.g., Australia and Canada). Several US bills also contain "leverage" provisions designed to prod China, India, and other large but reluctant emitting nations to take action. Both "leakage" and "leverage" measures could affect US exports and imports, especially two-way trade with countries that do not enforce comparable climate policies. Similar adverse trade impacts could result from national legislation enacted by other countries.

Against this background, the authors evaluate the consistency of climate policy options with core principles of the world trading system as set forth in the decisions of the General Agreement on Tariffs and Trade, the World Trade Organization (WTO), and its Appellate Body. Gary Clyde Hufbauer, Steve Charnovitz, and Jisun Kim argue that both import-restrictive measures and measures that appear to subsidize exports stand a fair chance of being challenged in the WTO. Unilateral import bans, border taxes, and comparability mechanisms could cause a drawn-out period of severe trade friction.

Given the uncertainties of the effectiveness of trade steps, their potential to interrupt trade, and their possible conflict with WTO rules, the authors argue that WTO members should attempt to negotiate a code that defines the "policy space" for climate control measures in ways consistent with core WTO principles. To encourage WTO negotiating efforts toward a Code of Good WTO Practice on Greenhouse Gas Emissions Controls, the authors suggest that the United States and other important emitting countries adopt time-limited "peace clauses" in national climate legislation. These clauses would suspend the application of border measures or other extraterritorial controls for a defined period while WTO negotiations are under way.

The Peter G. Peterson Institute for International Economics is a private, nonprofit institution for the study and discussion of international economic policy. Its purpose is to analyze important issues in that area and to develop and communicate practical new approaches for dealing with them. The Institute is completely nonpartisan.

The Institute is funded by a highly diversified group of philanthropic foundations, private corporations, and interested individuals. About 22 percent of the Institute's resources in our latest fiscal year were provided by contributors outside the United States, including about 9 percent from Japan. The Doris Duke Charitable Foundation provided generous support for this study.

The Institute's Board of Directors bears overall responsibilities for the Institute and gives general guidance and approval to its research program, including the identification of topics that are likely to become important over the medium run (one to three years) and that should be addressed by the Institute. The director, working closely with the staff and outside Advisory Committee, is responsible for the development of particular projects and makes the final decision to publish an individual study.

The Institute hopes that its studies and other activities will contribute to building a stronger foundation for international economic policy around the world. We invite readers of these publications to let us know how they think we can best accomplish this objective.

C. Fred Bergsten
Director
January 2009

Acknowledgments

This book benefited from the comments of many internal and external reviewers. We would particularly like to thank Trevor Houser, John Jackson, Sherman Katz, and Andrew Shoyer for their valuable and extensive suggestions and all the participants of the study group held at the Peterson Institute on October 30, 2008.

We deeply appreciate the efforts of Madona Devasahayam, Susann Luetjen, and Edward Tureen in producing this book in a timely manner. We wish to acknowledge the Doris Duke Charitable Foundation for its generous support, and finally, we thank C. Fred Bergsten for his interest in and advice on this project.

1

Introduction

Scientific opinion has coalesced around the view that human activity, through the emission of greenhouse gases, makes a major contribution to global warming, even though natural forces are also at work.[1] In 2006 a team led by the English economist Sir Nicholas Stern issued a striking report that sized up the economic dimensions of global climate change and called for immediate collective action to reduce greenhouse gas emissions. According to the Stern report, the danger of huge future costs can be reduced by incurring relatively modest costs over the next few decades.[2] In this vein, at the United Nations Climate Change Conference in Bali, Indonesia, in December 2007, representatives of 187 countries agreed on the so-called Bali Roadmap, which promises talks over the next two years

---

1. "Radiative forcing" measures how the energy balance of the earth-atmosphere system is influenced by various factors that affect climate. The Intergovernmental Panel on Climate Change (IPCC) has found that radiative forcing resulting from factors that are affected by human activity has been much larger than the radiative forcing resulting from natural processes. For more details, see IPCC (2007a). The report is also available at www.ipcc.ch (accessed on January 12, 2009).

2. The Stern report argued that the risk of the worst effects of climate change can be substantially reduced if greenhouse gas levels in the atmosphere are stabilized between 450 and 550 parts per million (ppm) CO_2 equivalent (CO_2e). The current level is 430 ppm CO_2e, and the concentration is rising at more than 2 ppm each year. Stabilization in the range advocated by Stern (450 to 550 ppm CO_2e) would require a drop in emissions at least 25 percent below current levels by 2050. Ultimately, annual emissions would need to be brought down by more than 80 percent below current levels. The report estimated annual costs of about 1 percent of global GDP to achieve stabilization between 500 and 550 ppm CO_2e if strong action is taken now. The full Stern (2006) report is available at www.hm-treasury.gov.uk (accessed on January 12, 2009).

to develop a new treaty that would replace the Kyoto Protocol after 2012.[3] At the United Nations Climate Change conference held in Poznan, Poland in December 2008, countries reaffirmed their commitment to the post-Kyoto regime and asserted that the economic downturn should not be an excuse for delaying action on climate change. While countries addressed technical details and presented proposals for elements in a post-Kyoto agreement, the Poznan conference failed to address key issues such as bound targets for emissions reduction by developing countries and technical and financial assistance from developed countries. Moreover, the current financial turmoil raises doubts that countries will reach agreement on a comprehensive new international climate regime in Copenhagen by December 2009.

In the midst of the climate change debate, the United States has been roundly criticized for its reluctance to take action. Although the United States ranked among the largest emitters of greenhouse gases, the US Senate passed the Byrd-Hagel Resolution by a 95–0 vote in 1997, effectively rejecting the Kyoto Protocol.[4] The Bill Clinton administration signed the Kyoto Protocol in 1998, but it never submitted the protocol to the Senate, acknowledging the force of the resolution. The George W. Bush administration rejected the Kyoto Protocol in 2001 and only grudgingly agreed to the Bali Roadmap.[5] However, some state governments (notably Califor-

---

3. The United Nations first called for collective action on climate change when it adopted the Framework Convention on Climate Change (UNFCCC) in 1994. After years of talks, in 1997, the Kyoto Protocol, which requires developed countries to reduce their greenhouse gas emissions below levels specified for each of them in the treaty, was adopted at the third Conference of the Parties to the UNFCCC in Japan. The Kyoto Protocol is scheduled to expire in 2012.

4. The Byrd-Hagel Resolution (S. Res. 98) stated: "Whereas the Senate strongly believes that the proposals under negotiation, because of the disparity of treatment between Annex I Parties and Developing Countries and the level of required emission reductions, could result in serious harm to the United States economy, including significant job loss, trade disadvantages, increased energy and consumer costs, or any combination thereof; and.... That it is the sense of the Senate that (1) the United States should not be a signatory to any protocol to, or other agreement regarding, the United Nations Framework Convention on Climate Change of 1992, at negotiations in Kyoto in December 1997, or thereafter, which would—(A) mandate new commitments to limit or reduce greenhouse gas emissions for the Annex I Parties, unless the protocol or other agreement also mandates new specific scheduled commitments to limit or reduce greenhouse gas emissions for Developing Country Parties within the same compliance period, or (B) would result in serious harm to the economy of the United States...." The full text of the resolution is available at http://thomas.loc.gov.

5. In a statement following the Bali conference, the White House expressed its dissatisfaction: "The United States does have serious concerns about other aspects of the Decision as we begin the negotiations.... Accordingly, for these negotiations to succeed, it is essential that the major developed and developing countries be prepared to negotiate commitments, consistent with their national circumstances, that will make a due contribution to the reduction of global emissions. A post-2012 arrangement will be effective only if it reflects such contributions" (quoted from the statement by White House Press Secretary Dana Perino on December 15,

nia) have enacted their own measures over the past six years, and several bills are now on the congressional agenda. Box 1.1 discusses core elements of current US climate policy.

While scientific and economic uncertainties are often cited in climate change debates, another enormous obstacle to collective action is the chasm between competing conceptual standards for setting greenhouse gas limits.[6] The chasm would exist even if all countries agreed on target levels for global greenhouse gas concentrations—which, of course, they do not. Even if a target for global levels could be agreed upon, however, a debate would still rage: Should national limits be based on "per capita comparability" or "carbon price equivalency"? Per capita comparability rests on the argument that the United States, Europe, and Japan emitted billions of tons of CO_2 on their path to industrialization and that China, India, and Brazil should not now be denied the same route. An approach based on "historic emissions," often advocated by developing countries arguing that targets should reflect cumulative emissions, draws on the same tenets. If per capita comparability or a historic emissions approach is to be the accepted standard, then developed countries would have to enforce tremendous reductions, while developing countries could vastly increase their greenhouse gas emissions (see table 1.1).

The argument for carbon price equivalency rests on the proposition that an additional billion tons of CO_2 does the same damage to the globe whether it comes from New York or New Delhi. If bygones are bygones, and the standard for collective action is to be carbon price equivalency, then a short list of major nations would need to impose very similar limits (see table 1.2, panel b). The explicit or implicit tax on greenhouse gas emissions, per ton of CO_2 equivalent (CO_2e) emissions, would then reach roughly the same high level in all major countries.[7]

Based on the debates surrounding the original Kyoto Protocol and the Bali Roadmap, US climate negotiators have harbored grave doubts that important developing countries (notably China and India) will accept carbon price equivalency as the working standard. In turn, the US Congress is very worried that, by taking the lead and imposing national

---

2007, www.whitehouse.gov [accessed on January 12, 2009]).

6. Climate change skepticism has diminished but not disappeared, as uncertainties still exist in climate change science and economic analysis. Michaels (2006) of the Cato Institute, for example, argues that many studies on climate change are seriously flawed and exaggerate the negative impact of global warming. Appendix A discusses four major uncertainties that are embedded in climate change debates.

7. An unmentioned but powerful undertone in the debate between per capita comparability and carbon price equivalency is the footprint of damage caused by climate change. All countries will be adversely affected, but some much more than others. As the science of climate change improves, and severe as opposed to modest losers are identified, that will influence the lineup between countries advocating one standard or the other.

Ethanol subsidies. At both the federal and local levels, the United States has subsidized ethanol (mostly corn-based) and other biofuels. The federal government currently provides a 51 cent tax credit per gallon of ethanol, and the states provide a wide array of policies to support ethanol and other biofuel industries. Economists have criticized the cost of ethanol and biofuel production, and scientists have questioned the environmental benefits, especially when CO_2 emissions from cleared land are taken into account. Issues related to biofuels are discussed in appendix B.

Energy standards. In December 2007 President George W. Bush signed an energy bill establishing higher fuel economy standards for new cars and light trucks and other conservation measures. New vehicles are mandated to increase their fuel efficiency by 40 percent, setting a standard of an average of 35 miles per gallon (mpg) by 2020, instead of the prior target of 25 mpg.

State climate policy. States have enacted tougher state laws to regulate greenhouse gas emissions. California became an environmental pioneer among states when Governor Arnold Schwarzenegger signed the Global Warming Solution Act into law on September 26, 2007. This is the first statewide cap on greenhouse gas emissions, mandating a 25 percent cut by 2020. Despite the denial by the Environmental Protection Agency in December 2007 of California's petition to adopt its own CO_2 guidelines, California has pledged to go further in a green direction. Other states have engaged in cooperative efforts by initiating regional programs such as the Regional Greenhouse Gas Initiative, the Western Climate Initiative, and the Midwestern Greenhouse Gas Reduction Accord (the Midwest Accord).

limits on greenhouse gas emissions, affected US industries will suffer a severe competitive disadvantage in the global marketplace. This would happen if China, India, and other developing countries were to insist on a per capita comparability or an historic emissions standard and impose few if any limits on their own carbon emissions.[8] To address this concern, several US climate bills introduced in the 110th Congress contain competitive provisions that, in one way or another, extend domestic greenhouse gas policies to US merchandise imports and foreign greenhouse gas control systems.

---

8. While China has pushed historic emissions or per capita comparability standards in international negotiations over the past several years, China has also aggressively pursued a combination of measures to control air, water, and soil pollution, using industrial and energy policies, among others. See Leggett, Logan, and Mackey (2008).

Table 1.1 CO$_2$ emissions from fuel combustion, 2006 (millions of tons)

Fuel type/sector	United States	China	EU-27	Russia	Japan	India	Brazil	Total	World total
Total	5,697	5,607	3,983	1,587	1,213	1,250	332	19,669	28,003
Percent change, 1990–2006	17	154	–2	–27	13	112	73		33
By fuel type									
Coal	2,090	4,641	1,263	445	431	844	47	9,761	11,686
Oil	2,411	864	1,682	321	587	339	246	6,450	10,768
Gas	1,169	101	999	805	190	67	40	3,371	5,445
Other[a]	27	n.a.	40	17	5	n.a.	n.a.	89	103
By sector									
Electricity and heat	2,421	2,796	1,461	913	459	702	34	8,786	11,509
Manufacturing industries and construction	633	1,764	656	222	292	284	98	3,949	5,477
Transportation	1,809	367	952	227	245	101	141	3,842	6,453
Residential	309	247	476	123	63	72	16	1,306	1,860
Other[a]	524	434	439	102	153	90	44	1,786	2,705
CO$_2$ per unit of GDP (kg/2000 US dollars)	0.51	2.68	0.42	4.25	0.24	1.78	0.43	0.74	
CO$_2$ per capita (tons/capita)	19.00	4.27	8.07	11.14	9.49	1.13	1.76	4.28	
Cumulative CO$_2$ emissions, 1950–2004 (percent of world total)[b]	26.70	9.90	21.70[c]	9.40	4.80	2.60	1.00	76.10	100

n.a. = not available

a. "Other" includes industrial waste and nonrenewable municipal waste.
b. Cumulative CO$_2$ emissions (energy) data for the period of 1950–2004 from World Resources Institute, Climate Analysis Indicators Tool (CAIT) Version 5.0, 2008.
c. Figure for EU-25.

Note: The Organization for Economic Cooperation and Development noted that CO$_2$ emissions are calculated using International Energy Agency energy balances, the sectoral approach of the Intergovernmental Panel on Climate Change, and the default emissions factors from the Revised 1996 IPCC Guidelines for National Greenhouse Gas Inventories. The calculations may differ from the national communication submitted by the parties to the UN Framework Convention on Climate Change.

Sources: International Energy Agency, *CO$_2$ Emissions from Fuel Combustion*, 2008; Organization for Economic Cooperation and Development; World Resources Institute, Climate Analysis Indicators Tool (CAIT) Version 5.0, 2008.

Statistical Overview

Before discussing US climate policy options and their consistency with the World Trade Organization (WTO), this section takes a quick look at some statistical evidence. Yes, climate change is happening. Scientists have found that since the mid-1970s, the average surface temperature has warmed about 1°F (Fahrenheit) and that the earth's surface is currently warming at a rate of about 0.32°F per decade, or 3.2°F per century. The top 10 warmest years in recorded history have all occurred since 1990.[9]

According to the IPCC, most of the observed increase in globally averaged temperatures since the mid-20th century likely reflects the observed increase in anthropogenic greenhouse gas concentrations.[10] Greenhouse gas concentrations in the atmosphere have historically varied as a result of natural processes. However, when industrialization accelerated after the Second World War, the human use of fossil fuels added great amounts of greenhouse gases to the atmosphere.

Tables 1.1 through 1.4 summarize greenhouse gas emissions by the largest emitters in the world—namely, the United States, European Union, China, Russia, Japan, India, and Brazil. In 2000 the United States ranked first among large greenhouse gas emitters (table 1.2, panel a), accounting for more than 20 percent of total world greenhouse gas emissions, and China and the European Union took the second and the third places, respectively. China probably surpassed the United States in total tonnage in 2007. Among the six major greenhouse gases—carbon dioxide (CO_2), methane (CH_4), nitrous oxide (N_2O), hydrofluorocarbons (HFCs), perfluocrocarbons (PFCs), and sulfur hexafluoride (SF_6)—emissions of carbon dioxide accounted for about 73 percent of world total greenhouse gas emissions in 2000 (table 1.2, panel a). In terms of sectors, the production and use of energy represents the largest source of total greenhouse gas emissions, contributing about 76 percent to the world total in 2000 (table 1.3, panel a).

Table 1.1 illustrates just CO_2 emissions from fuel combustion in 2006. Electricity and heat are the largest source of CO_2 emissions, accounting for about 41 percent of such emissions worldwide. In 2006 CO_2 emissions from the manufacturing sectors that lie at the center of the US competitive-

---

9. For more details, see annual climate reports by the National Oceanic and Atmospheric Administration's (NOAA), available at www.ncdc.noaa.gov, and surface temperature analysis by the National Aeronautics and Space Administration (NASA), available at http://data.giss.nasa.gov/gistemp.

10. The atmospheric concentration of carbon dioxide (CO_2) in 2005 was recorded at 379 ppm (estimated to be about 455 ppm CO_2e), which exceeds the natural range over the last 650,000 years (180 to 300 ppm), as determined from ice cores. The annual growth rate of CO_2 concentration was faster during the last decade than earlier, with an annual average increase of 1.9 ppm. The primary source of the increase since the preindustrial period is the growing use of fossil fuels. For more details, see IPCC (2007a, 2007c).

Table 1.2 Greenhouse gas emissions by gas and hypothetical carbon taxes

Gas	Equivalent factors (GWP)[a]	United States	EU-25	China	Russia	Japan	India	Brazil	World total
a. By gas, 2000 (million metric tons of CO_2 equivalent; percent of world total in parentheses)									
CO_2	1	5,791 (22)	3,843 (15)	3,400 (13)	1,533 (6)	1,266 (5)	1,034 (4)	337 (0)	26,351
CH_4	21	546 (9)	444 (7)	788 (13)	307 (5)	21 (0)	499 (8)	366 (6)	6,020
N_2O	310	396 (13)	408 (13)	645 (21)	55 (2)	37 (1)	67 (2)	241 (8)	3,114
HFCs	140 to 11,700	101 (39)	39 (15)	42 (16)	4 (2)	34 (13)	5 (2)	4 (2)	259
PFCs	6,500 to 9,200	14 (18)	10 (13)	6 (7)	8 (10)	6 (8)	1 (1)	2 (2)	81
SF_6	23,900	19 (48)	3 (7)	2 (5)	2 (5)	2 (5)	1 (2)	1 (2)	40
Greenhouse gas total		6,868 (19)	4,747 (13)	4,883 (14)	1,909 (5)	1,366 (4)	1,607 (5)	950 (3)	35,865
b. Hypothetical carbon taxes (billions of dollars)									
CO_2		158.1	104.9	92.8	41.9	34.6	28.2	9.2	719.4
CH_4		14.9	12.1	21.5	8.4	0.6	13.6	10.0	164.3
N_2O		10.8	11.1	17.6	1.5	1.0	1.8	6.6	85.0
HFCs		2.8	1.1	1.1	0.1	0.9	0.1	0.1	7.1
PFCs		0.4	0.3	0.2	0.2	0.2	0.0	0.1	2.2
SF_6		0.5	0.1	0.1	0.1	0.1	0.0	0.0	1.1
Greenhouse gas total		187.5	129.6	133.3	52.1	37.3	43.9	25.9	979.1

a. All emissions are expressed in CO_2 equivalents using 100-year global warming potentials (GWP), found at the website of the United Nations Framework Convention on Climate Change (http://unfccc.int). For HFCs and PFCs, GWPs are shown in range values, since HFCs and PFCs include several gases that differ in their GWP values.

Note: Table excludes CO_2 emitted through changes in land use. Hypothetical carbon tax equivalent amounts in panel b calculated based on greenhouse gas emissions by gas in panel a. The table uses an arbitrary price of $100 per metric ton of carbon equivalent, which converts to about $27 per metric ton of CO_2 equivalent (based on the conversion method used by the Environmental Protection Agency and the IPCC, which derives the quantity of carbon by multiplying the quantity of CO_2 by the factor 12/44).

Source: World Resources Institute, Climate Analysis Indicators Tool (CAIT) Version 5.0, 2008.

Table 1.3 Greenhouse gas emissions by sector and hypothetical carbon taxes

Sector	United States	EU-25	China	Russia	Japan	India	Brazil	World total
a. By sector, 2000 (million metric tons of CO_2 equivalent; percent of country total in parentheses)								
Electricity and heat[a]	2,685 (39)	1,477 (31)	1,466 (31)	917 (48)	466 (35)	556 (35)	50 (5)	11,582 (33)
Transportation[a]	1,714 (25)	879 (19)	219 (5)	176 (9)	257 (19)	92 (6)	126 (13)	5,098 (14)
Manufacturing and construction[a]	661 (10)	649 (14)	903 (19)	218 (11)	270 (20)	225 (14)	94 (10)	4,748 (13)
Industrial processes	208 (3)	226 (5)	377 (8)	32 (2)	87 (7)	57 (4)	31 (3)	1,369 (4)
Residential and other fuel combustion[a]	720 (11)	780 (17)	463 (10)	210 (11)	202 (15)	139 (9)	45 (5)	3,964 (11)
Agriculture	444 (7)	493 (10)	1,041 (22)	110 (6)	34 (3)	375 (24)	549 (58)	5,729 (16)
Fugitive emissions[a] and waste	416 (6)	225 (5)	290 (6)	243 (13)	10 (1)	150 (9)	47 (5)	2,958 (8)
Greenhouse gas total	6,846	4,730	4,759	1,906	1,326	1,595	942	35,440
Memorandum:								
Energy generation and use (percent of country total)	88	82	67	90	90	66	34	76
b. Hypothetical carbon taxes (billions of dollars)								
Electricity and heat	73.3	40.3	40.0	25.0	12.7	15.2	1.4	316.2
Transportation	46.8	24.0	6.0	4.8	7.0	2.5	3.4	139.2
Manufacturing and construction	18.0	17.7	24.7	6.0	7.4	6.1	2.6	129.6
Industrial processes	5.7	6.2	10.3	0.9	2.4	1.6	0.8	37.4
Residential and other fuel combustion	19.7	21.3	12.6	5.7	5.5	3.8	1.2	108.2
Agriculture	12.1	13.5	28.4	3.0	0.9	10.2	15.0	156.4
Fugitive emissions and waste	11.4	6.1	7.9	6.6	0.3	4.1	1.3	80.8
Greenhouse gas total	186.9	129.1	129.9	52.0	36.2	43.5	25.7	967.5

a. Sector included in "Energy generation and use" in the memorandum row.

Note: Table excludes CO_2 emitted through changes in land use. Hypothetical carbon tax equivalent amounts in panel b calculated based on greenhouse gas emissions by sector in panel a. The table uses an arbitrary price of $100 per metric ton of carbon equivalent, which converts to about $27 per metric ton of CO_2 equivalent (based on the conversion method used by the Environmental Protection Agency and the IPCC, which derives the quantity of carbon by multiplying the quantity of CO_2 by the factor 12/44).

Source: World Resources Institute, Climate Analysis Indicators Tool (CAIT) Version 5.0, 2008.

ness debate accounted for under 11 percent of total CO_2 emissions by the United States.[11] Also, the last row of table 1.1 shows the historical share of cumulative world CO_2 emissions by country from 1950 to 2004. The United States and the EU-25 accounted for about 27 and 22 percent of cumulative emissions, respectively, while China and India accounted for about 10 and 3 percent, respectively. These figures support the argument made by developing countries as to who is most responsible for climate change, since warming is generated by the cumulative stock of greenhouse gases in the atmosphere. On the other hand, if positive as well as negative contributions to human well-being are going to be tallied in a fanciful exercise to settle historical scores, the developed countries can list many technological innovations that benefited the developing world free of charge.

Compared with the 1990 level, total world CO_2 emissions increased by about 33 percent in 2006. China and India, two of the fastest industrializing countries, show huge increases in their CO_2 emissions of about 154 and 112 percent, respectively (table 1.1). In coming decades, these two countries are expected to continue on a path of faster growth in CO_2 emissions (table 1.4).

Serious limits on greenhouse gas emissions—of the sort proposed by Peterson Institute economist William Cline, Yale economist William Nordhaus, and Nicholas Stern—will entail heavy costs.[12] While estimates vary across a wide range depending on baselines and assumptions, experts agree that costs will sharply rise if actions to tackle greenhouse gas emissions are delayed. A principal reason is that valuable time will be lost both in implementing relatively easy control measures and in spurring new technologies that will enhance energy efficiency.

Panel b in tables 1.2 and 1.3 illustrates the cost/value implication if moderate measures are taken in the near future. These tables use an arbitrary price of $100 per metric ton of carbon equivalent, which converts to about $27 per metric ton of CO_2 equivalent. This figure can be interpreted as a "cost" if a uniform carbon tax is imposed on all emission sources. Alternatively, it can be interpreted as a "value" if emissions are rigorously capped and tradable emissions permits are distributed free of charge to established firms. A price of $100 per metric ton of carbon equivalent is well within the range of estimates made by the economists mentioned above. However, it is above the current value of EU emissions permits.[13] A control system that,

---

11. The figure of 11 percent includes emissions from both manufacturing industries and the construction sectors. Therefore, the manufacturing sector alone would account for less than 11 percent.

12. For references to these economists and others, see Stern (2006) and Cline (2004). The latter paper is available at www.copenhagenconsensus.com (accessed on January 12, 2009).

13. In December 2008 and January 2009, the EU allowance unit (EUA) contract for December 2009 delivery was traded at prices around €15 per metric ton of CO_2 in the European over-the-counter market (about $20 per metric ton of CO_2). The price of EUA can be found at

Table 1.4 CO_2 emissions projections by selected countries, 2005–30
(million metric tons of CO_2)

Country/region	2005 actual	2010	2020	2030	Average annual percent change (2005–30)
United States	5,982	6,011	6,384	6,851	0.5
OECD Europe[a]	4,383	4,512	4,760	4,834	0.4
China	5,323	6,898	9,475	12,007	3.3
Russia	1,696	1,789	1,984	2,117	0.9
Japan	1,230	1,196	1,195	1,170	−0.2
India	1,164	1,349	1,818	2,238	2.6
Brazil	356	451	541	633	2.3
Memorandum: World	28,051	31,100	37,035	42,325	1.7

OECD = Organization for Economic Cooperation and Development

a. Includes 23 countries: Austria, Belgium, the Czech Republic, Denmark, Finland, France, Germany, Greece, Hungary, Iceland, Ireland, Italy, Luxembourg, the Netherlands, Norway, Poland, Portugal, Slovakia, Spain, Sweden, Switzerland, Turkey, and the United Kingdom.

Source: US Energy Information Administration, *Annual Energy Outlook 2008.*

in terms of effect, equates to $100 per metric ton of emitted carbon-equivalent would generate costs/values of around $190 billion annually for the United States alone, at current emission levels. For the European Union or China, the costs/values would be around $130 billion annually.

Issues in Controlling Greenhouse Gas Emissions

Ramp Up Speed

While there is general agreement that world greenhouse gas emissions should be reduced to slow global warming, other important questions in addition to the "per capita" versus "carbon price" debate need to be answered, and these involve both economics and science. The critical question is how much emissions should be reduced and along what time path. Fundamentally, the answer must balance costs and benefits and give due weight to very low-probability but very high-damage scenarios. Using various models, economists have estimated the implied costs of reducing

www.pointcarbon.com (accessed on January 12, 2009).

emissions to defined levels on prescribed paths. These economists generally agree that if the emission targets are either quite modest or extremely ambitious, the policies adopted would be severely suboptimal—either the costs incurred would fall far short of the likely benefits from reducing the extent of climate change, or the costs would vastly exceed the likely benefits.[14]

Other participants in the debate argue that reasonable reductions in greenhouse gas emissions will only be accomplished with the creation of new technologies and their active deployment; therefore, severe public action to tackle climate change should be delayed until new technologies emerge or barriers to existing technologies (e.g., nuclear power plants, electric cars) are swept aside. In that way, the decline in emissions could be structured in a manner consistent with technological availability and public action could be implemented at lower cost. In a recent study, the respected McKinsey & Company strongly emphasized the new technology angle and suggested that dramatic reduction of greenhouse gas emissions may not be as costly as frequently cited if tested approaches and high-potential emerging technologies are implemented.[15]

While the importance of new technologies is not arguable, other studies have voiced strong calls for immediate international action with tough targets. In a report commissioned by Australia's federal, state, and territory governments and released in September 2008, distinguished economist Ross Garnaut (2008) warned that the world is heating up faster than previous climate models suggested because of rapid economic growth in developing countries—led by China and India—and that this growing amount of emissions makes mitigation both more urgent and more costly.[16] Damon H. Matthews and Ken Caldeira (2008) argue in the journal *Geophysical Research Letters* that holding the world's climate constant at present average temperatures will require near-zero future carbon emissions. According to these scientists, any future anthropogenic emissions will commit the climate system to warming that is essentially irreversible on a centennial time scale.[17]

---

14. See Cline (2004), Stern (2006), and Nordhaus (2007).

15. McKinsey & Company (2007) concluded that the United States could reduce greenhouse gas emissions by 2030 by 3.0 to 4.5 gigatons (1 gigaton equals 1 billion metric tons) of CO_2e using tested approaches and high-potential emerging technologies. These reductions would involve a wide array of abatement options available at marginal costs less than $50 per ton of CO_2e, with the average net cost to the economy being much lower if sizable gains in energy efficiency are achieved. This report even suggested that about 40 percent of abatement could be accomplished at "negative" marginal costs, meaning that investing in the options would generate positive economic returns from energy saved over the relevant life cycle.

16. The *Garnaut Climate Change Review* is available at www.garnautreview.org.au (accessed on January 12, 2009).

17. See Juliet Eilperin, "Carbon Output Must Near Zero To Avert Danger, New Studies Say," *Washington Post*, March 10, 2008, www.washingtonpost.com (accessed on January 12, 2009).

Competitiveness

A major US objection to taking stringent action on emissions controls is a fear that heavy costs would weaken the position of US producers, leading to the "leakage" of production and jobs to foreign firms. US measures might inflict competitive damage on the country's manufacturing firms, especially by comparison with China and India. A related concern is that, in the end, US controls will make no difference to climate change if emissions activity simply migrates to other countries. Moreover, US legislation would miss an opportunity if it does not create maximum leverage so that China, India, and other developing countries feel obligated to reduce their own emissions not only in the manufacturing sector but throughout the economy.[18] In the absence of parallel international commitments that result in approximately the same implicit tax per ton of CO_2e emissions, mandatory US programs would impose heavier costs on US industries than their foreign competitors. The extra costs in turn would put US producers at a price disadvantage.[19]

To level the playing field for vulnerable manufacturing firms, policymakers have tried to include specific provisions in climate bills, such as the allocation of free allowances, special exemptions, and border measures. The political parallel with trade legislation is obvious, in that compensatory measures for severely impacted industries may be required to forge a coalition prepared to enact controls on greenhouse gas emissions. To address leakage and leverage concerns—both of which are aspects of the broader competitiveness agenda—trade-related rules in the form of border adjustment schemes have gained political support. On the down side, however, trade measures could easily interrupt the broad agenda of trade liberalization that has proven enormously successful in boosting world economic growth since the Second World War and could also hinder international negotiations to design a global climate framework. At the Bali Roadmap conference in December 2007, US Trade Representative Susan Schwab expressed worries that efforts to address climate change

---

18. According to the *New York Times*, "In an alliance of denial, China and the United States are using each other's inaction as an excuse to do nothing [on climate change issue]." See "Warming and Global Security," *New York Times*, April 20, 2007, www.nytimes.com (accessed on January 12, 2009).

19. A competing line of thinking is that actions to reduce carbon emissions will reduce production costs through a more efficient and sustainable use of energy and the development of new technologies. From this perspective, the US government should require substantial domestic reductions in carbon emissions to further its own economic interests, regardless whether major developing countries reciprocate. The logical implication of this view is that no trade or border measures are needed to protect US competitiveness because a strong climate policy enhances rather than undermines US competitiveness.

through trade measures could lead to tit-for-tat trade restrictions and reduce global economic growth.[20]

Besides, any performance standards that the United States imposes on foreign firms, and any "comparability" tests it imposes on foreign greenhouse gas control systems, can be turned around and imposed on the United States. An example will illustrate. The United States might impose its own carbon tax or performance standards on imports of steel rebar products from India, citing an exceptionally high level of carbon emissions per ton of Indian rebar production. In turn, India might impose a duty on all imports from the United States, citing the exceptionally high figure of US per capita CO_2 emissions compared with the world average (table 1.1).

In addition, trade data show that the largest foreign suppliers to the United States of carbon-intensive goods are countries such as Canada and those of the European Union, and these countries emit considerably less carbon than the United States either on a national basis or a per capita basis. Moreover, restrictive US trade measures might serve as an excuse for other countries to erect barriers against imports from the United States but not serve as an effective incentive to convince developing countries to reduce their own greenhouse gas emissions. In 2007 imports from China made up an average of about 11 percent of US carbon-intensive imports in five main product groups combined, accounting for 15 percent of US steel imports, 6 percent of US aluminum imports, practically no US chemical imports, 12 percent of US paper imports, and 19 percent of US cement imports (see table 1.5).[21] It is not obvious that these trade shares create substantial leverage for the United States to shape Chinese greenhouse gas policies. Regarding leakage concerns, the International Energy Agency (IEA 2008b) found no meaningful changes in trade flows and production patterns in EU sectors affected by the first phase (2005–07) of the EU Emission Trading Scheme. However, emission controls during the first phase were relatively light.

Major Bills Introduced in the 110th Congress

The major bills introduced to the 110th Congress are summarized in tables 1A.1 and 1A.2 at the end of this chapter.[22] The legislative proposals embody two main incentive approaches: carbon taxes and cap-and-trade

---

20. Schwab warned that countries should not restrict imports based on the carbon intensity of production, because such measures easily lead to covert protectionism. See *Inside US Trade* 25, no. 49, December 14, 2007.

21. Table 1.5 does not show US import data from China for chemicals. The value of US imports of chemicals from China in 2007 was small, only $13 million.

22. New climate bills are being introduced in the 111th Congress.

Table 1.5   US imports by origin of selected carbon-intensive products, 2007

	Steel[a]				Cement[b]		
Rank	Country	Value (millions of US dollars)	Percent share	Rank	Country	Value (millions of US dollars)	Percent share
1	Canada	5,430	17.6	1	Canada	387	29.2
2	China	4,473	14.5	2	China	246	18.6
3	Mexico	2,530	8.2	3	Korea	121	9.1
4	Japan	1,794	5.8	4	Mexico	116	8.8
5	Germany	1,704	5.5	5	Colombia	105	7.9
6	Korea	1,610	5.2	6	Taiwan	99	7.5
7	Brazil	1,415	4.6	7	Brazil	39	2.9
8	Taiwan	1,324	4.3	8	Greece	36	2.7
9	India	1,227	4.0	9	Thailand	33	2.5
10	Italy	1,076	3.5	10	Sweden	25	1.9
Memorandum:				*Memorandum:*			
EU-27		7,643	24.7	EU-27		111	8.4
OECD		19,728	63.8	OECD		751	56.7
Total imports from world		30,909	100.0	Total imports from world		1,324	100.0

	Paper[c]				Aluminum[d]		
Rank	Country	Value (millions of US dollars)	Percent share	Rank	Country	Value (millions of US dollars)	Percent share
1	Canada	9,509	53.1	1	Canada	7,769	55.7
2	China	2,093	11.7	2	Russia	1,467	10.5
3	Finland	1,063	5.9	3	China	826	5.9
4	Germany	906	5.1	4	Germany	655	4.7
5	Mexico	858	4.8	5	South Africa	344	2.5
6	Japan	502	2.8	6	Brazil	336	2.4
7	Korea	443	2.5	7	United Arab Emirates	317	2.3
8	Indonesia	299	1.7				
9	United Kingdom	219	1.2	8	Venezuela	190	1.4
				9	Argentina	184	1.3
10	Brazil	210	1.2	10	Bahrain	174	1.2
Memorandum:				*Memorandum:*			
EU-27		3,231	18.0	EU-27		1,246	8.9
OECD		14,769	82.4	OECD		9,716	69.6
Total imports from world		17,917	100.0	Total imports from world		13,958	100.0

systems. Each of these approaches has several nuances. While both approaches will impose costs on the US economy, one major difference in approaches is whether permits are assigned to private companies, thereby conferring valuable "quota rents" on the recipients, or whether limits are imposed by way of auction or taxes so that the government collects substantial revenues. Another major difference is the choice of activity where

Table 1.5   US imports by origin of selected carbon-intensive products, 2007 *(continued)*

Rank	Country	Chemicals[e] Value (millions of US dollars)	Percent share
1	Trinidad & Tobago	1,033	22.6
2	Canada	919	20.1
3	Korea	556	12.1
4	Brazil	405	8.8
5	Venezuela	285	6.2
6	Netherlands	230	5.0
7	Equatorial Guinea	207	4.5
8	India	129	2.8
9	Argentina	110	2.4
10	Mexico	95	2.1
Memorandum:			
EU-27		459	10.0
OECD		2,047	44.7
Total imports from world		4,579	100.0

OECD = Organization for Economic Cooperation and Development

a. Standard International Trade Classification (SITC) 3-digit (672, 673, 674, 675, 676, 677, 678, 679).
b. SITC 4-digit (6612).
c. SITC 3-digit (641,642).
d. SITC 4-digit (6841, 6842).
e. SITC 5-digit (51111, 51112, 51113, 51122, 51123, 51124, 51211, 52251).

Note: US general imports based on general customs value. US general imports represent goods that arrive in the United States from foreign countries, whether such goods enter consumption channels immediately or are entered into bonded warehouses or foreign trade zones under customs custody.

Source: US International Trade Commission, Interactive Tariff and Trade Database, available at http://dataweb.usitc.gov (accessed on September 17, 2008).

limits are designed to "bite"—for example, on power generation and refineries, or also on transportation and manufacturing. Other parameters also differ between approaches, including the trading of permits, domestically and internationally; banking and borrowing of permits; and special auctions to curtail price spikes.

Carbon Tax Systems

These systems would levy charges in proportion to the carbon content of fuels and products. Economists generally favor carbon tax systems for three reasons. First, by contrast with cap-and-trade systems, which typically target only the larger sources of CO_2 emissions, a carbon tax would curtail emissions throughout the economy—importantly including electricity generation and transportation (the two US sectors that account for about three-quarters of total CO_2 emissions; see table 1.1). Second, in principle a carbon tax system can be fairly simple, easing the administrative burden. Third, the revenue raised through carbon taxes can be used to enlist the support of recalcitrant publics—for example, by financing Medicare.[23]

Offsetting these arguments is a powerful liability: the fact that a carbon tax is literally a "tax." This is the main reason why carbon tax systems have gained little political support in Congress. Moreover, a uniform tax per ton of carbon emitted would exert a highly differential price impact in percentage terms, depending on the fuel. For example, a tax of $100 per metric ton of carbon equivalent would increase the cost of residual fuel from petroleum by around 12 percent and the cost of bituminous coal by about 74 percent (table 1.6).[24]

Another argument against carbon taxes, perhaps unpersuasive to economists but often compelling to politicians, is that taxes do not set hard limits either on annual emissions or the stock of atmospheric CO_2. Environmental groups, inspired by apocalyptic visions and drawing on some scientific reports,[25] believe the time to enact hard limits is now, and anything less will pave the road to disaster.

Among the major bills listed in tables 1A.1 and 1A.2, two are based on carbon tax systems. One is the Save Our Climate Act (H.R. 2069), sponsored by Representative Fortney Pete Stark (D-CA); the other is the America's Energy Security Trust Fund Act (H.R. 3416), sponsored by Representative John Larson (D-CT). Both bills address the competitiveness concern by requiring equivalent taxes on imported goods (table 1A.2). Later we will examine the international dimension of the proposed border tax adjustments.

Cap-and-Trade Systems

Cap-and-trade systems enjoy far more support in Congress than carbon taxes, and the majority of bills reflect this fact. There are two reasons for this preference. First, cap-and-trade systems can be advertised as

---

23. As a similar inducement, former Vice President Al Gore has argued that carbon tax revenue can be used to lower payroll tax rates. See "Al Gore Suggests Carbon Tax Replace Payroll Taxes," Tax Foundation, December 19, 2006, www.taxfoundation.org (accessed on January 12, 2009).

24. For this comparison, as a baseline price of coal, we used the spot price of Illinois basin coal—$83 per short ton on August 29, 2008 (table 1.6). However, since electric utilities typically purchase on long-term contracts, the average delivered coal price in 2008 is likely to be lower than the spot price. Therefore, the 74 percent increase in the cost of bituminous coal due to a tax of $100 per metric ton of carbon equivalent is very likely an understatement.

25. For one example, see Matthews and Caldeira (2008).

Table 1.6 Carbon emissions and projected carbon taxes, by selected types of fuel

Fuel	Amount of CO_2 per unit[a] (pounds)	Amount of carbon per unit		Carbon tax per unit (in dollars) for following arbitrary tax amounts (assuming the same tax rate per metric ton of carbon emitted)			
		In pounds[b]	In metric tons[c]	$50	$100	$200	$400
Petroleum products (per barrel)							
Aviation gasoline	771	210	0.10	4.77	9.54	19.08	38.16
Distillate fuel	940	256	0.12	5.82	11.63	23.27	46.53
Jet fuel	886	242	0.11	5.48	10.96	21.93	43.85
Kerosene	905	247	0.11	5.60	11.19	22.39	44.77
Liquified petroleum gases	538	147	0.07	3.33	6.65	13.31	26.62
Motor gasoline	823	224	0.10	5.09	10.18	20.37	40.73
Petroleum coke	1,356	370	0.17	8.39	16.79	33.57	67.14
Residual fuel	1,093	298	0.14	6.76	13.53	27.06	54.12
Coal (per short ton)							
Anthracite	5,685	1,550	0.70	35.17	70.35	140.69	281.39
Bituminous	4,931	1,345	0.61	30.51	61.02	122.04	244.08
Subbituminous	3,716	1,013	0.46	22.99	45.98	91.96	183.93
Lignite	2,792	761	0.35	17.27	34.54	69.09	138.18

(table continues on next page)

Table 1.6 Carbon emissions and projected carbon taxes, by selected types of fuel *(continued)*

Memoranda:	
US price per unit (dollars)	
Petroleum, barrel (crude oil, as of August 29, 2008)	$110
Coal, short ton, spot price (Illinois basin, as of August 29, 2008)[d]	$83
CO_2 per million BTU used for electricity generation	
Petroleum (residual fuel)	174 pounds[e]
Coal (bituminous)	205 pounds[f]
Natural gas (pipeline)	117 pounds

a. Emission coefficients from US Energy Information Administration (EIA), available at www.eia.doe.gov.

b. To convert a quantity of CO_2 to a quantity of carbon, multiply by 12/44 (by definition used by the Environmental Protection Agency and the Intergovernmental Panel on Climate Change). See www.epa.gov.

c. 1 metric ton = 1.102 short ton = 2,204 pounds.

d. Spot price data from the EIA website at www.eia.doe.gov (accessed on September 8, 2008). Since electric utilities typically purchase on long-term contracts, the average delivered coal price in 2008 is lower than the spot price.

e. 1 metric ton of crude oil = 42.5 million BTU of crude oil.

f. 1 metric ton of coal = 23 million BTU of coal.

Sources: US Energy Information Administration, www.eia.doe.gov; US Environmental Protection Agency, www.epa.gov; Copenhagen Consensus Center, www.copenhagenconsensus.com. All websites accessed on January 12, 2009.

relatively painless, entailing little sacrifice from the general public. Second, meaningful caps will ripen into very valuable licenses, eventually worth hundreds of billions of dollars (see panel b in tables 1.2 and 1.3), and firms that are potentially affected want to claim part of the "quota rent," rather than see it entirely collected by the US Treasury in the form of carbon taxes or auctioned permits.

Under cap-and-trade systems, the federal government would establish a cap on total emissions and either assign or auction CO_2 and other greenhouse gas permits. Industrial holders of rights could emit annually at the specified levels. Moreover, holders could buy and sell permits. The core idea is that firms that are less able to cut greenhouse gas emissions will use all of their assigned rights and buy additional rights on the market; meanwhile, firms that are better able to cut emissions will sell some of their assigned rights.

Among the current climate bills, the Climate Security Act (S. 2191) sponsored by Senators Joe Lieberman (I-CT) and John Warner (R-VA) has received the most attention in Congress. In its original form, this bill was introduced in October 2007; after several amendments, it was reported favorably by the Senate Environment and Public Works Committee in December 2007. The Lieberman-Warner bill, based on a cap-and-trade system, requires a 70 percent reduction (from 2005 levels) in greenhouse gas emissions from covered sources by 2050. While the bill envisages the auction of some allowances, it includes transition assistance in the form of free allowances to certain industries, such as power plants and manufacturing firms, for the period between 2012 and 2030. The bill addresses concerns over the possible price volatility of allowances by including three provisions: auctioning some allowances; allowing firms to borrow permits from future periods; and establishing an "international reserve allowance" program. After adding a measure to ensure budget neutrality, the version of the act reported by the Environment and Public Works Committee was introduced in the Senate as S. 3036 on May 20, 2008. Shortly after, the Boxer substitute amendment to S. 3036 was introduced, but a cloture motion to limit debate on the Boxer amendment failed in June 2008.

In October 2008 House Energy and Commerce Chairman John Dingell and Energy and Air Quality Subcommittee Chairman Richard Boucher released their 461-page draft climate change bill. The draft proposed an 80 percent greenhouse gas emissions cut compared with 2005 levels by 2050. It covers roughly 88 percent of US emissions, including those from power plants, petroleum producers, and other major industrial polluters. As with many other proposed bills, the Dingell-Boucher bill would enable the Environmental Protection Agency (EPA) to regulate industrial emissions. Box 1.2 discusses the EPA and climate change. Table 1A.2 summarizes the draft.

The Lieberman-Warner bill and other cap-and-trade systems have

Box 1.2   The Environmental Protection Agency and climate change

In April 2007 the US Supreme Court ruled 5-4 in favor of petitioners in the case of *Massachusetts vs. EPA*.[1] In 1999 private organizations petitioned the Environmental Protection Agency (EPA) to regulate emissions of four greenhouse gases, including CO_2, from new motor vehicles, citing the EPA's duty described in Section 202 (a)(1) of the Clean Air Act.[2] However, in 2003 the EPA denied the Section 202 petition, asserting that it was not given the authority under the Clean Air Act to regulate CO_2 or other greenhouse gases, claiming they do not fall within the statutory definition of pollutants; moreover, even If the EPA had the authority to set greenhouse gas emissions standards, it would be "unwise to do so" owing to the scientific uncertainty in linking greenhouse gases to global warming. In response to the EPA's denial, Massachusetts along with other states, cities, and organizations sued the EPA.

Disagreeing with the EPA's assertions, the Supreme Court held: (1) EPA's action was not in accordance with law; (2) the Clean Air Act authorizes the EPA to regulate emissions from new motor vehicles based on their possible impact on climate change; and (3) Section 202 constrains EPA discretion once it determines that greenhouse gases contribute to climate change.

This ruling is very important in that it admonished the EPA to determine whether greenhouse gases are a dangerous pollutant to public health or welfare under the current law. Despite the court's ruling, however, the Bush administration and the EPA delayed the rule-making process. In July 2008 the EPA released an Advanced Notice of Public Rule-Making (ANPR), the first formal response to the Supreme Court's ruling in the *Massachusetts vs. EPA* case.[3] In the ANPR, the EPA stated that the Clean Air Act is "ill-suited" for the task of regulating greenhouse gases and urged Congress to enact comprehensive climate change legislation. Rather than making an "endangerment" finding that would in turn lead to regulating greenhouse gas emissions, the EPA in its ANPR further delayed the rule-making process by calling for a 120-day public comment period.

Despite the reluctant attitude of the Bush administration and the EPA, many discussions on Capitol Hill have centered on using the EPA and the Clean Air Act to regulate greenhouse gas emissions. In September 2008 the Senate Environment and Public Works Committee held a full committee hearing entitled "Regulation of Greenhouse Gases under the Clean Air Act." Several climate change bills introduced in the 110th Congress proposed to amend the Clean Air Act to regulate greenhouse gas emissions. Moreover, the Obama administration may use the Clean Air Act to regulate CO_2 emissions, a possibility expressed during the presidential campaign.[4]

evolved in the direction of hybrid systems with various market-based measures (notably auctions). They promise to be complex for three reasons:

- They guarantee a series of intense lobbying battles over initial permit allocations, subsequent renewals, and systems for auctioning licenses.
- How they would interact with state and regional limits on greenhouse gas emissions is not clear.
- How they would interact internationally with the climate policies of other nations is far from obvious.

A central concern of this study is the international dimension of cap-and-trade systems.

Appendix 1A

Table 1A.1 Major climate change bills of the 110th Congress (without competitiveness provisions)

	S 485: Global Warming Reduction Act	HR 1590: Safe Climate Act
Sponsor	Senators John Kerry and Olympia Snowe	Representative Henry Waxman
Status in Congress	Introduced on February 1, 2007	Introduced on March 20, 2007
Scope	All six greenhouse gases economywide	All six greenhouse gases economy-wide
First year of emissions cap	2010	2010
Emissions reduction targets	Mandatory caps ■ 2010: 2010 level ■ 2020: 1990 level ■ 2021–30: reduce by 2.5 percent per year ■ 2031–50: reduce by 3.5 percent per year ■ 2051: 62 percent below 1990 levels Long term: 2°C or less above preindustrial temperature level	Mandatory caps ■ 2010: 2009 levels ■ 2011–20: reduce by 2 percent per year ■ 2021–50: reduce by 5 percent per year ■ 2050: 80 percent below 1990 levels Long term: no targets
Allowance allocation	The president determines allocation/auction split	The president determines allocation/auction split
Offset provisions	■ Banking permitted and no specific provision on borrowing ■ Offsets generated from biological sequestration	■ No explicit provision on use of domestic and international offsets ■ Banking permitted and no specific provision on borrowing
Technology incentives	■ Funds and incentives for technology R&D, consumer impacts, and adaptation ■ Standards for vehicles, efficiency, and renewables	■ Standards for vehicles, efficiency, and renewables
Other key provisions	■ Establishes a Climate Reinvestment Fund and a national Climate Change Vulnerability and Resilience Program ■ Periodic evaluations	■ Establishes a Climate Reinvestment Fund and Renewable Portfolio Standards ■ Periodic evaluations

Table 1A.1   Major climate change bills of the 110th Congress (without competitiveness provisions) *(continued)*

	S 280 (related to HR 620): Climate Stewardship and Innovation Act	S 317: Electric Utility Cap and Trade Act
Sponsor	Senators Joseph Lieberman and John McCain	Senators Diane Feinstein and Tom Carper
Status in Congress	Introduced on January 12, 2007	Introduced on January 17, 2007
Scope	■ All six greenhouse gases econo-mywide ■ Upstream for transportation sector; downstream for electric utilities and large sources[a]	All six greenhouses, electricity sector cap (only power plants)
First year of emissions cap	2012	2011
Emissions reduction targets	Mandatory caps ■ 2012: 2004 level ■ 2020: 1990 level ■ 2030: 20 percent below 1990 level ■ 2050: 60 percent below 1990 level Long term: no targets	Mandatory caps ■ 2014: 2006 levels ■ 2015: 2001 levels ■ 2016–20: reduce by 1 percent per year ■ After 2020: reduce by 1.5 percent per year Long term: no targets
Allowance allocation	Administrator determines allocation/auction split	■ 85 percent free to industry, based on generation (updated annually), and phased out by 2036
Offset provisions	■ 30 percent limit on use of international credits and domestic reduction or sequestration offsets ■ Borrowing for five-year periods with interest; banking permitted	■ International offsets up to 25 percent of cap ■ Extensive domestic biological offsets ■ Banking and limited borrowing of allowances permitted
Technology incentives	■ Funds for research and development (R&D) on advanced coal, renewable electricity, energy efficiency, advanced technology vehicles, etc. ■ Incentives for mitigating impact on poor	■ Funds for technology programs, including a low-carbon technologies program; a clean coal technologies program; and an energy efficiency technology program ■ Funds for adaptation and mitigation activities
Other key provisions	■ Establishes a Climate Change Credit Corporation to reduce costs to consumers and a Climate Technology Financing Board ■ Periodic evaluations to determine whether emissions targets are adequate	■ Establishes a Climate Science Advisory Panel; a safe climate level; and a Climate Action Trust Fund to carry out this act ■ Periodic evaluations

(table continues on next page)

Table 1A.1   Major climate change bills of the 110th Congress (without competitiveness provisions) *(continued)*

	S 309: Global Warming Pollution Reduction Act
Sponsor	Senators Bernard Sanders and Barbara Boxer
Status in Congress	Introduced on January 16, 2007
Scope	All six greenhouse gases economywide
First year of emissions cap	2010
Emissions reduction targets	Mandatory caps ■ 2010–20: reduce by 2 percent per year to 1990 level ■ 2030: 27 percent below 1990 level ■ 2040: 53 percent below 1990 level ■ 2050: 80 percent below 1990 level Long term: stable at 450 ppm
Allowance allocation	■ Cap and trade permitted but not required ■ Allocation criteria include transition assistance and consumer impacts
Offset provisions	■ No limit on use of domestic biological sequestration ■ No specific provisions on borrowing and banking
Technology incentives	■ Funds for R&D on geologic sequestration ■ Standards for vehicles, power plants, efficiency, renewables, and bio sequestration
Other key provisions	■ Establishes a task force on international clean, low-carbon energy cooperation; a renewable portfolio standard and credit program; and a new low-carbon generation requirement and trading program ■ Periodic evaluations

a. An upstream approach is the one that requires fuel producers to submit allowances or pay a tax for emissions attributable to their products. By contrast, a downstream approach requires the final emission source (e.g., a manufacturing firm) to submit allowances or pay a tax.

Sources: Pew Center on Global Climate Change, "Economy-wide Cap-and-Trade Proposals in the 110th Congress as of October 20, 2008" (available at www.pewclimate.org); Resources for the Future, "Summary of Market-Based Climate Change Bills Introduced in the 110th Congress" (available at www.rff.org); Lieberman and Beach (2007); GovTrack website (www.govtrack.us); Congressional Research Service (2008). All websites accessed on January 12, 2009.

Table 1A.2   Major climate change bills of the 110th Congress (with competitiveness provisions)

	S 1766: Low Carbon Economy Act	HR 6316: Climate Matters Act of 2008
Sponsor	Senators Jeff Bingaman and Arlen Specter	Representative Lloyd Doggett
Status in Congress	Introduced on July 11, 2007	Introduced on June 19, 2008
Scope	▪ All six greenhouse gases economywide ▪ Upstream for natural gas and petroleum; downstream for coal	▪ All six greenhouse gases economywide ▪ Upstream for transport fuels and natural gas; downstream for large sources and large coal users
First year of emissions cap	2012	2012
Emissions reduction targets	Mandatory caps ▪ 2012: 2012 level ▪ 2020: 2006 level ▪ 2030: 1990 level	Mandatory caps ▪ 2012: 2012 level ▪ 2020: 1990 level ▪ 2050: 80 percent below 1990 level
Allowance allocation	▪ Increasing use of auctions: 24 percent from 2012–17, rising to 53 percent in 2030 ▪ Sector allocations are specified, including 9 percent to states, 53 percent to industry, declining 2 percent per year starting in 2017 ▪ 5 percent set-aside of allowances for agriculture	▪ Increases use of auctions: 85 percent at beginning and rising to 100 percent in 2020 ▪ Beginning in 2012, 5 percent of allowances to power plants and 10 percent to energy intensive manufacturers, phased out by 2020
Offset provisions	▪ President may implement use of international offsets subject to 10 percent limit ▪ $12 per ton of CO_2 equivalent "technology accelerator payment" starting in 2012 and increasing 5 percent per year above inflation ▪ Banking permitted and no specific provision on borrowing	▪ Limits on use of offsets: 10 percent domestic offsets; 15 percent international allowances; and 15 percent international forest allowances ▪ Banking permitted; the Carbon Market Efficiency Board may permit borrowing
Technology incentives	▪ Bonus allocation for carbon capture and storage ▪ Funds and incentives for research and development (R&D)	▪ Funds for energy efficiency and transportation

(table continues on next page)

Table 1A.2   Major climate change bills of the 110th Congress (with competitiveness provisions) *(continued)*

Other key provisions	■ Establishes an Energy Technology Deployment Fund; a Climate Adaptation Fund; and an Energy Assistance Fund ■ Periodic evaluations	■ Amends the Internal Revenue Code to establish a system for accounting of greenhouse gas emission allowances ■ Establishes a Carbon Market Efficiency Board to analyze information on the greenhouse gas emission allowance market ■ Establishes the Deficit Reduction Trust Fund and the Citizen Protection Trust Fund
Competitiveness provisions	■ Establishes an interagency group to review comparable action by foreign countries with respect to greenhouse gas emissions ■ Beginning in 2019, requires a US importer of greenhouse gas–intensive goods from a country that does not take comparable emission reduction action to buy these allowances, unless the importer proves a sufficient number of "international reserve allowances" (denominated in units of metric tons of CO_2 equivalent), or the importer shows that the goods are not subject to the program	■ Directs the Secretary of the Treasury to establishes an International Reserve Allowance Program and requires a US importer of greenhouse gas intensive goods to buy and submit required amount of allowances ■ Establishes the International Climate Change Commission to determine annually whether a World Trade Organization (WTO) participant country has taken certain action to limit its greenhouse gas emissions ■ Under the international reserve allowance program, allowance sales proceeds shall be used to mitigate the negative impacts of global change on disadvantaged communities in WTO participant countries

	HR 2069: Save Our Climate Act	**HR 3416: America's Energy Security Trust Fund Act**
Sponsor	Representative Fortney Pete Stark	Representative John Larson
Status in Congress	Introduced on April 26, 2007	Introduced on August 3, 2007
Scope	Economywide tax: fossil fuels taxed by CO_2 content at the point of production and import	Economywide tax: fossil fuels taxed by CO_2 content at the point of production and import
Emissions regulations	■ Amends the Internal Revenue Code to impose a tax on primary fossil fuels based on their carbon content ■ Imposes carbon tax at $10 per ton of carbon content when the fuel is either extracted or imported ■ The tax would increase $10 per ton every year until the Energy Department and Internal Revenue Service determine that US emissions of CO2 have dropped 80 percent from 1990 levels	■ Amends the Internal Revenue Code to impose an excise tax on any taxable carbon substance sold by a manufacturer, producer, or importer ■ Imposes taxes at $15 per ton in its first year for every ton of carbon dioxide emissions from the oil, gas, and coal industries, with the tax rising 10 percent annually faster than the cost of living adjustment each year

Table 1A.2 Major climate change bills of the 110th Congress (with competitiveness provisions) *(continued)*

Allowance allocation	100 percent revenue to US Treasury	1/6 of revenues to R&D, 1/12 to industry transition assistance with phase-out, remainder to payroll tax rebates
Offset provisions	Tax refunds for fuel CO_2 sequestered downstream: carbon capture and storage[a] or used to make plastics	Tax refunds for domestic sequestration and HFC destruction projects
Technology incentives	No provisions	1/5 of tax revenues up to $10 billion annually goes to clean technology R&D
Other key provisions	No provisions	Creates a trust fund (known as America's Energy Security Trust Fund) in the Treasury
Competitiveness provisions	■ Imposes equivalent taxes on imported products ■ No tax shall be imposed on the sale by the manufacturer or producer of any taxable fuel for export	■ Imposes equivalent taxes on imported products ■ No tax shall be imposed on the sale by the manufacturer or producer of any taxable fuel for export

	S 3036: Lieberman-Warner Climate Security Act of 2008	Discussion Draft: Dingell-Boucher Bill (as released on October 7, 2008)
Sponsor	Senator Barbara Boxer	Representatives John Dingell and Richard Boucher
Status in Congress	■ Introduced in the Senate on May 20, 2008 ■ Replaced S 2191: S 2191 was introduced on October 18, 2007 and the version was passed by the Senate Environment & Public Works Committee on December 5, 2007 ■ Cloture motion on the Boxer substitute was rejected on June 6, 2008	■ A discussion draft released on October 7, 2008
Scope	■ All six greenhouse gases economy-mywide ■ Upstream for transport fuels and natural gas; downstream for large coal users; separate cap for hydrofluorocarbons (HFC) consumption	■ All six greenhouse gases plus NF_3, economywide ■ Upstream for transport fuels and natural gas; downstream for electric utilities and large sources
First year of emissions cap	2012	Not specified
Emissions reduction targets	Mandatory caps ■ 2012: 4 percent below 2005 level ■ 2020: 19 percent below 2005 level ■ 2050: 71 percent below 2005 level	Mandatory caps ■ 2020: 6 percent below 2005 level ■ 2030: 44 percent below 2005 level ■ 2050: 80 percent below 2005 level

(table continues on next page)

Table 1A.2 Major climate change bills of the 110th Congress (with competitiveness provisions) *(continued)*

Allowance allocation	■ Increasing use of auctions: 24.5 percent in 2012 (includes 5 percent early auction), rising to 58.8 percent from 2032–50 ■ Free allowances totaling 75.5 percent in 2012 are specified, including 18 percent to power plants and 11 percent to manufacturers (both transition to zero in 2031), 12.75 percent to electricity and natural gas local distribution companies for consumers, and 15 percent to states ■ 4.25 percent set-aside of allowances for domestic agriculture and forestry	Four options for allocating allowance value: 1) most value to regulated entities; 2) less value to regulated entities and more value to complementary greenhouse gas reduction programs; 3) some value to adaptation and international programs; 4) most value to consumer rebates
Offset provisions	■ International offsets up to 15 percent and domestic offsets up to 15 percent ■ Banking permitted and borrowing up to 15 percent per company	■ Increasing use of offsets, including both domestic and international offsets: 5 percent initially, rising to 35 percent by 2024 ■ Borrowing up to 15 percent per company
Technology incentives	■ Funds and incentives for zero- or low-carbon energy technologies, advanced coal and sequestration technologies, production of fuel from cellulosic biomass, advanced technology vehicle manufacturing, and sustainable energy	■ Funds for energy efficiency and clean technologies, including carbon capture and storage and renewables
Other key provisions	■ Establishes a domestic offset program to sequester greenhouse gases, the Bonus Allowance Account for carbon capture and sequestration projects; the Carbon Market Efficiency Board; Climate Change Credit; and the Deficit Reduction Fund ■ Establishes and provides for the deposit of auction proceeds to and allocations from the (1) Energy Assistance Fund; (2) Climate Change Worker Training Fund; (3) Adaptation Fund; (4) Climate Change and National Security Fund; (5) Bureau of Land Management Emergency Firefighting Fund; (6) Forest Service Emergency Firefighting Fund; and (7) Climate Security Act Management Fund ■ Performance and targets subject to three-year National Academy of Sciences review	■ Establishes Bonus Allowance Accounts for carbon capture and storage, renewables projects ■ Establishes a Renewable Energy Worker Training Program; an Industrial Energy Engineer Apprenticeship program to provide industrial energy efficiency expertise; and a Natural Resources Adaptation Program ■ Establishes several funds such as the Climate Change Management Fund; National Energy Efficiency Fund; Low-Income Consumer Climate Change Rebate Fund; Consumer Climate Change Rebate Fund; Supplemental Greenhouse Gas Reduction Fund; Green Jobs Fund; National Climate Change Adaptation Fund; and International Clean Technology and Adaptation Fund

Table 1A.2 Major climate change bills of the 110th Congress (with competitiveness provisions) *(continued)*

Competitiveness provisions	▪ Establishes an interagency group to review comparable action by foreign countries with respect to greenhouse gas emissions and an Interagency Climate Change Task Force ▪ Establishes an International Reserve Allowance Program during the one-year period beginning on January 1, 2019 ▪ Beginning in 2019, requires a US importer of greenhouse gas–intensive goods to buy and submit required amount of allowances. The proceeds from sales of such allowances to be used to mitigate the negative impacts of climate change on other countries' disadvantaged communities ▪ Requires a US importer to submit, in lieu of international reserve allowances issued under the section, a foreign allowance or similar compliance instrument distributed by a foreign country pursuant to a cap-and-trade program that represents a comparable action, or a foreign credit or a credit for an international offset project that the administrator has authorized ▪ Not later than January 1, 2023, and annually thereafter, the president shall prepare and submit to Congress a report that assesses the effectiveness of the applicable international reserve allowance requirements under section 6006 with respect to the covered goods of each covered foreign country	▪ Establishes an International Climate Change Commission to review comparable action by foreign countries with respect to greenhouse gas emissions, on an annual basis starting no later than 2013 ▪ Establishes an International Reserve Allowance Program ▪ Requires a US importer of covered products to buy and submit required amount of allowances, or cash, bonds or other security in an amount sufficient to cover purchase of the required amount of international reserve allowances; the proceeds from sales of such allowances to be used to mitigate the negative impacts of climate change on other countries' disadvantaged communities ▪ Requires a US importer of covered product to declare to US Customs and Border Protection either that the imported products were not produced or processed in any foreign country on the covered list, or that the imported products are subject to the international reserve allowances requirements ▪ Requires a US importer of covered product to submit, in lieu of international reserve allowances issued under the section, a foreign allowance or similar compliance instrument distributed by a foreign country

a. Carbon capture and storage refers to technologies that remove carbon from the exhaust streams of fossil fuel burning plants and store the carbon underground indefinitely.

Sources: Pew Center on Global Climate Change, "Economy-wide Cap-and-Trade Proposals in the 110th Congress as of October 20, 2008" (available at www.pewclimate.org); Resources for the Future, "Summary of Market-Based Climate Change Bills Introduced in the 110th Congress" (available at www.rff.org); Lieberman and Beach (2007); GovTrack website (www.govtrack.us); Congressional Research Service (2008). All websites accessed on January 12, 2009.

2

Overview of Applicable World Trade Organization Rules

Under the World Trade Organization (WTO), countries have great flexibility in adopting environmental regulations within their territories, but the same discretion does not apply to environment-related trade or domestic measures with transborder economic effects. Accordingly, trade and domestic measures—whether adopted to meet multilateral environmental agreement commitments or to carry out domestic policies—have the potential to conflict with WTO rules. Moreover, when greenhouse gas trade measures are mixed with mechanisms designed to alleviate the burden of emission controls on domestic firms, the possibility arises of multiple collisions with WTO law. This chapter reviews the WTO and General Agreement on Tariffs and Trade (GATT) articles that might be cited in potential disputes over the greenhouse gas trade measures now favored in congressional bills. The legal texts of key GATT articles and short summaries on environmental aspects of other WTO agreements are found in tables 2.1 and 2.2, respectively. Appendix C provides summaries of several environmental dispute cases that have arisen within the multilateral trading system.

Several GATT provisions might have a bearing on environmental trade measures. However, since they were drafted long before climate change was on the horizon, their ultimate application will depend either on negotiated clarifications (e.g., a new Code of Good WTO Practice on Greenhouse Gas Emissions Controls) or on WTO Appellate Body decisions when one member's environmental controls are contested by other members. The case law does not create a landscape of "anything goes," provided only that the measure purports to address climate change. Hence, US emission controls, based either on carbon taxes or on cap-and-trade systems, may

Table 2.1   Articles applicable to environmental issues in the General Agreements on Tariffs and Trade (GATT) and on Trade in Services (GATS)

Article	Text language
GATT Article I:1 General Most Favored Nation Treatment	"1. With respect to customs duties and charges of any kind imposed on or in connection with importation or exportation or imposed on the international transfer of payments for imports or exports, and with respect to the method of levying such duties and charges, and with respect to all rules and formalities in connection with importation and exportation, and with respect to all matters referred to in paragraphs 2 and 4 of Article III, any advantage, favour, privilege or immunity granted by any contracting party to any product originating in or destined for any other country shall be accorded immediately and unconditionally to the like product originating in or destined for the territories of all other contracting parties...."

GATT Article II:1 (a), (b), and 2(a) Schedules of Concessions	"1. (a) Each contracting party shall accord to the commerce of the other contracting parties treatment no less favourable than that provided for in the appropriate Part of the appropriate Schedule annexed to this Agreement.
	    (b) The products described in Part I of the Schedule relating to any contracting party, which are the products of territories of other contracting parties, shall, on their importation into the territory to which the Schedule relates, and subject to the terms, conditions or qualifications set forth in that Schedule, be exempt from ordinary customs duties in excess of those set forth and provided therein. Such products shall also be exempt from all other duties or charges of any kind imposed on or in connection with the importation in excess of those imposed on the date of this Agreement or those directly and mandatorily required to be imposed thereafter by legislation in force in the importing territory on that date.
	2. Nothing in this Article shall prevent any contracting party from imposing at any time on the importation of any product:
	    (a) a charge equivalent to an internal tax imposed consistently with the provisions of paragraph 2 of Article III in respect of the like domestic product or in respect of an article from which the imported product has been manufactured or produced in whole or in part...."

GATT Article III:1, 2, and 4 National Treatment on Internal Taxation and Regulation	"1. The contracting parties recognize that internal taxes and other internal charges, and laws, regulations and requirements affecting the internal sale, offering for sale, purchase, transportation, distribution or use of products, and internal quantitative regulations requiring the mixture, processing or use of products in specified amounts or proportions, should not be applied to imported or domestic products so as to afford protection to domestic production. 2. The products of the territory of any contracting party imported into the territory of any other contracting party shall not be subject, directly or indirectly, to internal taxes or other internal charges of any kind in excess of those applied, directly or indirectly, to like domestic products. Moreover, no contracting party shall otherwise apply internal taxes or other internal charges to imported or domestic products in a manner contrary to the principles set forth in paragraph 1. (See also the Ad Note.)"

Table 2.1   Articles applicable to environmental issues in the General Agreements on Tariffs and Trade (GATT) and on Trade in Services (GATS) *(continued)*

	4. The products of the territory of any contracting party imported into the territory of any other contracting party shall be accorded treatment no less favourable than that accorded to like products of national origin in respect of all laws, regulations and requirements affecting their internal sale, offering for sale, purchase, transportation, distribution or use. The provisions of this paragraph shall not prevent the application of differential internal transportation charges which are based exclusively on the economic operation of the means of transport and not on the nationality of the product...."
GATT Article XI:1 and 2(a), (b), and (c) General Elimination of Quantitative Restrictions	"1. No prohibitions or restrictions other than duties, taxes or other charges, whether made effective through quotas, import or export licences or other measures, shall be instituted or maintained by any contracting party on the importation of any product of the territory of any other contracting party or on the exportation or sale for export of any product destined for the territory of any other contracting party. 2. The provisions of paragraph 1 of this Article shall not extend to the following: (a) Export prohibitions or restrictions temporarily applied to prevent or relieve critical shortages of foodstuffs or other products essential to the exporting contracting party; (b) Import and export prohibitions or restrictions necessary to the application of standards or regulations for the classification, grading or marketing of commodities in international trade; (c) Import restrictions on any agricultural or fisheries product, imported in any form, necessary to the enforcement of governmental measures which operate...."
GATT Article XX:(b) and (g) General Exceptions	"Subject to the requirement that such measures are not applied in a manner which would constitute a means of arbitrary or unjustifiable discrimination between countries where the same conditions prevail, or a disguised restriction on international trade, nothing in this Agreement shall be construed to prevent the adoption or enforcement by any contracting party of measures: "...(b) necessary to protect human, animal or plant life or health; "...(g) relating to the conservation of exhaustible natural resources if such measures are made effective in conjunction with restrictions on domestic production or consumption;...."
GATS Article XIV: General Exceptions	"Subject to the requirement that such measures are not applied in a manner which would constitute a means of arbitrary or unjustifiable discrimination between countries where like conditions prevail, or a disguised restriction on trade in services, nothing in this Agreement shall be construed to prevent the adoption or enforcement by any Member of measures; "...(b) necessary to protect human, animal or plant life or health;...."

Source: World Trade Organization, www.wto.org (accessed on January 12, 2009).

Table 2.2   Environmental aspects of other WTO agreements

Agreement	Contents
Agreement on Technical Barriers to Trade (TBT)	The TBT agreement supervises the application of governmental regulations and voluntary standards to imported products. Such measures are not to be more trade restrictive than necessary to fulfill a legitimate objective. The agreement lists the protection of the environment as a legitimate objective. In addition, the agreement requires that regulations be based on international standards except when such standards would be an ineffective or inappropriate means for the fulfillment of the legitimate objective pursued. Another part of the TBT agreement supervises conformity assessment practices. (The TBT agreement does not apply to SPS measures.)
Agreement on the Application of Sanitary and Phytosanitary Measures (SPS)	The SPS agreement supervises measures aimed at protecting humans, animals, or plants (inside the importing country) from listed risks, mainly food safety and shielding animals and plants from diseases and insect pests. A WTO member government is permitted to set its own appropriate level of health protection subject to a requirement on internal consistency unless different levels of protection are arbitrary and lead to a disguised restriction on trade. The measure that a government proposes to use to achieve its level of protection is subject to several disciplines, including that the measure not be more trade restrictive than necessary to achieve the chosen level of health protection and that the measure be based on scientific principles. Another discipline provides that an SPS measure applying to imports has to be based on a risk assessment that may include ecological and environmental conditions.
Agreement on Trade-Related Aspects of Intellectual Property Rights (TRIPS)	The TRIPS agreement requires that nationals of WTO member countries be accorded the intellectual property rights listed in the agreement. The TRIPS agreement has implications for the environment in several respects, including technology transfer and patenting of biodiversity. The agreement provides that WTO members may exclude inventions from patentability when necessary to avoid serious prejudice to the environment.
Agreement on Subsidies and Countervailing Measures (ASCM)	The SCM agreement supervises the use of subsidies. Export subsidies are prohibited per se, and other subsidies are prohibited if they cause serious prejudice to other countries. The agreement also contains disciplines on the use of countervailing measures. As originally negotiated, the agreement provided that certain subsidies to promote the adaptation of existing facilities to new environmental requirements would be nonactionable. These public policy carve-outs for nonactionable subsidies expired at the end of 1999.
General Agreement on Trade in Services (GATS)	The GATS supervises domestic measures that affect international trade in services. The GATS contains a general exception for measures necessary to protect human, animal, or plant life or health but does not contain an exception for the conservation of natural resources. Although the GATS recognizes that subsidies may have a distortive effect on services, the GATS does not contain disciplines on subsidies.
Agreement on Agriculture (AoA)	The AoA agreement seeks to reform trade in agricultural products and provide a basis for market-oriented policies by disciplining subsidies and quantitative restrictions. In its preamble, the agreement takes note of food security objectives and the need to protect the environment. The agreement recognizes the right of members to adopt domestic support measures with minimal impact on trade (known as "green box" policies and listed in Annex 2). Many environmental measures might qualify as "green box" supports.

Source: World Trade Organization, www.wto.org (accessed on January 12, 2009).

well spark conflicts in the WTO system with respect to how the measures affect international trade.

National Treatment

The principle of national treatment in GATT Article III holds that an imported product is to be treated no less favorably than a like domestic product. This purpose is carried out in two principal provisions: the first sentence of Article III:2 with respect to internal taxes or charges on products, and Article III:4 with respect to taxes and regulations not covered by Article III:2. The Appellate Body has explained that the broad and fundamental purpose of Article III is to avoid protectionism in the application of internal tax and regulatory measures. Article III covers taxes and regulations applied both within borders and at the time of importation. Although Articles III:2 and III:4 are parallel provisions and share some common jurisprudence, it should be noted that the term "like" is interpreted differently in the two provisions. Furthermore, an imported product may be treated less favorably than a like domestic product if the imported product is priced at a level that qualifies as "dumping" under GATT Article VI and the WTO Antidumping Agreement.

First Sentence of GATT Article III:2

The first sentence of GATT Article III:2[1] states: "The products of the territory of any contracting party imported into the territory of any other contracting party shall not be subject, directly or indirectly, to internal taxes or other internal charges of any kind in excess of those applied, directly or indirectly, to like domestic products." As interpreted by the *Argentina— Hides and Leather* panel, for an infringement of this provision, there must be an affirmative conclusion as to three matters: (1) that the measure is the type of tax or charge covered, (2) that the taxed imported and domestic products are "like," and (3) that the imported product is taxed in excess of the like domestic product.[2] In the *Japan—Alcohol* case, the Appellate Body explained that when doing "like" product comparisons, the term "like" should be "construed narrowly" and that the factual information used could include the product's end use in a given market, consumers' tastes and habits in the importing country, and the product's properties, nature,

---

1. An additional discipline exists in the second sentence of GATT Article III:2, but it is not discussed here as it would seem to have little applicability to climate change measures.

2. Panel Report, *Argentina—Measures Affecting the Export of Bovine Hides and the Import of Finished Leather*, WT/DS155/R, adopted on February 16, 2001, paragraph 11.131. The panel also explained that a comparison has to be made of the "actual tax burdens" imposed on the import and the like domestic product (paragraph 11.184).

and quality, and tariff classification.[3] With regard to the meaning of "excess," the Appellate Body held that even the smallest amount of excess is too much and that a complainant need not show trade impact of the higher taxation nor a protective purpose. The scope of the first sentence of Article III:2 covers not only taxes but also "other internal charges of any kind," including those collected at the border. In *Argentina—Hides and Leather*, the panel explained that a "charge" involves a "pecuniary burden" and a "liability to pay money laid on a person."[4] In *China—Auto Parts*, the Appellate Body held that Article III:2 covers charges imposed on goods that have already been imported, with the obligation to pay triggered by something that takes place within the customs territory.[5]

GATT Article III:4

GATT Article III:4 states: "The products of the territory of any contracting party imported into the territory of any other contracting party shall be accorded treatment no less favourable than that accorded to like products of national origin in respect of all laws, regulations and requirements affecting their internal sale, offering for sale, purchase, transportation, distribution or use." In the *European Communities (EC)—Asbestos* case, the Appellate Body explained that "like" in Article III:4 has a "relatively broad product scope" and is broader than "like" in the first sentence of Article III:2. Moreover, the likeness test is fundamentally a determination of the nature and extent of a competitive relationship in the marketplace between imported and domestic products.[6] The factors to be considered by a panel are the same as those in Article III:2, although this is not a closed list. Panels are to determine whether the evidence, as a whole, indicates that the products are "like." In *Asbestos*, the Appellate Body reversed the panel for having excluded the health risks associated with asbestos from its examination of the physical properties of the product. In the first compliance review in *United States—Foreign Sales Corporations*, the panel was considering an income tax exemption linked to a minimum amount of US origin for goods and services purchased by firms benefiting from the tax exemption. The panel ruled that, with a measure of general application that applies horizontally and is "solely and explicitly based on origin,"

---

3. Appellate Body Report, *Japan—Taxes on Alcoholic Beverages*, WT/DS8,10,11/AB/R, adopted on November 1, 1996, 20–21.

4. Panel Report, *Argentina—Hides and Leather*, paragraph 11.143.

5. Appellate Body Report, *China—Measures Affecting Imports of Automobile Parts*, WT/DS339,340,342/AB/R, adopted on January 12, 2009, paragraph 161, 171.

6. Appellate Body Report, *European Communities—Measures Affecting Asbestos and Asbestos-Containing Products*, WT/DS135/AB/R, adopted on April 5, 2001, paragraphs 98–100, 103.

the "like products" element was satisfied.[7] As a result of this ruling, the US attempt at compliance was found to be unsatisfactory because it discriminated against foreign origin goods.

The word "affecting" in GATT Article III:4 was interpreted by the Appellate Body in the *United States—Foreign Sales Corporations* first compliance review. The Appellate Body explained that "affecting" serves to define the scope of Article III:4 and operates as a link between the identified types of government actions covered by this rule ("laws, regulations and requirements") and the specific transactions, activities, and uses relating to products in the marketplace ("internal sale, offering for sale, purchase, transportation, distribution or use"). In view of that function, the Appellate Body held that the word "affecting" has a "broad scope of application."[8]

The meaning of "no less favorable treatment" has been explicated in several cases. In *Korea—Beef*, the Appellate Body explained that less favorable treatment is detected by considering whether the fundamental thrust of the measure is that it "modifies the conditions of competition in the relevant market to the detriment of imported products.[9] In the *Dominican Republic—Import and Sales of Cigarettes* case, the Appellate Body explained that "a detrimental effect on a given imported product resulting from a measure does not necessarily imply that the measure accords less favourable treatment to imports if the detrimental effect is explained by factors or circumstances unrelated to the foreign origin of the product...."[10] In *European Communities—Asbestos*, the Appellate Body noted that a government may draw distinctions between products that have been found to be "like" without, for this reason alone, according the group of "like" imported products less favorable treatment than accorded to "like" domestic products.[11] In the first compliance review of the *United States—Foreign Sales Corporations* case, the Appellate Body explained that an adjudication of Article III:4 must be founded on a careful analysis of the contested measure and of its implications in the marketplace. The Appellate Body cautioned, however, that such an analysis did not need to be based on the

---

7. Panel Report, *United States—Tax Treatment for Foreign Sales Corporations*, Recourse to Article 21.5 of the Dispute Settlement Understanding (DSU) procedures by the European Communities, WT/DS108/RW, adopted on January 29, 2002, paragraphs 8.133–8.135.

8. Appellate Body Report, *United States—Tax Treatment for Foreign Sales Corporations*, Recourse to Article 21.5 of the DSU procedures by the European Communities, WT/DS108/AB/RW, adopted on January 29, 2002, paragraph 210.

9. Appellate Body Report, *Korea—Measures Affecting Imports of Fresh, Chilled and Frozen Beef*, WT/DS161,169/AB/R, adopted on January 10, 2001, paragraphs 137, 142.

10. Appellate Body Report, *Dominican Republic—Measures Affecting the Importation and Internal Sale of Cigarettes*, WT/DS302/AB/R, adopted on May 19, 2005, paragraph 96.

11. Appellate Body Report, *European Communities—Asbestos*, paragraph 100.

actual effects in the marketplace.[12] In the *Dominican Republic—Import and Sales of Cigarettes* case, the panel agreed that the tax stamp requirement at issue provided formally identical treatment between domestic and imported cigarettes. Nevertheless, the panel found less favorable treatment for imports because importers had additional processes and costs.[13]

Domestic Subsidies and National Treatment

Under GATT Article III:8(b), the prohibitions in GATT Article III do not apply to payments of subsidies "exclusively to domestic producers, including payments to domestic producers derived from the proceeds of internal taxes or charges applied consistently with the provisions" of Article III.[14] For example, in the *European Communities—Commercial Vessels* case, the panel found that a shipbuilding subsidy given to domestic ship producers but not to foreign producers was precisely the kind of different treatment that is allowed by Article III:8(b), and thus not inconsistent with Article III.[15] In the *Canada—Periodicals* case, the Appellate Body ruled that Article III: 8(b) only covers the payment of subsidies that involve "the expenditure of revenue by a government" and suggested that a reduction in government fees or tax preferences would not be covered by this provision.[16]

Charges Equivalent to Internal Taxes Applied to Imports

GATT Article II:1(a) and (b) contain the core disciplines in the GATT on the imposition of ordinary customs duties. In addition, Article II:1(b) prohibits the imposition of newly applied charges (on items having bound tariffs) by extending the coverage to "all other duties or charges of any kind imposed "on or in connection with" importation.[17] The scope of Article II is limited, however, by Article II:2(a), which states that nothing in the

---

12. Appellate Body Report, *United States—Foreign Sales Corporations* (Article 21.5–EC), paragraph 215.

13. Panel Report, *Dominican Republic—Measures Affecting the Importation and Internal Sale of Cigarettes*, WT/DS302/R, adopted on May 19, 2005, paragraph 7.196. This was an instance of de facto discrimination.

14. GATT Article III:8(b). The meaning of "domestic producers" in terms of corporate ownership and control has not been clarified in GATT/WTO dispute settlement.

15. Panel Report, *European Communities—Measures Affecting Trade in Commercial Vessels*, WT/DS301/R, adopted on June 20, 2005, paragraph 7.69. Domestic in this context appears to mean corporate location rather than nationality.

16. Appellate Body Report, *Canada—Certain Measures Concerning Periodicals*, WT/DS31/AB/R, adopted on June 30, 1997, pp. 34–35.

17. See the WTO Understanding on the Interpretation of Article II:1(b) of the GATT, 1994.

article shall prevent a government from imposing at any time on the importation of any product "a charge equivalent to an internal tax imposed consistently with the provisions of paragraph 2 of Article III in respect of the like domestic product or in respect of an article from which the imported product has been manufactured or produced in whole or in part." Little WTO case law exists on the meaning of Article II:2(a). In *Chile—Price Band System*, the Appellate Body opined that "charges equivalent to internal taxes" are not included within the "other duties or charges" disciplined by GATT Article II:1.[18]

The only WTO case applying Article II:2(a) to charges imposed at the border is the recent case filed by the United States against India. In that dispute, the Appellate Body explained that the concept of "equivalent" in Article II:2(a) includes elements of "effect" and "amount," and that a panel needs to make a comparative assessment of the charge and the internal tax that is both qualitative and quantitative.[19] The Appellate Body also held that a charge coming within the terms of Article II:2(a) could not be in excess of the corresponding internal tax.[20] With regard to India's additional duties and extra-additional duties, the Appellate Body found that these charges could not be justified under GATT Article II:2(a) insofar as they result in the imposition of charges on imports in excess of the domestic excise, sales, value-added, and local taxes imposed on the like domestic products.

Border Tax Adjustments on Products

WTO rules allow members to adjust product taxes at the border. Governments can impose product taxes on imports and rebate these taxes on exports. Symmetry is not required: a government can choose to adjust its product taxes on imports but not on exports, or vice versa.

No one questions that border tax adjustments (BTAs) on imports are permitted by trade rules on a consumption tax imposed on a product, such as a sales tax, or an environmental tax imposed directly on a product. But the potential adjustability of environmental taxes levied on the producer of a product—for example, a tax on the energy used or the pollution emitted—remains an uncertain and debated issue in trade law.

The role of BTA in the trading system was examined in a GATT Working Party on Border Tax Adjustments, whose report was adopted in 1970. The working party defined BTAs as fiscal measures that enable exported

---

18. Appellate Body Report, *Chile—Price Band System and Safeguard Measures Relating to Certain Agricultural Products*, WT/DS207/AB/R, adopted on October 23, 2002, paragraph 276.

19. Appellate Body Report, *India—Additional and Extra-Additional Duties on Imports from the United States*, WT/DS360/AB/R, adopted on November 17, 2008, paragraphs 172, 175.

20. Appellate Body Report, *India—Additional Import Duties*, paragraph 180.

products to be relieved of some or all of the tax charged in the exporting country with respect to similar domestic products and that enable imported products sold to consumers to be charged with some or all of the tax charged in the importing country with respect to similar domestic products.[21]

The working party report is an unusual GATT-era report in that it expresses positions on matters of consensus and on matters on which there were differences of opinion. For example, the report states that most delegations agreed that the philosophy behind BTAs is to ensure "trade neutrality."[22] The report also states: "It was agreed that GATT provisions on tax adjustment applied the principle of destination identically to imports and exports" and that the GATT rules "set maxima limits for adjustment (compensation) which were not to be exceeded," but below which governments were "free to differentiate in the degree of compensation applied."[23] In addition, the report states that some delegations believed that "GATT provisions on tax adjustment did not provide for any form of protection but rather for the possibility for governments to create equality in treatment between imported and domestically-produced goods."[24]

With regard to eligibility for BTAs, the report states that there was a "convergence of views to the effect that taxes directly levied on products were eligible for tax adjustment," and it was "agreed in principle that for composite goods, it was administratively sensible and sufficiently accurate to give export rebates by average rates for a given class of goods."[25] There was also a "convergence of views to the effect that certain taxes that were not directly levied on products were not eligible for tax adjustment," with examples given of social security charges.[26] For taxes in between, the working party reported that there was a "divergence of views." One example of such taxes were so-called taxes occultes, and several such taxes

---

21. Working Party Report, *Border Tax Adjustments*, BISD 18S/97, adopted on December 2, 1970, paragraph 4. The definition came from the Organization for Economic Cooperation and Development (OECD). The GATT report is available at www.worldtradelaw.net (accessed on January 12, 2009).

22. Working Party Report, *Border Tax Adjustments*, paragraph 9.

23. Working Party Report, *Border Tax Adjustments*, paragraphs 10–11. The supposed symmetry between tax adjustments on imports and exports, stated in the report, is no longer required by the GATT, even if it was accepted practice in 1970. Under the destination principle, indirect taxes on goods that move in international trade are levied by the country of destination and are remitted by the country of exportation.

24. Working Party Report, *Border Tax Adjustments*, paragraph 13.

25. Working Party Report, *Border Tax Adjustments*, paragraphs 14, 16. The report also noted that some taxes, such as cascade taxes, which were generally considered eligible for adjustment, presented a problem because of the difficulty in tracing exactly the amount embodied in the final products.

26. Working Party Report, *Border Tax Adjustments*, paragraph 14.

were listed, among them taxes on "energy" and "transportation."[27] This means that in 1970 GATT law was unclear as to whether an adjustment at the border for energy taxes was permitted.

The rules for BTAs on imports are found in GATT Articles II and III, which were discussed above. With respect to BTAs on imports, the most important trade law case on BTAs was the GATT case of 1987, *United States—Taxes on Petroleum and Certain Imported Substances (Superfund)*.[28] In that dispute, the United States was imposing a tax on imported substances made from specific chemicals that were subject to US tax. In principle, the amount of tax on imported substances was set equal to the amount of US tax that would have been imposed on incorporated chemicals if those chemicals had been sold in the United States. The United States defended this tax before the GATT panel as a BTA fully consistent with GATT Articles II:2(a) and III:2. The panel agreed with the United States but expressed concern about a provision in the US Superfund Act that would permit an additional tax on imports when the importer fails to furnish necessary information. The panel suggested that this penalty provision would violate Article III:2 if it were actually imposed.

The European Economic Community had challenged the tax on imported substances as a violation of GATT because, according to them, the environmental tax conflicted with the OECD's "polluter-pays principle" when applied to imports, since the pollution created in the production of the imported substances did not occur in the United States. The panel ruled that the purpose of the tax was not relevant in determining whether the tax complied with GATT rules. The panel also noted that the GATT rules did not oblige the United States to impose a border adjustment on the imported product, but that the United States was free to do so.

With respect to BTAs on exports, the WTO rules are found in GATT Article XVI and the Agreement on Subsidies and Countervailing Measures (ASCM). The ASCM may have widened the scope for export rebates on energy taxes from what was available under the plurilateral Tokyo Round Subsidies Code (Hufbauer 1996, 49–50). The matter is not clear, however, as there is ambiguity in the ASCM.

The pertinent provisions in the ASCM are detailed in box 2.1. To un-

---

27. Working Party Report, *Border Tax Adjustments*, paragraph 15. Taxes on pollution are not specifically mentioned. No general definition of "taxes occultes" was provided by the working party; however, an OECD definition of "taxes occultes" includes taxes on capital equipment, auxiliary supplies (such as energy), and services used in the transportation and production of other taxable goods.

28. GATT Panel Report, *United States—Taxes on Petroleum and Certain Imported Substances*, BISD 34S/136, adopted on June 17, 1987. This dispute, known as the Superfund case, involved a complaint by Canada and the European Economic Community (and Mexico, in part) against the United States regarding US taxes on petroleum and certain imported substances levied under the Superfund Amendments and Reauthorization Act of 1986. The panel report is available at www.wto.org (accessed on January 12, 2009).

Box 2.1 Selected text from the Agreement on Subsidies and Countervailing Measures (ASCM)[1]

ASCM

ANNEX I

ILLUSTRATIVE LIST OF EXPORT SUBSIDIES

(e) The full or partial exemption, remission or deferral specifically related to exports, of direct taxes[58] or social welfare charges paid or payable by industrial or commercial enterprises.

(g) The exemption or remission, in respect of the production and distribution of exported products, of indirect taxes[58] in excess of those levied in respect of the production and distribution of like products when sold for domestic consumption.

(h) The exemption, remission or deferral of prior-stage cumulative indirect taxes[58] on goods or services used in the production of exported products in excess of the exemption, remission or deferral of like prior-stage cumulative indirect taxes on goods or services used in the production of like products when sold for domestic consumption; provided, however, that prior-stage cumulative indirect taxes may be exempted, remitted or deferred on exported products even when not exempted, remitted or deferred on like products when sold for domestic consumption, if the prior-stage cumulative indirect taxes are levied on inputs that are consumed in the production of the exported product (making normal allowance for waste). This item shall be interpreted in accordance with the guidelines on consumption of inputs in the production process contained in Annex II.

ANNEX II

GUIDELINES ON CONSUMPTION OF INPUTS IN THE PRODUCTION PROCESS

1. Indirect tax rebate schemes can allow for exemption, remission or deferral of prior-stage cumulative indirect taxes levied on inputs that are consumed in the production of the exported product (making normal allowance for waste)....

2. The Illustrative List of Export Subsidies in Annex I of this Agreement makes reference to the term "inputs that are consumed in the production of the exported product" in paragraphs (h) and (i). Pursuant to paragraph (h), indirect tax rebate schemes can constitute an export subsidy to the extent that they result in exemption, remission or deferral of prior-stage cumulative indirect taxes in excess of the amount of such taxes actually levied on inputs that are consumed in the production of the exported product.

**Box 2.1   Selected text from the Agreement on Subsidies and
Countervailing Measures (ASCM)** *(continued)*

Pertinent ASCM Footnotes

1. In accordance with the provisions of Article XVI of GATT 1994 (Note to Article XVI) and the provisions of Annexes I through III of this Agreement, the exemption of an exported product from duties or taxes borne by the like product when destined for domestic consumption, or the remission of such duties or taxes in amounts not in excess of those which have accrued, shall not be deemed to be a subsidy.

5. Measures referred to in Annex I as not constituting export subsidies shall not be prohibited under this or any other provision of this Agreement.

58. For the purpose of this Agreement:

    The term "direct taxes" shall mean taxes on wages, profits, interests, rents, royalties, and all other forms of income, and taxes on the ownership of real property;

    The term "import charges" shall mean tariffs, duties, and other fiscal charges not elsewhere enumerated in this note that are levied on imports;

    The term "indirect taxes" shall mean sales, excise, turnover, value added, franchise, stamp, transfer, inventory and equipment taxes, border taxes and all taxes other than direct taxes and import charges;

    "Prior-stage" indirect taxes are those levied on goods or services used directly or indirectly in making the product;

    "Cumulative" indirect taxes are multi-staged taxes levied where there is no mechanism for subsequent crediting of the tax if the goods or services subject to tax at one stage of production are used in a succeeding stage of production;

    "Remission" of taxes includes the refund or rebate of taxes.

61. Inputs consumed in the production process are inputs physically incorporated, energy, fuels and oil used in the production process and catalysts which are consumed in the course of their use to obtain the exported product.

---

1. The footnotes in the text of this box are from the ASCM itself and are explained in the subsection entitled "Pertinent ASCM Footnotes."

pack these provisions, start with ASCM footnote 1, which states that "In accordance with the provisions of Article XVI of GATT 1994 (Note to Article XVI) and the provisions of Annexes I through III of this agreement, the exemption of an exported product from duties or taxes borne by the like product when destined for domestic consumption, or the remission of such taxes in amounts not in excess of those which have accrued, shall not be deemed a subsidy [under the ASCM]." What is clear in this provision is that some policies to remit taxes on exports do not constitute subsidies, but which taxes qualify is not clear. The descriptor "taxes borne by the like product" takes us no further than the lack of conclusion reached in the 1970 Working Party on Border Tax Adjustments regarding which taxes are in fact borne by the product. But the new ASCM footnote 5 may help to clear up some of the ambiguity. That footnote states that: "Measures referred to in Annex I as not constituting export subsidies shall not be prohibited under this or any other provision of this Agreement." Thus, unlike the Tokyo Round Subsidies Code, which was an optional agreement, the ASCM Annex I may be able to resolve authoritatively that certain practices referred to as not constituting export subsidies are permitted by the ASCM.[29]

Annex I clarifies the scope of allowable BTAs through its definitions in footnote 58—definitions that do not exist in the GATT (although many of them were in the Tokyo Round Code). Indirect taxes are defined broadly to embrace specific types of taxes, including for purposes here both "excise" taxes and "border taxes," as well as "all other taxes other than direct taxes and import charges." The category of "tax occultes" is not mentioned, which raises the intriguing question of whether the authors of the ASCM assumed that "tax occultes" qualified as indirect taxes. An alternative explanation is that "taxes occultes" come within the term "import charges" as "other fiscal charges not elsewhere enumerated." Looking only at the definitions, energy taxes or pollution taxes could be either indirect taxes or fiscal charges. However, they are not direct taxes, akin to income taxes or social security charges.

The text and context of Annex I may help further to clarify the matter. Item (h) on "prior-stage cumulative indirect taxes on goods and services used in the production of exported products" provides a special rule for taxes levied on "inputs that are consumed in the production of the exported product" and refers to Annex II. Footnote 61 in Annex II defines such inputs as "inputs physically incorporated, energy, fuels and oil used in the production process and catalysts which are consumed in the course of their use to obtain the exported product."[30] Thus, item (h) would appear to

---

29. This reasoning assumes that GATT Article XVI has been superseded by the ASCM to the extent of an inconsistency.

30. ASCM, footnote 61. In that regard, it is interesting to note that the WTO Valuation Agreement recognizes "materials consumed in the production of the imported goods," and

cover taxes on energy, fuels, and oil that are used in the production process but that are *not* physically incorporated inputs. The advent of the ASCM Annex II was, of course, unknown to the 1970 Working Party on Border Tax Adjustments. Thus, the ASCM would seem to be saying that taxes on energy qualify as indirect taxes and are subject to the discipline in item (h). If so, there is an authoritative answer to the definitional uncertainty noted above as to whether energy taxes are indirect taxes or instead are fiscal charges. And the inclusion of energy taxes within indirect taxes would settle the status of energy taxes that puzzled the 1970 working party.

The inclusion of taxes on energy in ASCM Annexes I and II would therefore seem to mean that a border adjustment on energy exports is a legal possibility. We know from Annex II, paragraph 2 that an indirect tax rebate on exports would constitute an export subsidy if it were to result in a remission of "prior-stage cumulative indirect taxes in excess of the amount of such taxes actually levied on inputs that are consumed in the production process." Logically, therefore, an export rebate that exactly matches the taxes levied on inputs, such as energy consumed in the production process, would not be an export subsidy. Of course, by its own terms, item (h) applies only to "prior-stage cumulative indirect taxes."[31] The carbon taxes being proposed are not designed to be cumulative (de Cendra 2006, 140), although it may be possible to make them so. But providing energy tax rebates on exports does not depend solely on item (h). If energy taxes are indirect taxes under Annex I, then item (g) would permit the use of export BTAs on energy taxes, provided the exemption or remission does not exceed taxes levied on production and distribution for domestic use.

A counterargument against the foregoing analysis might run as follows: although energy taxes are indirect taxes, the ASCM deals with such taxes under item (h) and footnote 61 rather than item (g). Seen in that way, export rebates are only allowed under item (h) and then only for prior-stage cumulative indirect taxes and for inputs consumed in production. During the implementation of the Uruguay Round, the US government went on record suggesting that item (h) and footnote 61 were *not* meant to allow export BTAs on energy inputs (WTO 1997, paragraph 76). If the interpretation offered by the United States is correct, then one might assume that such energy BTAs were not meant to be authorized by item (g) either. The meaning of footnote 61 has been analyzed by the WTO Secre-

---

requires that the value of those materials be included in the customs value when such goods are supplied by the buyer at a reduced cost. Agreement on the Implementation of Article VII of the 1994 GATT, Article 8.1(b)(iii).

31. Note also that item (h) permits a tax exemption for exported products even when the same tax continues to be imposed on domestic products when the objects being taxed are inputs consumed in the production of the exported product. Such a tax exemption would not be a prohibited export subsidy under the ASCM, as per Article 3.1(a) and footnote 5.

tariat and the Committee on Subsidies and Countervailing Measures, but no clarity has emerged. If this question were to come before a WTO panel, little weight would probably be accorded to the unilateral US interpretation (Biermann and Brohm 2005, 297).

In summary, one could argue that the ASCM has clarified that status of energy taxes—as compared with the GATT era, when they were mysterious "taxes occultes"—and that energy taxes can now be rebated upon export. Conversely, one could also argue that the possibility for such an export rebate remains uncertain in the ASCM or that the ASCM actually prohibits energy BTAs on exports. Future WTO dispute settlement or negotiations may clarify these matters.

Most Favored Nation Treatment

The principle of most favored nation treatment in GATT Article I holds that any advantage accorded to an imported product has to be accorded to a "like" product from any WTO member country. Article I:1 states:

> With respect to customs duties and charges of any kind imposed on or in connection with importation or exportation or imposed on the international transfer of payments for imports or exports, and with respect to the method of levying such duties and charges, and with respect to all rules and formalities in connection with importation and exportation, and with respect to all matters referred to in paragraphs 2 and 4 of Article III, any advantage, favour, privilege or immunity granted by any contracting party to any product originating in or destined for any other country shall be accorded immediately and unconditionally to the like product originating in or destined for the territories of all other contracting parties.

Thus Article I applies to customs duties and charges, import and export formalities, and measures covered by Article III:2 and III:4. Note, however, that if a measure is covered by GATT Article III but is not a violation of Article III because of the domestic subsidy exclusion in GATT Article III:8(b), such a measure would not come within the discipline of GATT Article I:1.[32]

GATT Article I:1 has been explicated in several WTO disputes. In *Canada—Autos*, the Appellate Body explained that Article I:1 covers not only de jure discrimination but also de facto discrimination involving ostensibly origin-neutral measures.[33] In *European Communities—Bananas*, the Appellate Body noted approvingly the broad interpretation of "advantage" followed in pre-WTO adjudication and upheld the panel's decision that the differing rules on imports did constitute an advantage, even though competition policy considerations may have been the basis for the EC

---

32. Panel Report, *European Communities—Commercial Vessels*, paragraph 7.90.

33. Appellate Body Report, *Canada—Certain Measures Affecting the Automotive Industry*, WT/DS139,142/AB/R, adopted on June 19, 2000, paragraph 78.

Box 2.2   How GATT rules apply to border measures for climate change

- Other duties and charges on imported products   Article II:1(b)
- Charge equivalent to an internal tax   Article II:2(a)
- Internal taxes or charges on products   Article III:2
- Regulations affecting internal sale   Article III:4
- Import bans and quotas   Article XI:1

rules. In addition, the Appellate Body agreed with the panel that the initial allocation of export certificates to some countries gave those countries an advantage in violation of Article I:1.[34] In the *European Communities—Tariff Preferences* case, the panel held that the term "unconditionally" meant that the treatment is "not limited by or subject to any conditions."[35]

Quantitative Restrictions on Goods

The GATT prohibits complete import bans as well as quantitative restrictions. GATT Article XI:1 states: "No prohibitions or restrictions other than duties, taxes or other charges, whether made effective through quotas, import or export licenses or other measures, shall be instituted or maintained by any contracting party on the importation of any product of the territory of any other contracting party...." This provision interrelates with the provisions discussed above that supervise the use of duties, taxes, or other charges, as shown in box 2.2.

WTO panels have interpreted Article XI:1 broadly to include any form of import restriction. For example, in the *Korea—Beef* case, the panel found that action by the state trading agency to purchase grain-fed beef, while excluding the purchase of grass-fed beef, constituted a de facto import restriction on such purchase in violation of GATT Article XI:1.[36] In *Brazil—Tyres*, the panel held that a prohibition on the issuance of an import license violated Article XI:1.[37]

---

34. Appellate Body Report, *European Communities—Regime for the Importation, Sale, and Distribution of Bananas*, WT/DS27/AB/R, adopted on September 25, 1997, paragraphs 206–207.

35. Panel Report, *European Communities—Conditions for the Granting of Tariff Preferences to Developing Countries*, WT/DS246/R, adopted on April 20, 2004, paragraph 7.59.

36. Panel Report, *Korea—Measures Affecting Imports of Fresh, Chilled and Frozen Beef*, WT/DS161,169/R, adopted on January 10, 2001, paragraphs 774, 777.

37. Panel Report, *Brazil—Measures Affecting Imports of Retreaded Tyres*, WT/DS332/R, adopted

Domestic Regulations and the Agreement on Technical Barriers to Trade

In addition to the GATT, another WTO agreement supervising governmental regulation is the Agreement on Technical Barriers to Trade (TBT). The scope of the TBT agreement includes both mandatory and voluntary measures. Mandatory measures are termed "technical regulations" and are defined as any measure that "lays down product characteristics or their related processes and production methods."[38] In *European Communities—Asbestos*, the Appellate Body explained that product characteristics are "any objectively definable 'features,' 'qualities,' 'attributes,' or other 'distinguishing mark' of a product" and noted that they might relate, *inter alia*, to a product's "composition, size, shape, colour, texture, hardness, tensile strength, flammability, conductivity, density, or viscosity."[39] The Appellate Body also stated that product characteristics include "not only features and qualities intrinsic to the product itself, but also related 'characteristics.'"[40] But the Appellate Body did not discuss the language in the definition on "related processes and production methods." Whether the term "related" can be stretched to include the energy used in making a product is unclear.

If a regulation about the energy footprint of a product is not covered by the TBT agreement, it would be covered by GATT Articles III:4 or XI. At the time that the TBT agreement was drafted, the conventional wisdom was that it covers regulations about the physical product and does not cover regulations about the way a product is made. Whether that understanding would survive the text-oriented approach to interpretation now used in the WTO dispute settlement (which gives little consideration to negotiating history) remains to be seen.

For regulations within the scope of the TBT agreement there are a host of TBT rules. For example, TBT Article 2.3 states that "Technical regulations shall not be maintained if the circumstances or objectives giving rise to their adoption no longer exist or if the changed circumstances or objectives can be addressed in a less trade-restrictive manner." Article 2.4 requires the use of international standards in certain circumstances.[41] Article

---

on December 17, 2007, paragraph 7.15.

38. Agreement on Technical Barriers to Trade, Article 1.2 and Annex 1, paragraph 1. The TBT agreement does not apply to sanitary or phytosanitary measures (see Article 1.5).

39. Appellate Body Report, *European Communities—Asbestos*, paragraph 67.

40. Appellate Body Report, *European Communities—Asbestos*, paragraph 67.

41. It is interesting to note that there are International Organization for Standardization (ISO) standards on climate related to the quantification and reporting of greenhouse gas emissions and reductions (e.g., ISO 14064 and 14065). At present, no ISO climate standards exist for particular products or emission levels.

2.5 states that when a technical regulation is applied for one of the legitimate objectives listed in the TBT agreement, which includes the environment, and is in accord with an international standard, the measure shall be rebuttably presumed not to create an unnecessary obstacle to international trade (Howse 2006, 393–94).

General Exceptions

A measure violating any provision of the GATT can be excused if it qualifies for an exception under GATT Article XX.[42] Under the heading "General Exceptions," Article XX states in part:

> Subject to the requirement that such measures are not applied in a manner which would constitute a means of arbitrary or unjustifiable discrimination between countries where the same conditions prevail, or a disguised restriction on international trade, nothing in this Agreement shall be construed to prevent the adoption or enforcement by any contracting party of measures:...(b) necessary to protect human, animal or plant life or health;...(g) relating to the conservation of exhaustible natural resources if such measures are made effective in conjunction with restrictions on domestic production or consumption....

The Appellate Body has explained that the exceptions are "limited and conditional" and that the analysis is two-tiered.[43] A panel will look first to see whether the measure comes within the scope of one of the paragraphs in Article XX and then, if so, will consider whether the measure meets the terms of the specific exception. When a measure is provisionally justified under one of the specific exceptions, the next step for a panel will be to see if the measure meets the legal standard set forth in the chapeau of Article XX. The list of public policy purposes under Article XX is a closed list. Clearly, the list does not include measures necessary to avoid adverse competitive impact from environmental laws imposed on the domestic economy.

Fifteen years ago, there was uncertainty as to whether the GATT outlawed import bans linked to the content of another country's environmental policy (Esty 1994). Since then, the case law of the WTO has clarified that GATT rules do not necessarily preclude such environmental measures. In a central ruling in the *United States—Shrimp* case, the Appellate Body explained that "conditioning access to a Member's domestic market on whether exporting Members comply with, or adopt, a policy or policies unilaterally prescribed by the importing Member may, to some degree, be

---

42. Importantly, however, Article XX does not excuse violations of the TBT agreement.

43. Appellate Body Report, *United States—Import Prohibitions of Certain Shrimp and Shrimp Products*, WT/DS58/AB/R, adopted on November 6, 1998, paragraph 157 (emphasis deleted).

a common aspect of measures falling within the scope of one or another of the exceptions (a) to (j) of Article XX."[44] In the follow-up compliance litigation, the panel stated that the WTO agreement "does not provide for any recourse" to an exporting country in a situation where another WTO member requires "as a condition of access of certain products to its market, the exporting countries commit themselves to a regulatory program deemed comparable to its own."[45] The Appellate Body seemed comfortable with that conclusion. On the other hand, it should be noted that in the final *United States—Shrimp* ruling, the complaining country (Malaysia) had not even applied for US certification of its shrimping regulations.[46] The Appellate Body might have reached a different conclusion if Malaysia had applied to export shrimp to the United States but been turned down by the US authorities.

Article XX contains several exceptions that could be relevant to climate change, but the one most discussed is paragraph (g), which provides an exception for measures "relating to the conservation of exhaustible natural resources if such measures are made effective in conjunction with restrictions on domestic production or consumption." Whether the (g) exception fits the climate change problem is not free from doubt. Climate is being affected by many factors, but the primary one is the emission of greenhouse gases into the upper atmosphere. The policy response of reducing greenhouse gas emissions is a classic pollution control policy, not a conservation policy.[47] Speaking very narrowly, climate change policies do not seek to conserve the atmosphere itself; instead they seek to preserve a certain balance of gases within the atmosphere.

If WTO adjudicators were to hold that greenhouse gas mitigation programs do not fit the (g) exception (a surprising determination), then there could be recourse to the Article XX(b) exception for measures "necessary to protect human, animal or plant life or health" (Bhagwati and Mavroidis 2007, 308).[48] Our study, however, does not address the (b) exception because we assume that WTO adjudicators will agree that climate change can be treated as an "exhaustible natural resource" within the (g) exception. After all, in the first WTO case, *United States—Gasoline*, a case about

---

44. Appellate Body Report, *United States—Shrimp*, paragraph 121.

45. Panel Report, *United States—Import Prohibitions of Certain Shrimp and Shrimp Products*, Recourse to Article 21.5 by Malaysia, WT/DS58/RW, adopted on November 21, 2001, paragraph 5.103.

46. Panel Report, *United States—Import Prohibitions of Certain Shrimp and Shrimp Products*, paragraph 148.

47. As a stretch, climate policies might be characterized as efforts to conserve terrestrial carbon and keep it from going into the atmosphere.

48. If it were in litigation, the United States would likely invoke both the (b) and (g) exceptions.

air pollution, the panel ruled that clean air was a resource, had value, was natural, and could be depleted.[49] In *Gasoline*, the US law sought to prevent further deterioration of the level of air pollution prevailing in 1990. For a future panel to refuse to apply this precedent to climate change seems highly unlikely. In the *United States—Shrimp* case, the Appellate Body stated that the term "exhaustible natural resources" had to be "read by a treaty interpreter in the light of contemporary concerns of the community of nations about the protection and conservation of the environment."[50] Furthermore, the Appellate Body said that "natural resources" is not "static" but rather "by definition, evolutionary."[51]

That said, it is interesting to note that in the *Brazil—Tyres* case (a dispute about the health effects of waste tires), the Appellate Body interjected a discussion of climate change into its analysis of Article XX(b). Was the Appellate Body signaling something? The point made by the Appellate Body was that a measure being proposed for justification under Article XX(b) had to bring about "a material contribution to the achievement of its objective."[52] Yet for measures adopted to attenuate global warming and climate change, the Appellate Body explained that results "can only be evaluated with the benefit of time."[53] In our view, the Appellate Body did not intend to suggest that climate change had to be justified under the (b) exception in Article XX rather than the (g) exception.

Article XX(g)

Once a panel concludes that a climate measure falls within the scope of Article XX(g), the panel will consider the two prongs of the (g) exception: first, whether the measure challenged is one "relating" to conservation of exhaustible natural resources, and second, whether the measure is "made effective in conjunction with restrictions on domestic production or consumption." Important case law exists on both of these points.

Regarding the first prong, in *United States—Gasoline*, the Appellate Body held that there was a "substantial relationship" between the US measures and the goal of "conservation of clean air."[54] In *United States—*

---

49. Panel Report, *United States—Standards for Reformulated and Conventional Gasoline*, WT/DS2/R, adopted on May 20, 1996, paragraph 6.37. The Appellate Body did not review this holding but did analyze the US measure under Article XX(g) and not Article (b).

50. Appellate Body Report, *United States—Shrimp*, paragraph 129.

51. Appellate Body Report, *United States—Shrimp*, paragraph 130.

52. Appellate Body Report, *Brazil—Measures Affecting Imports of Retreaded Tyres*, WT/DS332/R, adopted on December 17, 2007, paragraph 151.

53. Appellate Body Report, *Brazil—Tyres*, paragraph 151.

54. Appellate Body Report, United States—Standards for Reformulated and Conventional

Shrimp, the Appellate Body found that the sea turtles being protected by US law were "exhaustible" and that they had "sufficient nexus" to the United States.[55] The Appellate Body then considered the relationship between the "general structure and design" of the measure and the legitimate policy of conserving natural resources.[56] The measure at issue was an import ban, and the Appellate Body saw it as being designed to influence other countries to adopt national regulatory programs requiring the use of turtle excluder devices and requiring that such programs be comparable to US programs. In examining the US measure, the Appellate Body concluded that the means used "are, in principle, reasonably related to the ends," and, therefore, the measure qualified under the first prong.[57]

The second prong is whether the measure is "made effective in conjunction with restrictions on domestic production or consumption." In *United States—Gasoline*, the Appellate Body interpreted this clause as requiring "even-handedness in the imposition of restrictions."[58] The Appellate Body further noted that the clause speaks disjunctively of "domestic production *or* consumption."[59]

Article XX Chapeau

A measure that is provisionally justified by one of the GATT Article XX exceptions is then further appraised to see whether it is consistent with the chapeau of Article XX. The chapeau states that recourse to a GATT exception for challenged measures is "[s]ubject to the requirement that such measures are not applied in a manner which would constitute a means of arbitrary or unjustifiable discrimination between countries where the same conditions prevail, or a disguised restriction on international trade." The standards in the chapeau may vary as between different paragraphs in Article XX.[60] Whatever paragraph is invoked, the burden of proof is on the defendant government.

Before discussing the chapeau, it should be noted that its norms have been internalized into the United Nations Framework Convention on Climate Change (UNFCCC). Article 3.5 of the UNFCCC states, in part, that "Measures taken to combat climate change, including unilateral ones,

---

Gasoline, WT/DS2/AB/R, adopted on May 20, 1996, p. 19.

55. Appellate Body Report, *United States—Shrimp*, paragraphs 133–134.

56. Appellate Body Report, *United States—Shrimp*, paragraph 138.

57. Appellate Body Report, *United States—Shrimp*, paragraphs 141–142.

58. Appellate Body Report, *United States—Gasoline*, p. 21 (emphasis omitted). The Appellate Body also explained that "made effective" is not a reference to an "effects test."

59. Appellate Body Report, *United States—Gasoline*, p. 21.

60. Appellate Body Report, *United States—Shrimp*, paragraph 120.

should not constitute a means of arbitrary or unjustifiable discrimination or a disguised restriction on international trade." GATT Article XX thus exemplifies the way that some fundamental norms of environmental regulation have been incorporated into the GATT through interpretation and some fundamental norms of the GATT have been incorporated into the climate regime (Runnalls 2007).

According to the Appellate Body, the function of the chapeau is to prevent abuse of the Article XX exceptions and to ensure that governments use the Article XX exceptions "in good faith."[61] Thus a measure being reviewed under the chapeau "must be applied reasonably."[62] Explaining further, the Appellate Body has stated that the task of interpreting and applying the chapeau (by panels and the Appellate Body) is a "delicate one of locating and marking out a line of equilibrium" between the rights of the WTO member invoking the exception and the rights of the member lodging the case.[63] The Appellate Body has further noted that the preamble to the WTO agreement "gives colour, texture, and shading" to the chapeau and that the preamble demonstrates a recognition by the negotiators drafting the WTO agreement that "optimal use of the world's resources should be made in accordance with the objective of sustainable development."[64] This jurisprudence suggests, and the Article XX cases confirm, that adjudicators exercise a great deal of discretion in using the chapeau to discipline national measures.

In its first case, the *United States—Gasoline* decision, the Appellate Body suggested that the chapeau addresses the manner in which the challenged measure "is applied" and not so much the measure itself or its contents.[65] The Appellate Body has repeated this principle in several cases. In *United States—Shrimp*, the Appellate Body stated that a violation of the chapeau could occur "where a measure, otherwise fair and just on its face, is actually applied in an arbitrary and unjustifiable manner."[66] The Appellate Body has suggested that "the general design and structure" of a measure are examined under an Article XX paragraph rather than the chapeau.[67]

Yet in the same case, the Appellate Body stated that there could be a violation of the chapeau "when the detailed operating provisions of

---

61. Appellate Body Report, *Brazil—Tyres*, paragraphs 215, 224.

62. Appellate Body Report, *United States—Gasoline*, p. 22.

63. Appellate Body Report, *Brazil—Tyres*, paragraph 224.

64. Appellate Body Report, *United States—Shrimp*, paragraphs 153, 155.

65. Appellate Body Report, *United States—Gasoline*, p. 22.

66. Appellate Body Report, *United States—Shrimp*, paragraph 160.

67. Appellate Body Report, *United States—Shrimp*, paragraph 149.

the measure prescribe the arbitrary or unjustifiable activity."[68] Thus one should not read too strictly the suggestion that only the application of the measure is examined under the chapeau and not a measure's design.[69] Indeed, in *United States—Gambling*, the Appellate Body reversed part of the panel's analysis of the chapeau for having focused on isolated instances of nonenforcement rather than on the statutory wording of the measure at issue.[70] The Appellate Body also upheld one panel finding of a chapeau violation based solely on an ambiguity of a law (not being challenged) that affected the measure being challenged.[71] Based on this jurisprudence, one can expect WTO adjudicators to look not only at how a measure has actually been implemented but sometimes also its design in order to determine whether the chapeau is violated.

The Appellate Body has held that the standards of the chapeau "project both substantive and procedural requirements."[72] For example, a procedural requirement could be whether the challenged measure gives the affected party a right of appeal to the government imposing a regulation. A substantive requirement could be discrimination that arises in the implementation of the measure being challenged.

The Appellate Body has expounded the "arbitrary or unjustifiable discrimination" clause in several cases and has recently refined its jurisprudence in the *Brazil—Tyres* case. In that case, the Appellate Body stated that "analyzing whether discrimination is arbitrary or unjustifiable usually involves an analysis that relates primarily to the cause or rationale of the discrimination."[73] Elaborating further, the Appellate Body suggested that the key questions are whether the discrimination has a legitimate cause and whether the rationale put forward can justify the discrimination.

The first step in the analysis is to consider whether the application of the measure results in discrimination. The Appellate Body has said that this language "cannot logically refer to the same standard(s) by which a violation of a substantive rule has been determined to have occurred."[74]

68. Appellate Body Report, *United States—Shrimp*, paragraph 160.

69. Furthermore, in its review of the appeal in the compliance proceeding in *United States—Shrimp*, the Appellate Body endorsed the panel's chapeau analysis of the "design and application" of the revised US measure. Appellate Body Report, *United States—Import Prohibitions of Certain Shrimp and Shrimp Products*, Recourse to Article 21.5 of the DSU by Malaysia, WT/DS58/AB/RW, adopted on November 21, 2001, paragraph 140.

70. Appellate Body Report, *United States—Measures Affecting the Cross-Border Supply of Gambling and Betting Services*, WT/DS285/AB/R, adopted on April 20, 2005, paragraph 357. This case involves the chapeau of the General Exceptions in the GATS rather than the GATT.

71. Appellate Body Report, *United States—Gambling*, paragraphs 369, 371.

72. Appellate Body Report, *United States—Shrimp*, paragraph 160.

73. Appellate Body Report, *Brazil—Tyres*, paragraph 225.

74. Appellate Body Report, *United States—Gasoline*, p. 23.

This seems to mean that the discrimination entailed in a violation of national treatment or most favored nation treatment would not in itself be sufficient to be "discrimination" under the Article XX chapeau. But how much more is needed remains unclear. In *United States—Shrimp*, the Appellate Body explained that the "nature and quality" of chapeau discrimination "is different from the discrimination in the treatment of products" to be found under other GATT provisions.[75] The Appellate Body also stated that discrimination results "not only when countries in which the same conditions prevail are differently treated, but also when the application of the measure at issue does not allow for any inquiry into the appropriateness of the regulatory program for the conditions prevailing in those exporting countries."[76]

The second step is to judge whether the discrimination is "unjustifiable" or "arbitrary." There is important case law on both provisions. Little case law exists on when the same conditions prevail between countries, but the Appellate Body has accepted the assumption of litigants that such discrimination could occur between foreign countries and between a foreign country and the domestic market.[77]

With regard to "unjustifiable" discrimination, the Appellate Body has considered how the measure treats other countries with different regulatory programs. In *United States—Shrimp*, the Appellate Body held that it is not acceptable in trade relations, and hence a violation of the chapeau, to "use an economic embargo to require other Members to adopt essentially the same comprehensive regulatory program...without taking into consideration different conditions which may occur in the territories" of other countries.[78] In *United States—Shrimp*, the Appellate Body also sharply criticized the US measure for excluding shrimp from fishing vessels from uncertified countries even when those shrimp were caught using methods identical to those employed in the United States.[79] In the follow-up compliance review in *United States—Shrimp*, however, the Appellate Body explicitly stated that the chapeau permits a government to condition market access by requiring the governments of exporting countries to put in place regulatory programs "comparable in effectiveness" to that

---

75. Appellate Body Report, *United States—Shrimp*, paragraph 150.

76. Appellate Body Report, *United States—Shrimp*, paragraph 164.

77. Appellate Body Report, *United States—Shrimp*, paragraph 150. In one case, the panel rejected the defendant Argentina's claim that the same conditions did not prevail between it and the complainant, the European Communities. Panel Report, *Argentina—Hides and Leather*, paragraph 11.315, n. 570.

78. Appellate Body Report, *United States—Shrimp*, paragraph 164. The jurisprudence is silent as to whether the same standard would apply to a measure that is not a trade embargo—for example, an import charge.

79. Appellate Body Report, *United States—Shrimp*, paragraph 165.

of the importing country.[80] Even so, the Appellate Body cautioned that "a measure should be designed in such a manner that there is sufficient flexibility to take into account the specific conditions prevailing in *any* exporting Member....Yet this is not the same as saying that there must be specific provisions in the measure aimed at addressing specifically the particular conditions prevailing in *every individual* exporting Member."[81]

The issue of whether the defendant government pursued a cooperative approach has also come up in the analysis of unjustifiable discrimination. In the *United States—Shrimp* case, the Appellate Body found that it was unjustifiable discrimination for the United States to have neglected to negotiate with the complaining countries while having negotiated with other countries on turtle conservation issues.[82] In the *United States—Shrimp* compliance review, the Appellate Body explained that exporting countries should be given similar opportunities to negotiate an international agreement and that such agreements should be "comparable from one forum of negotiation to the other."[83]

Because of the inexact phraseology used by the Appellate Body, many commentators have perceived it to be saying that a quest for an international agreement was a prerequisite for invoking an Article XX exception.[84] This view receives further support from *United States—Gasoline*, where the Appellate Body seemed to suggest that one of the flaws in the US measure, in terms of the chapeau, was that the United States had not pursued cooperative agreements with foreign industry and government to collect

---

80. Appellate Body Report, *United States—Shrimp* (Article 21.5—Malaysia), paragraph 144.

81. Appellate Body Report, *United States—Shrimp* (Article 21.5—Malaysia), paragraph 149 (emphasis in original). The Appellate Body also noted approvingly that the revised US regulation took into account other measures being taken by the exporting country beyond those indicated by the United States (see paragraph 147).

82. Appellate Body Report, *United States—Shrimp*, paragraph 172. The Appellate Body also noted that the United States had failed to raise the issue of turtle conservation in one multilateral environmental agreement forum and had failed to ratify two environmental treaties relevant to the sea turtle problem. Appellate Body Report, *United States—Shrimp*, paragraph 171, n. 174. This was an interesting observation by the Appellate Body because the United States had no obligation in international law to ratify either of those treaties.

83. Appellate Body Report, *United States—Shrimp* (Article 21.5—Malaysia), paragraph 122. The Appellate Body seemed to endorse the panel's proviso that the defendant country be engaging in "serious good faith efforts to negotiate a multilateral agreement" (see paragraph 152, n.117).

84. For example, in a recent speech, WTO Director-General Pascal Lamy asserted that the Appellate Body in the *United States—Shrimp* case had established that, as a condition for unilateral measures to be greenlighted, "all efforts first be made to achieve a consensual multilateral accord." See Pascal Lamy, "A Consensual International Accord on Climate Change Is Needed," Temporary Committee on Climate Change, European Parliament, May 29, 2008.

information needed for US regulatory purposes.[85] Importantly, however, the Appellate Body also made clear that recourse to the chapeau was not contingent upon a successful result to the negotiation.[86]

The case law suggests some other possible causes for a finding of unjustifiable discrimination. In *United States—Gasoline*, the Appellate Body criticized the United States for taking account of costs to domestic industry in devising US regulations but having "disregard[ed] that kind of consideration when it came to foreign refiners."[87] In *United States—Shrimp*, the Appellate Body criticized the United States for having given some countries longer phase-in periods to meet US regulations and for having given some countries greater transfer of technology than others. It was unclear in *United States—Shrimp* whether each of those elements alone could trigger a violation. In *Brazil—Tyres*, the Appellate Body suggested that the effects of the discrimination can be a relevant factor in showing unjustifiable discrimination.[88] In *Argentina—Hides and Leather*, the panel found that even after refunding the higher prepayment of taxes required for imports, Argentina was engaging in discrimination because importers had to forego more interest on prepaid taxes than domestic competitors did. The panel concluded that Argentina had not justified this extra burden on importers because an alternative course of action—namely, refunding the interest—was available to Argentina.[89]

In some cases, unjustifiable and arbitrary discrimination have been considered of a piece. In *European Communities—Tariff Preferences*, the panel found that the EC did not satisfy its burden of proof by providing evidence to demonstrate that its country selection criteria for a program dealing with illicit drugs (known as "Drug Arrangements") did not entail arbitrary and unjustifiable discrimination.[90] The panel could see no justification for the EC's decision to name only 12 countries as beneficiaries, to the exclusion of other countries with the same prevailing conditions. For example, the EC had not included Iran within the list of beneficiary

---

85. Appellate Body Report, *United States—Gasoline*, pp. 27–28. The context was that the United States had rejected giving foreign industry individual baselines because of a lack of reliable information.

86. Appellate Body Report, *United States—Shrimp* (Article 21.5—Malaysia), paragraphs 123–124.

87. Appellate Body Report, *United States—Gasoline*, pp. 28–29.

88. Appellate Body Report, *Brazil—Tyres*, paragraph 230.

89. Panel Report, *Argentina—Hides and Leather*, paragraphs 11.315–11.331. The panel agreed that its suggested approach would entail some administrative costs for Argentina, but the panel was not convinced that the costs would be excessive.

90. Panel Report, *European Communities—Conditions for the Granting of Tariff Preference in Developing Countries*, WT/DS246/R, adopted on April 20, 2004, paragraphs 7.225–7.235. The panel's holding and reasoning on this point was not appealed.

countries even though Iran was a more seriously drug-affected country than the beneficiary Pakistan. In addition, according to the panel, the EC's explanations were unconvincing for why Pakistan had been excluded from the program before 2002 but included later even though there was no objective change in Pakistan's situation. The panel's solicitude for Iran is remarkable because Iran is not a WTO member.

The Article XX chapeau jurisprudence was further developed in the *Brazil—Tyres* case, where the EC challenged Brazil's import ban. There the Appellate Body considered arbitrary and unjustifiable discrimination together and suggested that both would exist if a measure is applied in a discriminatory manner between countries where the same conditions prevail, "and when the reasons given for this discrimination bear no rational connection to the objective falling within the purview of a paragraph of Article XX, or would go against that objective."[91] Explaining further, the Appellate Body stated that "we have difficulty understanding how discrimination might be viewed as complying with the chapeau of Article XX when the alleged rationale for discriminating does not relate to the pursuit of or would go against the objective that was provisionally found to justify a measure under a paragraph of Article XX."[92] Two findings by the Appellate Body illustrate this principle. In *Tyres*, Brazil was banning retreaded tires from most countries while permitting them from countries in the Southern Common Market (Mercosur). The Appellate Body found that such discrimination was arbitrary or unjustifiable because its justification (regional treaty compliance) "does not relate to the pursuit or would go against the objective" in Article XX(b) being claimed by Brazil.[93] Also in *Tyres*, Brazil was permitting the importation of used tires that would then be retreaded by domestic companies; at the same time, Brazil was prohibiting the importation of tires that had been retreaded in the European Union. The Appellate Body explained that this was discrimination, and that it was arbitrary or unjustifiable because the only rationale put forward by Brazil was that such importation, although ostensibly prohibited by law, was being permitted under various court injunctions. Such a rationale was unacceptable, according to the Appellate Body, because it "bears no relationship" to the objective of reducing exposure to the risks from the accumulation of waste tires.[94]

Brazil—Tyres provided an important test case for a classic conflict of law problem where a defendant country in a WTO dispute points to a non-WTO treaty obligation as a defense within the WTO. In *Tyres*, an in-

---

91. Appellate Body Report, *Brazil—Tyres*, paragraph 227.

92. Appellate Body Report, *Brazil—Tyres*, paragraph 227.

93. Appellate Body Report, *Brazil—Tyres*, paragraph 228. The Appellate Body reversed the panel that had found that the quantity of imports from Mercosur was not significant.

94. Appellate Body Report, *Brazil—Tyres*, paragraph 246.

ternational Mercosur tribunal had ruled that Brazil was obliged to allow imports from Uruguay. Nevertheless, the EC argued that taking such a treaty obligation into account would seriously undermine the effectiveness of the Article XX chapeau. The Appellate Body agreed and held that allowing imports from Uruguay while prohibiting them from the EC violated the chapeau. In winning this point, the EC solidified WTO jurisprudence that so far has refrained from giving legal weight to nontrade treaty obligations as an Article XX defense. It should be noted that in *Tyres*, the international obligation being offered as a defense by Brazil arose from a trade liberalization treaty. Whether the Appellate Body would be more deferential to an environmental treaty remains to be seen.

As noted above, the Appellate Body has held that there is a procedural dimension in the adjudication of "unjustifiable." In *United States—Shrimp*, the Appellate Body stated that the unjustifiability of the US measure was underscored by the unilateral way in which US regulators had acted. Specifically, the jurists criticized the fact that the operating details of the US policies were shaped without the participation of other WTO members.[95] Furthermore, the "system and processes of certification are established and administered by the United States agencies alone," and the decision making for the grant, denial, or certification of countries is also unilateral.[96]

With specific regard to "arbitrary" discrimination, the Appellate Body has held that "rigidity and inflexibility" in administration can be arbitrary discrimination when there is no inquiry in regulating countries as to the appropriateness of the regulatory program for conditions prevailing in exporting countries.[97] In addition, procedural inflexibilities can constitute arbitrary discrimination. For example, in *United States—Shrimp*, the Appellate Body stated that, in a country certification process, the lack of a formal opportunity for other countries to be heard and to respond to arguments against the process and the lack of a procedure for appeal would constitute arbitrary discrimination for a country denied certification.[98] The Appellate Body also criticized the nontransparent nature of the internal US government procedures being applied.

WTO adjudicators have expounded the "disguised restriction on international trade" condition in a few cases. In *United States—Gasoline*, the Appellate Body made clear that a concealed or unannounced restriction does not exhaust the meaning of a disguised restriction and that "disguised discrimination" would amount to a disguised restriction.[99] In line with the

---

95. Appellate Body Report, *United States—Shrimp*, paragraph 172.

96. Appellate Body Report, *United States—Shrimp*, paragraph 172.

97. Appellate Body Report, *United States—Shrimp*, paragraph 177.

98. Appellate Body Report, *United States—Shrimp*, paragraphs 180–181.

99. Appellate Body Report, *United States—Gasoline*, p. 25.

reasons that it found "unjustifiable discrimination," the Appellate Body in *United States—Gasoline* also found a "disguised restriction on international trade." In *European Communities—Asbestos*, the panel suggested that "intention" is an element of "disguised," and that discriminatory measures could violate this prong if they are "in fact only a disguise to conceal the pursuit of trade-restrictive objectives."[100] The panel also suggested that "protectionist objectives" of a measure can be ascertained from its "design, architecture, and revealing structure"[101] and called attention to the lack of evidence showing that the French import ban had benefited domestic industry to the detriment of foreign producers. In the *United States—Shrimp* compliance adjudication, the panel echoed this formulation in *European Communities—Asbestos* and examined the design, architecture, and revealing structure of the measure being contested to see if it was a "disguised restriction." The panel concluded that even though the US competing industry was probably in favor of the import ban, US domestic industry was "likely to incur little commercial gain from a ban" and thus there was no chapeau violation."[102] The panel also noted approvingly that the US government was offering technical assistance to exporting countries to develop the utilization of environmental-friendly technology. By contrast, in *Brazil—Tyres*, the panel found that the allowance of imported used tires made the tire import ban a "disguised restriction on international trade" because such importation benefited domestic retreaders while undermining the health purpose of the import ban.[103]

In summary, although the applicability of the Article XX exception to measures linked to the life cycle of a product was not clear from the Uruguay Round negotiation, the jurisprudence of the Appellate Body leaves no doubt that measures linked to the production processes used in foreign countries are not, per se, outside the scope of Article XX. If such a measure is challenged in the WTO and is found to be discriminatory or an import ban, the defending country may seek to justify the measure under Article XX. In such litigation, the defending country will have to show that its measure is provisionally justified by an Article XX exception such as XX(g) and then that the measure is applied consistently with the Article XX chapeau.

---

100. Panel Report, *European Communities—Measures Affecting Asbestos and Asbestos-Containing Products*, WT/DS135/R, adopted on April 5, 2001, paragraph 8.236.

101. Panel Report, *European Communities—Asbestos*, paragraphs 8.236, 8.238.

102. Panel Report, *United States—Shrimp* (Article 21.5—Malaysia), paragraph 5.143.

103. Panel Report, *Brazil—Tyres*, paragraph 7.348. The Appellate Body upheld this finding but reversed the panel in part because the panel had conditioned its analysis on the quantity of used tire imports.

Disciplines on Subsidies

The Agreement on Subsidies and Countervailing Measures governs the use of subsidies. Because many climate change proposals rely on subsidies, the ASCM will need to be examined to assure that any subsidies comply with the agreement. Certainly, a grant or tax exemption by a government is a "subsidy" under the ASCM, but the status of emissions allowances is not clear.

ASCM Article 1 defines a "subsidy" under the agreement, and if a measure does not fit within that definition, it is not covered by the agreement. A subsidy requires a "financial contribution" and a "benefit" to the recipient. The question of whether the free allocation of an emissions allowance is a subsidy does not have an obvious answer, and there has been no WTO jurisprudence on this point (Lodefalk and Storey 2005, 41–43). The same puzzle exists for the rebate of an emissions allowance upon export. Under the ASCM, a subsidy exists when there is a financial contribution by a government and a benefit conferred to the recipient. The granting of an emissions allowance is intended as a benefit and surely is one.[104] So the key question is whether such a grant is a financial contribution. The ASCM definition of financial contribution is broad and includes, among other points, "a direct transfer of funds" and a situation where "a government provides goods or services other than general infrastructure."[105] A "fiscal incentive" where revenue that is "otherwise due is foregone or not collected" is also a financial contribution.[106] None of these examples of financial contribution clearly match an emissions allowance given to a private economic actor by a government because such an allowance may not be a good or a service but rather an intangible property right.

The closest WTO case regarding property rights was *United States— Softwood Lumber IV*, where Canada challenged a US countervailing duty on lumber.[107] In that case, the Appellate Body was asked to decide whether

---

104. Under ASCM, Article 14(d), the provision of goods or services by the government confers a benefit if the provision is made for less than adequate remuneration under prevailing market conditions. Whether or not an emissions allowance is a good, the same principle should apply; since emissions allowances could be traded on the market, they would have a market price, and so providing them free to the recipient is a benefit. It does not matter whether the recipient of the subsidy uses it in a manner that promotes public policy objectives on climate. In other words, one might presume that a government subsidy generates a benefit to the government, but the ASCM does not take such private-sector performance into account in deciding whether the recipient has benefited from the subsidy.

105. ASCM, Article 1.1(a)(1)(i), (iii). Note that government grants for general infrastructure, such as a new electrical grid, are not treated as financial contributions under the ASCM.

106. ASCM, Article 1.1(a)(1)(ii).

107. Appellate Body Report, *United States—Final Countervailing Duty Determination with Respect to Certain Softwood Lumber from Canada*, WT/DS257/AB/R, adopted on February 17,

an intangible right to harvest timber was a good, and the Appellate Body decided that it was, stating that "we believe that, by granting a right to harvest standing timber, governments provide that standing timber to timber harvesters."[108] The principle in that case—that a right to a good translates for ASCM purposes into a good—might also carry forward to services such that a right to use a service is itself a service.

A greenhouse gas emissions allowance, however, would not appear to be a good or a service as those terms are generally understood.[109] Rather, such permits are government licenses to pollute within a regulatory scheme. Since the definition of subsidy in the ASCM was drawn narrowly to prevent the existence or nonexistence of government regulation from being considered a subsidy,[110] it might seem anomalous to pigeonhole government licenses into the definition of a subsidy. Moreover, unlike a right to timber where timber itself is a good, a right to generate greenhouse gas emissions is not a right to a good because greenhouse gas emissions are not a good as the term is commonly used.[111]

Nevertheless, there would be strong trade policy grounds for treating emissions allowances as subsidies covered by the ASCM because, if not, governments in the future carbon-conscious world would be able to avoid all subsidy disciplines by using the form of tradable emissions allowances to confer aid on favored industries or agricultural producers.[112] Thus, a panel faced with deciding whether carbon permits are subsidies would probably find that they are through an expansive interpretation of the definition of an ASCM subsidy. One possibility would be to call an emis-

---

2004 [known as *Softwood Lumber IV*].

108. Appellate Body Report, *United States—Softwood Lumber IV*, paragraph 75.

109. de Cendra (2006, 137) suggests that emissions allowances could be considered financial services under the GATS Annex on Financial Services because Article 5(a) of the annex includes trade in negotiable instruments. We do not agree with that argument. Although trading in negotiable instruments is a service, nothing in the annex suggests that the negotiable instrument itself is a service.

110. The negotiating history is discussed in the WTO Panel Report, *United States—Measures Treating Export Restraints as Subsidies*, WT/DS194/R, adopted on August 23, 2001, paragraphs 8.64-8.74.

111. Some international law experts (e.g., Murase 2008, 408) suggest that certified emissions credits are either a good or a service.

112. Treating the government grant of an emissions allowance as a financial contribution can be distinguished from other government acts that are not subsidies. For example, the ASCM would seem to permit a government to relax its regulations on exporters. The limited purview of the ASCM was noted in one WTO case when the panel explained that not every "government intervention that might in economic theory be deemed a subsidy with the potential to distort trade is a subsidy within the meaning of the SCM Agreement." Panel Report, *United States—Export Restraints*, paragraph 8.62.

sion allowance either a good or a service.[113] Another would be to use the "direct transfer of funds" definition of a financial contribution to include government permits that are convertible into cash through a government-approved auction. A third possibility would be to hold that the allocation of some subsidies freely while others are being auctioned by the government is tantamount to the foregoing of revenue by a WTO member.

If a free distribution of an emissions allowance is a subsidy, then it is subject to the disciplines of the ASCM. Under ASCM Article 3, the granting of a subsidy contingent upon export performance is prohibited. The other ASCM disciplines require that the subsidy be specific. When subsidies are limited to certain enterprises, such subsidies are specific (Green 2006, 400–401). Otherwise, specificity is judged based on several factors listed in ASCM Article 2. Under Article 5, the granting of a specific subsidy causing adverse effects to the interests of other WTO members is prohibited. The meaning of "adverse effects" is spelled out in Articles 5 and 6. Under Part V of the ASCM, when a specific subsidy causes injury to the import-competing domestic industry producing a like product to that being subsidized, the importing country may impose a countervailing duty on the imported product.

The adverse effect most applicable to climate subsidies is "serious prejudice" as defined in ASCM Article 6.3. Under that provision, one form of serious prejudice occurs when "the effect of the subsidy is to displace or impede the imports of a like product of another Member into the market of the subsidizing Member."[114] For example, if the United States subsidizes its domestic widget industry, and that subsidy causes a displacement of imports of widgets into the United States from China, then China could lodge a WTO case against the United States alleging an actionable subsidy. In the context of climate subsidies, an interesting question arises as to whether there is any legal significance when the domestic subsidy is part of a larger program imposing onerous domestic regulation. In other words, what is the baseline against which displacement should be measured? Is it the status quo ante before the subsidy or before both the subsidy and the domestic regulation? As far as we are aware, this exact question has not come up in WTO dispute settlement.

If the purpose of the ASCM provisions outlawing actionable subsidies is to prevent them, then it would be illogical to allow governments to defend such a subsidy on the grounds that it is linked to another domestic policy that has put the industry receiving the subsidy at a disadvantage. Generally, the motive for a subsidy is something that the ASCM does not

---

113. Whether electricity is a good or a service in WTO law is not specified. (Electricity is specifically excluded from the Convention on Contracts for the International Sale of Goods.) Traditionally, many trade experts have considered electricity a good (Voigt 2008, 58). So the right to use electricity could likewise be a good.

114. ASCM Article 6.3(a).

take into account; the agreement treats subsidies to prevent market failure with the same rules as it treats subsidies to redistribute income. The fact that the original ASCM specifically declared as nonactionable certain environmental subsidies connected to burdensome environmental regulations further suggests that without such an exception, environmental subsidies would be treated the same way as other subsidies in assessing the prejudice to other countries of a government's domestic subsidy.[115] Unfortunately, the WTO exception permitting environmental adaptation and general research subsidies has expired.[116] Thus, the proper baseline for determining the effects of a subsidy would seem to be the economic situation that would have existed but for the subsidy.

The WTO Agreement on Agriculture also contains disciplines on domestic subsidies linked to commitments made in trade negotiations. Article 6 forbids WTO members from providing greater subsidies than the commitments made in particular categories.[117] This provision also provides a policy exemption for developing countries for subsidies to producers to encourage diversification from growing illicit narcotic crops.[118] In addition, the agreement exempts qualifying subsidies that have at most minimal trade-distorting effects or effects on production.[119] Certain environmental subsidies are specifically noted as qualifying.[120]

---

115. The one exception in ASCM law shows the rule: Article 27.13 provides that ASCM Part III (Actionable Subsidies) does not apply to "subsidies to cover social costs" when such subsidies are granted as part of a privatization program of a developing country. This carve-out would not have been added by negotiators if the adverse effects of a subsidy to cover such social costs would have been automatically immunized, because the subsidies were in response to the economic effects of the government's privatization policy.

116. See ASCM, Articles 8.2. Among the nonactionable subsidies were grants to promote adaptation of existing facilities to new environmental requirements imposed by laws "which result in greater constraints and financial burdens on firms...."

117. Note that bioethanol is covered by the Agreement on Agriculture, but whether biodiesel is covered is a matter of debate.

118. Agreement on Agriculture, Article 6.2.

119. Agreement on Agriculture, Article 7 and Annex II (so-called green box subsidies).

120. Agreement on Agriculture, Annex II, paragraph 2(g), 8(a), 12.

3

Status of Climate Measures Under the Law of the World Trade Organization

In its first decision, the World Trade Organization (WTO) Appellate Body addressed the relationship between WTO rules and environmental measures, explaining that "WTO Members have a large measure of autonomy to determine their own policies on the environment (including its relationship with trade), their environmental objectives and the environmental legislation they enact and implement. So far as concerns the WTO, that autonomy is circumscribed only by the need to respect the requirements of the General Agreement [on Tariffs and Trade, GATT] and the other covered agreements."[1] Besides the GATT, some other relevant covered agreements are the Agreement on Subsidies and Countervailing Measures (ASCM), the Agreement on Technical Barriers to Trade (TBT), the General Agreement on Trade in Services (GATS), and the Agreement on Agriculture (AoA).

The requirements of WTO rules could potentially interact with climate change policies insofar as these policies apply to goods imported into or exported from a WTO member. The literature of trade and environment points out several reasons why the US and other governments would likely want to include trade-related measures in climate programs.

First, there is a concern that emissions reductions accomplished domestically would go for naught if production and emissions migrated to other countries that had lower regulation. This concern has been termed the "polluter haven" problem in environmental policy. In the context of climate change, the problem is called "leakage" or "carbon laundering." The concern is that a national climate program is undermined, and the

---

1. Appellate Body Report, *United States—Standards for Reformulated and Conventional Gasoline*, WT/DS2/AB/R, adopted on May 20 1996, 30.

international agenda loses coherence, if emissions are relocated from a country with higher standards to a country with lower standards.

Second, there is a possible adverse competitiveness impact on a country if it reduces emissions while its trade and investment partners do not. This concern, often given the moniker of a "level playing field," reflects a mixed motive of economics (the cost of strict greenhouse gas regulations) and politics (coalition-building). Concern about "fairness" in international commercial relations leads to various proposals to adjust for policy differences at the border.

Third, governments may seek to use trade measures to encourage other countries to cooperate in adopting equivalent environmental policies, encourage them to join multilateral environmental agreements (MEAs), or punish them for being free riders. The motive for using such leverage would be either coherence or competitiveness or both.

Figure 3.1 provides a quick view as to whether US climate policy options with respect to imports of goods can be justified under particular GATT articles, and this chapter examines in depth the status of various climate change proposals under the GATT and other WTO rules. The chapter s tarts with a discussion of key components of climate policy generically and then moves to a review of two specific proposals under consideration in the United States and Australia.

Border Adjustments on Imports

A border tax adjustment (BTA) on an import is the application of a charge or tax on the import aimed to match the domestic indirect taxes imposed on the like product and/or its inputs. Historically, of course, BTAs had nothing to do with environmental concerns; they were applied to level the playing field between domestically produced and imported goods. In the climate debate, analysts have sometimes used the BTA term imprecisely to refer to a tax imposed at the border designed to match the economic effects of a regulation on imports (Cosbey 2008a, 1, n. 2). But when there is no domestic tax, then the application of the supposedly corresponding tax or charge on imports is not a BTA.[2]

Only taxes on products can be border-adjusted. Thus taxes not applied to products are not susceptible to being border-adjusted. Whether taxes on energy consumed in making a product (sometimes called "embedded energy" or "carbon footprint" taxes) are border-adjustable on an import has not been considered in WTO dispute settlement. As noted

---

2. For example, one proposal being floated is to take the average cost of compliance for US companies and then impose that same charge on imported products. Such a measure would violate GATT Article III:2 because there would be no identified tax or charge on domestic production. The national treatment problem would not be cured by allowing the foreign exporter to prove that its own production is less carbon-intensive than the US average.

Figure 3.1 US climate policy options with respect to energy-intensive imports

Restriction on imports of goods		Justified under General Agreement on Tariffs and Trade (GATT) articles?				
		Article I (Most favored nation)	Article II (Tariff schedules)	Article III (National treatment)	Article XI (Quotas)	Article XX (Exceptions)
Import restriction applied to penalize "foreign-emitted carbon" (measures applied only against imports)	Import ban (quantitative restriction)	Status unclear		Covered under Article XI	No	Yes. If any provision or restriction on imports can be justified under Article XX, it is permitted even though it violates other GATT rules. Recourse to an Article XX exception is scrutinized carefully, and the burden of proof is on the country seeking to invoke the exception. The measure has to qualify under a specific exception in Article XX, such as Article XX(g) as a measure relating to the conservation of exhaustible natural resources. In addition, the measure must meet the test in the Article XX chapeau, namely, that the measure is not applied in a manner that constitutes arbitrary or unjustifiable discrimination or as a disguised restriction on international trade.
	Additional or punitive tariff	No, because punitive tariffs will differ between foreign countries	No, because it violates bound tariffs.			
	Antidumping or countervailing duties	No. Under present GATT rules, even if the exporting country does not restrict its carbon emissions, the social cost of carbon cannot be labeled as dumping or a subsidy. The failure to impose a carbon tax, or otherwise internalize the full price of carbon, does not currently give other World Trade Organization members the right to impose penalty duties on imports. Such measures would violate the Agreement on Subsidies and Countervailing Measures and the Antidumping Agreement for which no Article XX exception would be available.				
Competitiveness provision applied as an extension of domestic US climate policy (measures applied both to domestic production and imports)	Carbon tax on products	Yes, if the tax is imposed on the product and is not based on the country of origin		Not violated. Carbon taxes on products can be justified as an "internal tax" under GATT Articles III:2 and II:2(a) and thus can be adjusted at the border.		
	Cap-and-trade system with applicability to imports	No, if foreign countries are treated differently		A violation would occur if imported products are treated less favorably than like domestic products.		
	Carbon performance regulation applied to products and the production process	No, if foreign countries are treated differently		A violation would occur if imported products are treated less favorably than domestic products. (The Agreement on Technical Barriers to Trade may also be implicated.)		

Note: Cells are in grey when the referenced GATT articles are not likely to be relevant to the restriction in question. Pauwelyn (2007) contains an early summary of GATT provisions and climate policy options.

above, Annexes I and II of the ASCM can be read so as to permit the rebate of energy taxes on exports. Whether that would correspondingly allow the imposition of domestic energy taxes on imports remains unclear. Robert Howse and Antonia Eliason (2008, 24–25) have argued that ASCM Annex II would provide context for a panel's interpretation of GATT Article II as to permit the application of process-related energy taxes to imports.

It might seem straightforward to characterize carbon taxes as product taxes and impose them at the border when goods are imported. But things are not so simple. The core problem is that a product of a given physical description—say a ton of hot-rolled steel plate—will be responsible for different amounts of CO_2 emission depending on the manufacturing process. Emissions will differ from firm to firm and even within a firm. Moreover, if the border-adjustment scheme reflects carbon emissions of ancillary materials (e.g., scrap steel), the tracing challenge becomes an additional source of difficulty.

Consider this hypothetical policy as an illustration of a way to apply climate policies to imports that would probably comply with GATT rules. Suppose the United States required that any good sold be accompanied by a certificate stating its carbon footprint, meaning the quantity of greenhouse gas–producing substances used in its upstream production process (such certificates have been called a "carbon passport").[3] Suppose further that there is an internal carbon tax imposed on the product proportionate to the amount of greenhouse gas listed on the certificate. Although there is no precise trade law jurisprudence on this point, the language of GATT Article II:2(a) would seem to suggest that a BTA equivalent to the domestic tax could be imposed on imports. The language of Article II:2(a) allows the tax adjustment to be based on an "article from which the imported product has been manufactured or produced in whole or in part."[4] Thus, a certificate that adds up all of the carbon-based energy used in the

---

3. Whether two otherwise identical products differing only on the objective information about greenhouse gas emissions listed on a certificate are "like" products is an issue not yet determined in WTO dispute settlement. In 2003 the WTO granted a waiver for trade restrictions imposed on diamonds based on whether the diamond was accompanied by a certification that it was not a so-called conflict diamond used by rebel movements to finance conflict. The waiver applied to trade restrictions against WTO members that did not participate in the Kimberley Certification Scheme. The use of a waiver did not necessarily imply that the trade restrictions would otherwise have been WTO-illegal (Pauwelyn 2003). But that episode did show the possibility of regulating trade based on certificates that provide information about characteristics not discernible in the good (i.e., the diamond) itself.

4. It has been suggested that the equally authentic French text of GATT Article II:2(a) reads more restrictively to require that the input be incorporated into the imported product (Demaret and Stewardson 1994, 19). In that more restrictive reading, a BTA on coke consumed in steel production would be allowed by Article II:2(a), while a BTA on natural gas used to power steel furnaces would not be allowed.

production process—for example, coal, natural gas, and oil—could serve as a basis for the application of the domestic tax to the imported product. To be sure, there are administrative problems of verifying the accuracy of certificates attached to imports, or, for that matter, on certificates attached to domestic products. But this illustration shows that the parallel application of a product-specific carbon tax to domestic and imported products does not inevitably lead to a conflict with GATT rules.

Border Adjustments on Exports

As noted above, whether the ASCM permits the rebate of energy taxes on exportation has not yet been resolved. Rebating an energy or carbon tax on exports would seem to be environmentally perverse because exportation does not undo the environmental impact of the greenhouse gas emissions. Of course, as was seen in the *Superfund* case,[5] the WTO legality of a BTA does not hinge on an environmental justification.

The only sensible rationale for a rebate of climate taxes on exports would be to avoid double carbon taxation. In other words, in a world economy where nearly all governments are imposing BTAs on imports to match domestic carbon taxes, there could be an agreement to use the destination principle for energy taxes by taxing imports but not exports. (To be more precise, all domestic production would be taxed, but when a product is exported the tax would be rebated by the exporting country government.) As noted above, the ASCM is unclear as to whether energy taxes are susceptible to being remitted or rebated upon export.

Although GATT Article XX is not directly relevant to whether a BTA for outward shipments is an export subsidy, the rebate on an energy tax for exports could undermine the Article XX environmental justification for applying the BTA to imports. For example, consider how a panel might have appraised the US shrimp import ban if US law had allowed shrimp caught without turtle excluder devices to be exported by the United States. In those circumstances, the import ban would have appeared as arbitrary or unjustifiable discrimination.

Another border adjustment could occur if a domestic firm purchased a greenhouse gas emissions allowance to produce an exported good, and the payment was then rebated. The rebate of this emissions allowance would not be a rebate of a tax because the requirement to purchase an emissions allowance is a regulation, not a tax. Thus, the rebate of an emissions allowance on exportation is technically not a border tax adjustment. Rebating an emissions allowance would have WTO implications, however, if an emissions allowance is viewed by the WTO as the equivalent of

---

5. GATT Panel Report, *United States—Taxes on Petroleum and Certain Imported Substances*, BISD 34S/136, adopted on June 17, 1987. See chapter 2.

money. As noted in the previous chapter, if a government pays money to a firm in connection with an export, that payment constitutes a prohibited export subsidy.

Unilateral Countervailing Duties or Sanctions

A countervailing duty (CVD) is a trade penalty applied to an imported product to offset the competitive effect of a foreign subsidy. The prerequisite to a CVD is a subsidy that is specific to a firm or industry and causes material injury to the competing domestic industry producing the "like" product. Commentators have sometimes proposed applying CVDs on carbon-intensive imports as a "stick" against "carbon free riding."[6] The problem with this formulation is that free riding on carbon restrictions is not a subsidy, as currently defined by the ASCM, because the absence of a government regulation is not the legal equivalent to the presence of a financial contribution from that government.

If the intent of a proposed trade penalty is to sanction countries that are going slow on adopting climate measures, then it would violate GATT Articles I or XI or both and would not be justified by Article XX. The justification for the import ban in the *United States—Shrimp* case was that the imported products from certain producers were caught in a way that led to the killing of endangered sea turtles. The Appellate Body ultimately permitted that ban, even though it was unilateral, because conditioning market access on a foreign government's adoption of a program comparable in effectiveness to the US program gave sufficient latitude to that foreign government.[7] In our view, one cannot infer from this one case that the Appellate Body would approve a trade sanction levied against a target country proceeding at a different environmental speed than the sender country. The most prominent slowpoke on the climate issue over the past 10 years has been the United States, and there was never a serious suggestion that other countries could have legally imposed trade sanctions against the United States for that reason.

In commenting on the legal status of trade sanctions, it should first be repeated that border adjustment measures are not trade sanctions. The central purpose of a border adjustment measure is to equilibrate conditions between an imported product and a domestic product. As explained earlier, border adjustments can be legal or illegal under WTO rules, depending on the underlying economic circumstances. One motivation for a border

---

6. See Ralph Nader and Toby Heaps, "We Need a Global Carbon Tax," *Wall Street Journal*, December 3, 2008, A17.

7. Appellate Body Report, *United States—Import Prohibitions of Certain Shrimp and Shrimp Products*, Recourse to Article 21.5 of the DSU by Malaysia, WT/DS58/AB/RW, adopted on November 21, 2001, paragraph 144.

adjustment may be to influence the policy of another country. That is also the case for a countervailing duty, which is, in part, designed to dissuade foreign governments from subsidizing. But having the motivation to influence another government does not necessarily mean that a measure amounts to a "sanction." However, there are no officially agreed upon bright lines as to when a restrictive trade measure constitutes a sanction.

Finally, the WTO implications of multilaterally agreed upon trade sanctions on climate scofflaws have yet to be addressed. Multilaterally approved trade sanctions are virtually unknown outside of the UN Security Council and the WTO dispute system. Although enforcement actions have been taken through multilateral environmental agreements, trade sanctions, per se, are not authorized.

Greenhouse Gas Performance Standards

In contrast to a carbon tax, carbon intensity standards (or carbon footprint standards) could be devised for particular sectors that could be imposed equally on both imports and domestic production.[8] If the greenhouse gases emitted in production were to exceed the relevant performance standard, then the product could not be sold. For example, then European Commissioner for Trade Peter Mandelson suggested that environmental standards for biofuels should be the same for European and imported biofuels and should cover changes in land use.[9] The idea of performance standards was recently put forward in a staff paper published by the US House of Representatives Energy and Commerce Committee (2008, 11).

Although there is no WTO case law on this point, we assume that such standards would be reviewed under GATT Article III and, if necessary, under Article XX. If foreign products are treated less favorably—for example, by imputing to them artificial carbon footprint values—that would violate national treatment.

Whether a carbon performance standard would also be considered a TBT "technical regulation" and therefore subject to TBT disciplines remains an open question. That issue was not addressed by the Appellate Body in *European Communities—Asbestos*.[10] In our view, panels could decide that such performance measures are covered by the TBT agreement because

---

8. As used here, the term "standard" means a mandatory government regulation. In other words, we follow common usage rather than the TBT agreement nomenclature that defines standards as nonmandatory provisions.

9. See Peter Mandelson, "Keeping the Crop in Hand: By Imposing Rigorous Sustainability Standards, We Can Make a Global Market in Biofuels Work," *Guardian*, April 29, 2008, www.guardian.co.uk (accessed on January 12, 2009).

10. Appellate Body Report, *European Communities—Measures Affecting Asbestos and Asbestos-Containing Products*, WT/DS135/AB/R, adopted on April 5, 2001.

noncoverage would mean that the disciplines of that agreement would not apply. In other words, the definition of covered regulations in the TBT agreement—namely, regulations about "product characteristics or their related processes and production methods"[11]—could be interpreted broadly (Verrill 2008). It is true that the negotiating history of the TBT agreement would suggest an intent for narrower coverage, but in WTO jurisprudence, negotiating history takes a second place to textual and contextual analysis.

In 2007 a US law was passed to forbid federal government procurement of an alternative or synthetic fuel for a mobility-related use unless the contract specifies that the "lifecycle greenhouse gas emissions associated with the production and combustion of the fuel" is less than or equal to such emissions from equivalent conventional fuel produced from conventional petroleum sources.[12] This measure has not been challenged in the WTO. Although GATT Article III is not applicable to government procurement, the WTO Agreement on Government Procurement does embody most favored nation and national treatment principles.[13]

If a carbon performance standard were analyzed under the TBT agreement, one key question would be whether it was based on an international standard. If so, then the use of that standard would be "rebuttably presumed not to create an unnecessary obstacle to trade."[14] Whether such a standard could be imposed by the United States on developing countries is not clear under TBT rules, however, because the TBT agreement states that developing country WTO members should not be expected to use international standards that "are not appropriate to their development, financial and trade needs."[15] If a domestic carbon performance standard is not based on an international standard, then the domestic standard would be subject to the requirement in the TBT agreement that any application to imports "shall not be more trade-restrictive than necessary to fulfil a legitimate objective," such as protection of the environment.[16]

If a panel decides that a carbon performance standard is not a TBT measure, then it would be analyzed under Article III:4 of the GATT. The standard would violate Article III:4 if it treats the imported product less favorably than the like domestic product. Most commentators would say that a regulation based on the method of production would violate Article III,

---

11. TBT agreement, Article 1.2 and Annex 1, paragraph 1.

12. 42 USC § 17142.

13. WTO Agreement on Government Procurement, Article III. It should be noted that the agreement lacks a general exception for the environment or for measures relating to the conservation of exhaustible natural resources.

14. TBT agreement, Articles 2.4, 2.5.

15. TBT agreement, Article 12.4.

16. TBT agreement, Article 2.2.

but there is no WTO jurisprudence squarely on that point. A violation of Article III would not be fatal, however, as the regulating country could invoke Article XX(g). Assuming that the greenhouse gas performance standard is applied to all countries (including the domestic market) in the same way, we believe that the Article XX defense would succeed.[17]

"Food Miles" and Transport Emissions

A new idea that has emerged in recent years is to internalize the externalities from international transport into the cost of a product (Kejun, Cosbey, and Murphy 2008, 5). For agricultural products, this idea is referred to as "food miles." In a climate context, this might mean adding a charge at the border for the greenhouse gas emissions entailed in the transportation of that product to the importing country. Once such an import comes into a country, it could be treated the same as a domestic product with respect to internal transport-related emissions.

Certainly, any food mile charge would be a violation of GATT Article I because it is origin-specific. Moreover, food mile charges would be outside the scope of Article II:2(a), which permits border tax adjustments, because transportation is a service, not an "article." Nowhere does the GATT or the General Agreement on Trade in Services (GATS) authorize BTAs on services. Food mile charges would also be a violation of Article III because imports as a group would be treated less favorably.[18]

Using a Multilateral Climate Agreement as a Sword against Import Restrictions

Some commentators (e.g., Cosbey 2007, 16) have suggested that countries that are not listed in Annex I of the United Nations Framework Convention on Climate Change (UNFCCC) could argue that if they are in compliance with their (minimal) obligations under the UNFCCC or the Kyoto Protocol, then potential defendant importing countries would not be able

---

17. The possibility that such a measure could be defended under Article XX of the GATT is the reason why we believe that a parallel claim would be mounted to the effect that "food mile" charges also violate the TBT agreement, as discussed in the subsequent section. However, this claim would put complaining developing countries in an ironic posture of arguing that the TBT agreement covers process-based measures (so-called PPMs). A decade ago, developing countries argued that the TBT agreement did not cover PPMs because they thought coverage would legalize PPMs under the TBT agreement, even though the PPMs would otherwise be prohibited by the GATT. After the *United States—Shrimp* decision, it became clear that the GATT could allow PPMs but that the TBT agreement might instill discipline that the GATT lacks.

18. Note that the second sentence of Article III:4 permits "internal transportation charges" to be based on "the economic operation of the means of transport" so long as they are not based on the nationality of the product. The implication is that differential external transportation charges based on the nationality of the product would amount to less favorable treatment.

to justify trade restrictive measures under WTO rules. This is not a facetious argument, but since the WTO Appellate Body has not given weight to obligations under other international agreements (e.g., *Brazil—Tyres*),[19] it is difficult to imagine a panel would imbue greater legal significance to the lack of obligations under other international agreements. Moreover, the two existing climate MEAs do not contain provisions obliging developed countries to refrain from using trade or border measures against developing countries.

In upcoming negotiations in Copenhagen for the next climate protocol, it would be possible for developing countries to seek treaty language to forestall the use of border measures that would hamper their exports. In other words, there may be proposals that if developing countries accept some emissions reduction commitments, developed countries have to agree not to impose additional commitments through unilateral measures. A specific provision of that sort, if written into the next climate protocol, could perhaps be given legal effect in WTO dispute settlement.

Another proposition being offered in "trade and climate" debates is that, because it is a nonparty to the Kyoto Protocol, the United States could be disqualified from invoking an Article XX defense (Frankel 2008, 10) for a trade-related climate measure. Although the Appellate Body in *United States—Shrimp* never said that prior negotiations was a prerequisite for invoking Article XX, there is nevertheless a widespread perception that the Appellate Body did so, and one could imagine a panel finding fault with the United States for not being a Kyoto Protocol party.[20] Support for that outcome could be found in the Appellate Body's statement that "good faith" is required under the Article XX chapeau. Furthermore, in *United States—Shrimp*, the Appellate Body took note that the United States had not ratified three environmental MEAs that loosely relate to turtle conservation.[21]

Using a Multilateral Climate Agreement to Establish Rules for Trade

It would also be possible for a new climate protocol to establish a rule that all goods in international commerce have to carry an emissions permit ("carbon passport") obtained from an international facility. The permit could be issued free for production that meets an internationally determined performance standard or could be purchased at an internationally

---

19. Appellate Body Report, *Brazil—Measures Affecting Imports of Retreaded Tyres*, WT/DS332/AB/R, adopted on December 17, 2007, paragraphs 228, 234.

20. Of course, the United States was a major player in the negotiation of the Kyoto Protocol. Many countries objected to the United States not ratifying Kyoto, but the United States did not have any international law obligation to do so.

21. Appellate Body Report, *United States—Shrimp*, paragraph 171, n. 174.

set price. If all WTO member countries subscribe to this rule, then trade conflicts regarding the treatment of imports should not arise. If some WTO members were a party to this agreement and some refused to join, then the nonparties could complain if a party refused to allow an importation without such a permit. How a WTO panel would deal with such a case is not certain. Box 3.1 discusses the relation between WTO rules and MEAs. The most likely outcome is that the panel would find that the MEA norm does not override WTO rules. Yet the possibility exists that a panel could seek to internalize the climate norm into WTO rules and apply it against nonparties because the rule is multilateral. This situation did not arise in the *United States—Shrimp* case because the US measure was unilateral, not multilateral.

This hypothetical is put forward to show the possibility of constructive synergism between trade and climate law. We do not, however, see the climate regime moving in this direction, because carbon passports would only address the climate effects of production for exportation, not production for domestic consumption. Production for domestic consumption is by far the bigger problem. For example, only about 6 percent of cement production is traded internationally. This explains why almost all proposals for border adjustment hinge on the entire emissions profile of a foreign country, not just its exports.

Allocating Emissions Allowances to Other Countries

One idea being floated in climate talks is for an industrial country like the United States to give some free emissions allowances to developing countries that are taking early action to reduce greenhouse gases. Article 1.1(a)(1) of the ASCM is ambiguous as to whether a financial contribution by government A can be characterized as its subsidy when it gives the money to economic actors in government B. In any event, we are doubtful, however, that free subsidies given to other countries would cause sufficient adverse effects to be actionable, because the ASCM Part III discipline ("Actionable Subsidies") is on the donor country (country A in our example), not the recipient country (country B). One should also note that the ASCM does not have a most favored nation clause, so a donor country need not give the same subsidy to every WTO member.

Output-Based Rebates

Alan H. Price (2008) from Wiley Rein LLP has proposed temporary federal government payments to certain firms equal to their cost of purchasing

Box 3.1   WTO rules and multilateral environmental agreements

At the Doha Ministerial Conference in 2001, World Trade Organization (WTO) members agreed for the first time to launch negotiations that would address the trade-environment nexus. The Doha Declaration thus includes a negotiating mandate on clarifying the relationship between multilateral environmental agreements (MEAs) and WTO rules.[1] Like much else in the Doha Declaration, nothing has come from this mandate so far. However, existing WTO rules, past initiatives, and decisions by the Appellate Body are already shaping the WTO response to environmental issues.

In 1995 the WTO Ministerial Decision on Trade and Environment created the Committee on Trade and Environment. Among its works, the committee has examined the relationship between WTO provisions and trade measures for environmental purposes. At present, there are more than 250 MEAs in force, and over 20 of these incorporate trade measures.[2]

As the number of MEAs has increased, the committee has debated whether the WTO should change its rules to accommodate them. While the committee has never agreed on recommendations that would modify WTO rules, Sampson (2005) contends that its work has been useful in understanding the complexity of MEA issues, which may explain why no dispute related to an MEA has yet been brought to the WTO.

---

1. Paragraph 31 of the Doha Declaration states: "With a view to enhancing the mutual supportiveness of trade and environment, we agree to negotiations, without prejudging their outcome, on: (i) the relationship between existing WTO rules and specific trade obligations set out in multilateral environment agreements. The negotiations shall be limited in scope to the applicability of such existing WTO rules as among parties to the MEA in question. The negotiations shall not prejudice the WTO rights of any Member that is not a party to the MEA in question; (ii) procedures for regular information exchange between MEA Secretariats and the relevant WTO committees, and the criteria for the granting of observer status; (iii) the reduction or, as appropriate, elimination of tariff and non-tariff barriers to environmental goods and services."

2. Among MEAs with trade provisions are the Convention on International Trade in Endangered Species of Wild Fauna and Flora; Montreal Protocol on Substances that Deplete the Ozone Layer; Basel Convention; Convention on Biodiversity; and the Stockholm Convention and Rotterdam Convention. For more details, see the WTO website at www.wto.org (accessed on January 12, 2009). Trade measures in MEAs usually refer to one of the following actions: (1) reporting requirements; (2) labeling or other identification requirements; (3) requirements for transportation documents involving notification and consent by exporters and importers; (4) export and/or import bans (targeted or general); and (5) market measures such as taxes, charges, and subsidies.

climate emission permits.[22] The eligible industries would include iron, steel, aluminum, pulp/paper, bulk glass, cement, and certain chemicals. Eligibility would require that an industry be energy-intensive, produce a globally traded commodity, and face rising imports in response to higher domestic energy prices. Price recognizes that such payments would be subsidies under WTO rules but argues that "a rebate for added costs incurred under a domestic environmental policy would be unlikely to have any demonstrable impact on international competitors."

Our view is different. As we see it, if a direct payment to domestic producers is designed to protect domestic companies from the competitive effects of higher domestic regulation, then the payment may reasonably be expected to distort trade and cause serious prejudice to other WTO members. If so, the payments would violate the ASCM prohibition against granting subsidies that cause adverse effects on other countries.

Climate Safeguards

In a study group organized for this book, one analyst floated an interesting idea. Rather than compensate US firms ex ante with free distribution of emissions allowances, an ex post system should instead provide government assistance to companies upon a showing of injury from competing imports or reduced opportunities to export. This program would be distinguishable from safeguards permitted in the WTO Agreement on Safeguards. Under the Safeguards Agreement, importing country governments may respond to domestic injury by trade restrictions that entail the suspension of GATT obligations or the modification of GATT tariff concessions.[23] Although the point has not been litigated in the WTO, the Safeguard Agreement does not appear to relieve WTO members of their obligations under the ASCM. In other words, WTO law seems to insist that a safeguard be a trade restrictive measure (on an imported product) rather than a subsidy. This interpretation would be consistent with the position taken by the Appellate Body in ASCM jurisprudence, which ruled against countervailing subsidies to domestic companies that are hurt from foreign subsidies. Instead, the Appellate Body held that only countervailing duties could be used.[24] Perhaps WTO rules should be modified to permit the ex post relief suggested above.

---

22. The paper is available on the Environmental Law Institute website at www.eli.org (accessed on January 12, 2009).

23. Agreement on Safeguards, Article 1 and GATT Article XIX:1.

24. Appellate Body Report, *United States—Continued Dumping and Subsidy Offset Act of 2000*, WT/DS217/WT/AB/R, adopted on January 27, 2003, paragraphs 269–273.

Hybrid Systems

"Hybrid" measures are found not only within each approach to the competitiveness question—carbon taxes and cap-and-trade systems—but also within each country's overall policy framework to cope with climate change. Governments are legislating a mixture of subsidies (e.g., biofuels, solar, and wind power), performance standards for vehicles, and other greenhouse gas controls. Major nations find it congenial to design legislation in a way that fosters domestic producers, especially "national champions." The United States is well along this path with respect to biofuels, having enacted measures that generously support ethanol production by firms like Archer-Daniels-Midland. The US domestic auto industry is likewise on the threshold of more government assistance, which almost certainly will encourage CO_2 efficient engines. President Nicolas Sarkozy of France and other European leaders favor the same approach, especially in the current financial crisis.

Because of their complexity and variations from country to country, hybrid systems would need to be examined under several WTO agreements. A violation of WTO rules may arise when the measure to be applied to an imported product is not the same as the measure to be applied to a domestic product. For example, this could happen when the domestic measure to be matched is not a tax on products but rather is a regulation. In that case, the measure on imports cannot be immunized by GATT Article II:2(a), dealing with border tax adjustments. The measure would instead be reviewed under GATT Article III, and if a violation is found, a panel would inquire whether an exception is permitted by GATT Article XX. Another WTO violation could arise when a measure treats foreign countries differently depending on their climate policies. Although there are valid environmental reasons for discriminating between countries, such discrimination could run afoul of GATT Article I. If so, recourse to Article XX is possible, but measures will need to be carefully designed and applied to meet the various prerequisites of Article XX.

Boxer Amendment to Lieberman-Warner Climate Security Act of 2008

The amendment proposed by Senator Barbara Boxer (D-CA) on May 20, 2008 to the Climate Security Act (S. 3036) sponsored by Senators Joseph Lieberman (I-CT) and John Warner (R-VA) establishes a cap-and-trade program for greenhouse gas emissions in the United States.[25] Its stated purpose is to "reduce United States greenhouse gas emissions substantially enough to avert the catastrophic impacts of global climate change." For

---

25. This paragraph is based on Sections 3, 202, and 203 as well as various other sections of the bill. Boxer Amendment, S. Amdt. 4825, available at http://thomas.loc.gov.

domestic producers, the program works as follows: An operator of covered business entities in the United States would need to submit emissions allowances to cover its own greenhouse gas emissions. The US government would create emissions allowances and either distribute them freely or auction them. For example, in the first five years of the program, about 48 percent of the allowances would be given away free to domestic carbon-intensive manufacturers, fossil fuel–fired electricity generators, refiners of petroleum-based fuel, natural gas processors, carbon sequestration and renewable energy projects, and biofuels. Additional allowances could be made available to commercial recipients via the allocation of 13 percent of allowances to local energy distribution companies. Another 13 percent of allowances would be distributed freely to states and Indian tribes or used for clean fleets or buildings. These allowances could be transferred or sold to firms requiring emissions allowances. However, none of the emissions allowances could be used for imports.

Imports are instead covered in Title XIII Part A of the bill, which is titled "Promoting Fairness While Reducing Emissions." Its stated purposes include "to promote a strong global effort to significantly reduce greenhouse emissions"; "to ensure, to the maximum extent practicable, that greenhouse gas emissions occurring outside the United States do not undermine the objectives of the United States in addressing global climate change"; and "to encourage effective international action." Descriptions of the bill circulated by its private-sector authors state the purpose more candidly; for example, one description says that the bill "helps prevent the shifting of US jobs to foreign countries that would have lower manufacturing costs merely because they refuse to do their part to limit greenhouse gas emissions" (McBroom 2008, 2).

The Boxer bill also lays out US objectives for climate negotiations. One central idea is to prod other countries to take comparable action in reducing greenhouse gas emissions. The bill points toward a standard of "carbon tax comparability." The inclusion of explicit negotiating objectives would fill a significant gap under current US law.

As written up in the spring of 2008, the international program in the Boxer bill would be largely administered by the US Environmental Protection Agency (EPA). Some administrative determinations, however, would be made by an independent commission of US citizens appointed by the president. Of course, all of the details of the Boxer bill are subject to change in the 111th Congress in 2009.

The import provisions of the program apply to covered goods from covered countries (Section 1301). Covered goods are so-called primary products, such as steel and chemicals, and possibly manufactured goods when the production process generates a substantial quantity of greenhouse gas emissions. Covered imports also have to be closely related to a US good whose cost of production is affected by the new domestic climate requirements. Some examples of primary products listed in the bill are iron, steel, aluminum, cement, glass, pulp, paper, chemicals, and industrial ceramics. Covered countries are those that are not on the excluded list. To qualify for the excluded list, a country has to be either (1) taking action comparable to the United States to limit domestic greenhouse gas emissions from the 2005 base year, (2) a least-developed country, or (3) a country that is a de minimis emitter of greenhouse gases.

The determination as to whether a foreign country is taking comparable action is to be made by the independent commission (Sections 1306 and 322). Comparable action will be found if the foreign country reduces its greenhouse gas emissions from 2005 levels in terms of percentage at least as much as the United States did in the preceding year.[26] The commission can also find comparable action if a foreign government implements, verifies, and enforces state-of-the-art technologies that lead to actual emissions reductions and has greenhouse gas–limiting regulatory programs in place. A tie vote in the commission goes against the foreign country. The bill gives the commission considerable latitude, so it is impossible to know in advance what would qualify as comparable action and whether the commission would apply the same standard to every trading partner. However, according to the bill, "Any determination on comparable action made by the Commission...shall comply with applicable international agreements."[27]

Title XIII would require, two years after the US domestic program goes into effect, that an importer of a covered good purchase sufficient international reserve allowances to cover the corresponding greenhouse gas emissions (unless the good arrives from a country on the excluded list).[28] The price of the international reserve allowance would be set daily equal to the market price for a domestic emissions allowance. The quantity of international reserve allowances needed for an importation would be set according to a formula that takes into account (1) the national greenhouse gas intensity rate for each category of covered goods for covered countries,

26. There are many ways to define comparability. In a discussion draft, circulated as a prelude to a House bill that would be sponsored by Representatives John Dingell (D-MI) and Richard Boucher (D-VA), a foreign-issued emissions allowance would qualify in the United States only if the foreign law requires a mandatory absolute greenhouse gas tonnage limit that is at least as stringent as the US program, including comparable monitoring and compliance (p. 201–02).

27. Boxer Amendment, S. Amdt. 4825, p. S5091 §1301. The bill makes clear that international agreements include the WTO agreement. It should be noted, however, that the WTO does not have rules defining comparable action on climate change, so the statutory reference can only have meaning by reference to general WTO rules.

28. See Sections 202(a)(2) and 1306(d). As an alternative to purchasing an international reserve allowance from the United States, an importer could substitute an allowance from a foreign government cap-and-trade system that is deemed comparable to the US system or an offset allowance from an approved program. We do not see how this option ameliorates the WTO law problems, but we do not venture a separate analysis.

and both direct and indirect emissions (as determined by the administrator), (2) an allowance adjustment factor designed to adjust in each sector for the free distribution of allowances to the same industry in the United States (as determined by the administrator), and (3) an economic adjustment ratio for foreign countries that takes into account foreign programs to limit greenhouse gas emissions and use of state-of-the-art technology (as determined by the commission).[29] This brief exposition reveals that the determination of international reserve allowances entails considerable—and potentially contentious—discretion and complexity.

A few other trade-related provisions should be noted. First, the bill provides for an exclusion for petroleum-based liquid fuel imported from a North American Free Trade Agreement (NAFTA) country that has greenhouse gas reduction requirements no less stringent than those in the United States (see Section 202). Second, the bill provides (with some exclusions) that when a product is exported for which an emissions allowance was used in domestic production, the exporting entity will receive a compensatory allowance upon export (see Section 202). Third, the bill provides for financial assistance to certain countries and specifies that the proceeds of the sale of international reserve allowances would be used to carry out a program "to mitigate negative impacts of climate change on disadvantaged communities in foreign countries" (see Section 1306). Fourth, the bill authorizes the EPA administrator to adjust the requirements for imported goods so as to take action that the commission determines necessary to address greenhouse gas emissions in covered imports "in compliance with all applicable international agreements" (see Section 1307). Fifth, the bill would allow domestic producers to use emissions allowances issued by other governments that impose mandatory greenhouse gas limits when such programs are of "comparable stringency" to the US program, including administrative action that ensures monitoring, compliance, and enforcement.

Analyzing the WTO legality of the import provisions is difficult because a defense under Article XX would be required, the program has not been enacted, and implementation is some way off. So far, all of the cases involving Article XX have dealt with measures that have actually been applied. Thus applying the Article XX case law ex ante is necessarily a tentative exercise.

Before getting to Article XX, however, there has to be a violation of a GATT discipline. Such violations may exist under the Boxer bill for several reasons. The requirement that importers purchase an international reserve allowance seems to fit within "other duties and charges" on importation that are regulated by GATT Article II:1(b). If so, the requirement amounts to an automatic violation (Quick 2008, 166). It may be possible, howev-

29. The economic adjustment ratio is determined on an economywide basis. The commission would not be able to take into account differing facts at the company level.

er, for the authors of the bill to rewrite the requirement to be an internal charge rather than a charge on importation. If so, such a charge would be reviewed under GATT Article III:2. The panel might then ask whether the burden on imports exceeds the burden on domestic production. The answer to that would depend on a comparison of relative burdens.[30] Then, if the burdens are found to be the same, the panel might conclude that the requirement to purchase an international reserve allowance passes muster under the GATT national treatment rule.

If a panel were to consider the reserve allowance requirement to be a tax or charge on an entity rather than on the product itself, then the measure would be reviewed under Article III:4.[31] The key question would be whether the program modifies the conditions of competition between imported and domestic products in a way that is less favorable to imports. The answer would probably be affirmative because the formula for calculating the requisite quantity of international reserve allowances facially discriminates based solely on the origin of the products. The formula for imports is based on the national (i.e., foreign) greenhouse gas intensity rate, while the emissions allowances for domestic products are based on the emissions of the individual producer. Such discrimination would be to the detriment of at least some imported products. Of course, a panel would also want to find some quantitative evidence of probable discriminatory effect, and a conclusion on that would depend on the decisions made regarding the other two factors in the formula.

The program would clearly be a violation of GATT Article I:1 because of the inherent origin-based discrimination. Some WTO members would be covered countries and some would not. Article I:1 generally does not permit an importing government to condition trade treatment on the policies being followed by an exporting country government, and yet the program classifies countries into covered and uncovered categories based on the comparability of the foreign government's climate change policies with US policies. Of course, finding an Article I violation would depend on a conclusion that two otherwise identical products are "like" if the only difference between them is the country of origin. In our view, this conclusion is inescapable under contemporary tariff classifications that do not take carbon content during production into account. In the future, if WTO members renegotiate tariff classifications to create separate headings based on greenhouse gas emissions, that would be a different story (Wiers

---

30. If a panel determined that foreign steel produced without a government emissions program is not a like product to domestic steel produced under such a program, then there would not be a violation of GATT Article III:2. Such a panel determination is highly unlikely in our view and would conflict with existing precedents. Nonetheless, we note the evolving role of regulatory purpose and consumer preference in Article III:4 jurisprudence as to what constitutes a "like" product and less favorable treatment.

31. The points made in footnote 30 with respect to Article III:2 also apply to Article III:4.

2008, 22–23).[32] In such a scenario, two otherwise like products that differed on their carbon footprints would be considered as not "like" products for purposes of GATT rules.

Whatever the outcome in the GATT Article II and III analysis, the international allowance requirement is a violation of Article I and would need justification under Article XX(g). Based on the *United States—Gasoline* and the *United States—Shrimp* cases, a panel would first look to see whether the import measures being challenged are reasonably related to the ends. The panel would have to start by ascertaining the ends of the program, particularly its international dimension. The text of the bill suggests several purposes, as noted above. Since Article (g) only covers the policy goal of conservation, it might not be available to justify a program whose goal is to promote "fairness."[33] On the other hand, if the legislation was rewritten to make clear that the goal of the program is to encourage other countries to enact greenhouse gas emission controls because the atmosphere is shared by all countries, that could fit within the text of Article (g).[34] The US goal could also be stated as promoting the sustainability of US consumption by imposing emissions controls on domestic producers and applying parallel consumption policies to imported products (Carmody 2008). In view of the *United States—Shrimp* precedent, a trade measure that reduces US consumption of imports that are produced with environmentally unfriendly methods is a reasonable instrument[35] to achieve the conservation

---

32. Harmonized tariff categories typically differentiate goods by observable product characteristics. Sometimes goods are differentiated by nonobservable characteristics, such as how a good will be used. For example, see 4411.92.30 in the US Tariff Schedule.

33. The text of the bill does not explain precisely what kind of fairness is being sought. One person close to the drafting has suggested that the fairness being pursued is not the "level playing field" common in the trade policy context but rather the concept of "common but differentiated responsibilities" used in multilateral environmental agreements.

34. Encouraging other countries to adopt comparable conservation policies was the environmental logic behind the measures at issue in *United States—Shrimp* that were accepted by the Appellate Body as fitting within the (g) exception. The United States did not seek to defend its import ban as promoting fairness for US shrimp harvesters.

35. In the *United States—Shrimp* dispute, the instrument used by the United States was an import ban to keep out all shrimp imports from uncertified countries. In Title XIII of the Boxer program, imports would be allowed from uncertified countries so long as the importer paid for an allowance. The allowance requirement is less trade restrictive than an import ban, but ironically, by allowing trade, the environmental rationale for the import charge is undermined. After all, in *Shrimp*, the United States did not allow foreign producers of turtle-unsafe shrimp to buy their way into the US market. The best answer to this quandary is that the requirement of an import charge may boost political pressure in foreign supplier countries to enact greenhouse gas control measures and, as a second best consequence, assure that foreign polluters pay and that US consumers are faced with some cost-internalization of greenhouse gas effects when imports are bought from countries without comparable greenhouse gas control policies.

ends being sought.[36] One might question whether charging importers for an international reserve allowance promotes conservation; perhaps, instead, the charge simply transfers resources from foreign producers to the US government. However, the program provides a built-in answer: The funds collected from the sale of international reserve allowances will be expended by the US government in foreign countries for climate change prevention. Thus, the first prong of (g) could be satisfied.[37]

The second prong of (g) could be satisfied, as the program is even-handed in requiring greenhouse gas reductions for imported goods only when domestic production is also subject to greenhouse gas reductions. Nevertheless, an objection could be raised that, by rebating emissions allowances on exports, the United States would not be fully even-handed, since some domestic production would effectively escape climate regulation. One answer to this might be that the program is even-handed with respect to goods destined for domestic consumption, even if it is not even-handed with respect to all domestic production. That answer is not wholly satisfactory.

The most serious barrier to legality under GATT Article XX would be the Article XX chapeau. The first step in the legal analysis would investigate whether there was discrimination within the meaning of Article XX. The Appellate Body has expostulated that Article XX discrimination has to be of a different quality than what has already been found in the preceding analysis under Articles I and III. Recalling the Appellate Body's statement in *United States—Shrimp* that Article XX discrimination exists when the application of the measure at issue does not allow for any inquiry into the appropriateness of the regulatory program for the conditions prevailing in exporting countries, a panel could find that there is "discrimination" because the Boxer bill does not insist on an inquiry into

---

36. The "ends" to be defended by the United States need not be to prevent carbon leakage. Thus, although some analysts have suggested that a border charge might do little to actually reduce leakage (Bordoff 2008, 20), reducing leakage need not be the sole objective that the United States might seek.

37. Trevor Houser from the Peterson Institute for International Economics has raised the question of whether border measures would qualify for Article XX(g) if they carry insufficient leverage to convince foreign governments to adopt comparable greenhouse gas regulatory programs. The question of the standard of scrutiny by the international judge of environmental programs has been discussed in trade law literature, but there is little jurisprudence on that point. In our view, the Appellate Body in *United States—Shrimp* did not carefully scrutinize the actual utility of the challenged measure. The test applied by the Appellate Body was whether the means used were "reasonably related" to the ends. In parallel cases involving the exception in Article XX(b), the Appellate Body in *European Communities—Asbestos* and *Brazil—Tyres* did not carefully scrutinize the effectiveness of those measures either. Calling for a stricter attitude by the Appellate Body would put the WTO in the paradoxical position of insisting that climate demandeur nations impose tough surveillance on developing countries in order to justify their own measures under Article XX. We doubt that the Appellate Body would follow this course.

whether a greenhouse gas regulatory program is appropriate for each affected foreign country. Furthermore, a requirement that other countries use their 2005 emission level as a baseline could be found to discriminate against rapidly growing countries, particularly when those countries have emitted cumulatively much less greenhouse gas over past decades than the United States.

Next, the panel would consider whether the Article XX discrimination identified is arbitrary or unjustifiable, and the panel would do so by examining the rationale put forward by the United States. Given the ruling in the *United States—Shrimp* compliance review, a precedent exists for considering justifiable a program that makes import access contingent on whether the foreign government has a regulatory program "comparable in effectiveness" to that of the United States.[38] The flexibilities existing in the Boxer bill seem designed to achieve the standard set out by the Appellate Body of providing sufficient latitude to take into account the specific conditions in foreign countries. Whether they do so, in fact, could only be determined after implementation, especially the determination of comparable action and, for covered countries, the allowance adjustment factor and the economic adjustment ratio. The Appellate Body's concern with discrimination in negotiations is dealt with in the bill by calling for negotiations with all countries, but again a panel would look at implementation rather than congressionally written goals.

The bill also tries to address the Appellate Body's concern in *Brazil—Tyres* that the discrimination not go against the environmental objective of the program, but in our view that effort fails to meet the tests of the chapeau for several reasons. First, recall that the program discriminates against like products based on national origin. Thus an importer of steel produced in a company in India using clean energy would still have to purchase an international allowance. This could be viewed as unjustifiable discrimination because it would go against the objective of the program.[39] As explained by Trevor Houser et al. (2008, 36), there would be an

---

38. On the other hand, one should recall that in *United States—Shrimp*, the complaining countries had not offered a dueling metric for measuring turtle conservation. So there is some uncertainty as to what a panel would do if the United States were to present one metric—namely, reduction in emissions from a 2005 baseline—and other countries were to argue for other metrics, such as reduction in emissions per capita, or reduction from a cumulative baseline. Imagine a third country T facing one metric of comparability from the United States and a different metric from India. Country T could perhaps argue that the inconsistent metrics faced by its exports are arbitrary. Another difference is that, in the *United States—Shrimp* dispute, the domestic regulatory program was effective in saving sea turtles. By contrast, the effectiveness of a US cap-and-trade program in reducing US or global carbon emissions remains to be seen.

39. See Appellate Body Report, *United States—Shrimp*, paragraph 165 (discussing exclusion of shrimp solely from a particular firm solely because of its origin in uncertified countries) and Appellate Body Report, *Brazil—Tyres*, paragraph 246 (criticizing discrimination that

environmental benefit in using measures that require foreign producers to track their own emissions and take responsibility for them. Second, aside from the allowances distributed freely to covered US industries (which are reflected in the allowance adjustment factor), an additional one-quarter of the total allowances would be distributed without charge in the early years and would be sloshing around the US economy. Such allowances could only be used to enable domestic production and could not be used for imports. The handout of such allowances by the government could cause market distortions against imports that would not be justified by any environmental purpose. If all such allowances were traded in an arm's-length transaction, that might not cause a distortion because the price for the domestic emissions allowances would go down, which would correspondingly lower the price for the international reserve allowance. But if some of the domestic allowances reach covered producers through off-market arbitrage, it would, in effect, be a way for government to lower the regulatory burden on domestic industry to the detriment of foreign firms that would have to pay the official, higher price for an international reserve allowance.

The chapeau could also be violated because of procedural deficiencies in the bill. The Appellate Body in *United States—Shrimp* criticized the US program because its operating details were shaped without the participation of other WTO members and because the system of certification was established and administered by US agencies alone. The same flaw exists in the Lieberman-Warner-Boxer bill. This flaw could be remedied if there was an internationally agreed-upon approach being followed by the United States for how countries that adopt emissions control policies should treat imports. Another corrective would be to provide for foreign government participation on the commission that is set up in Title XIII. The Appellate Body in *United States—Shrimp* also criticized the lack of opportunities for foreign governments or companies to participate in administrative proceedings and to appeal the decisions. Such flaws appear to exist with respect to the key determinations by the commission; for example, there is no appeal mechanism indicated in the program. Indeed, the Boxer bill is so complex that its very complexity could be arbitrary discrimination against foreign producers.

With regard to the disguised restriction clause in the Article XX chapeau, a panel could look at the "intention" of US policymakers as well as the design of the program. If there was evidence that the intention of the program is to restrict foreign imports in order to level the playing field between US and foreign producers, that could be viewed as a protectionist motive that could run afoul of the chapeau, even if there would be some environmental benefit to the United States of discouraging production

---

bears no relationship to the environmental objective). On the other hand, it could be argued that allowing firm-specific imports would undermine the defense under Article XX.

and exports in countries with less extensive climate policies. One statutory design feature that a panel might consider is that the only imported goods that are covered are those that are closely related to a good whose cost of production in the United States is affected by the program. This selective concern about imports seems to operate against the environmental purpose of the program.

As noted above, the compliance panel in the *United States—Shrimp* dispute explained that the unlikelihood of any "commercial gain" from the US measure was a factor in favor of finding that there was no disguised restriction under the Article XX chapeau.[40] In a situation where the US measure does lead to a domestic commercial gain over foreign competitors, it would seem more likely that a panel would detect a disguised restriction and hence disqualify the measure under Article XX.

Another consideration would be the legislative title of the program, "Promoting Fairness While Reducing Emissions." The panel could point to the differences from the *United States—Shrimp* case, where the US measure was not being justified as a way to promote fairness for US shrimp harvesters. Rather, the country certification process in *United States—Shrimp* was designed to change turtle conservation policies of other countries. We anticipate that this and some other incriminating features of the Boxer bill may be cleaned up in the version to be introduced in 2009.[41]

In addition to failing to qualify for an exception under GATT Article XX, the program could run into WTO problems under the ASCM. The two main concerns are the free allocation of allowances and the rebate of emissions allowances on exports.

A threshold question would be whether the free grant of an emissions allowance is a subsidy. From a formal perspective, the emissions allowance would arguably fall outside the scope of an ASCM subsidy because it is not a financial contribution. But from a functional perspective, one can imagine a panel saying that an allowance is equivalent to cash because the bill has provisions for sale and for "auction on consignment" by the US government of emissions allowances.[42] In other words, if anyone with an allowance can exchange it for cash in an auction facilitated by the government, the panel will deem it to be a subsidy. By contrast, if the method of allocation were pure grandfathering, to allow an entity to continue to spew out some level of carbon emissions, and that right was not transferable to another, then such a permissive regulation would not be a "subsidy."

If an emissions allowance is considered as the equivalent of a govern-

40. Panel Report, *United States—Shrimp* (Article 21.5—Malaysia), paragraph 5.143.

41. The Boucher-Dingell draft bill, tabled on October 7, 2008, does not include a "fairness" purpose in its International Reserve Allowance Program (Part G).

42. Boxer Amendment, S. Amdt. 4825, p. S5062 §401, S5065 §441.

ment payment,[43] then there are two implications for WTO subsidy law: first, whether there are actionable subsidies, and second, whether there are export subsidies. Because over half of the emissions allowances in the Boxer program are distributed freely, there will be a question as to whether this causes an actionable subsidy. This question cannot be judged a priori because the ASCM disciplines are linked to the effects of the subsidy on competition.[44]

The other question is whether the export rebate of an emissions allowance is a prohibited subsidy under ASCM Article 3. A key test in determining whether an export rebate is a prohibited subsidy is ASCM footnote 1, which excludes from ASCM subsidies a BTA on exports that is consistent with WTO law. As discussed in chapter 2, WTO law is not clear on whether a requirement to purchase an emissions allowance is a domestic tax or charge on a product that could serve as a basis for a rebate on exports.[45]

Another issue that could arise is a hypothetical decision by foreign governments to purchase international reserve allowances and give them freely to companies that want to export to the United States. If the free allocation of an emissions allowance within the United States is a subsidy, then a free allocation of a US-created international reserve allowance outside the United States would also be a subsidy. Indeed, even if all emissions allowances within the United States were auctioned, and therefore not subsidies, a foreign government program to buy an international reserve allowance may be considered a "financial contribution" under ASCM Article 1. Therefore, if domestic injury to a US industry could be shown, the US government would be able to countervail imports from countries that bought international reserve allowances for the benefit of their exporters.

In summary, the Lieberman-Warner-Boxer provisions on imports seem to have been written with a roadmap of WTO law in mind, and some of the potential legal conflicts were nicely dealt with in the design of the legislation. Nevertheless, there remain GATT violations that would require defense under Article XX, and an adjudication would probably find that the program fails to comply with the chapeau of Article XX. We have doubts about the assumption made by the proponents of the bill that a WTO panel would apply the *United States—Shrimp* precedent approvingly to a climate program that, after all, involves astronomically more trade

---

43. Jason E. Bordoff (2008, 23) has observed that under US budget scorekeeping, free allocation of permits will be scored as a budget outlay.

44. Article 5, footnote 13 of the ASCM permits a cause of action for a threat of serious prejudice, but WTO panels have not yet clarified how such a threat could be demonstrated in litigation.

45. In other words, the only way that ASCM footnote 1 could help is if the requirement to deposit an emissions allowance is viewed as a tax on a product, not a tax on the producer.

than was involved in the *Shrimp* dispute.[46] In addition, the ASCM would also come into play, and the panel would need to decide how emissions allowances are treated under the relevant subsidy disciplines.

Australia's Carbon Pollution Reduction Scheme

In July 2008 the Australian government released a Green Paper presenting a cap-and-trade scheme. To deal with the problem of competition "against firms that do not at this stage have comparable carbon constraints," the paper proposes special assistance for "emissions-intensive trade-exposed industries" (Australian Government 2008, 27). The assistance would come in the form of freely allocated carbon pollution permits to those industries. The amount allocated would be large, about 30 percent of the total carbon pollution permits issued. The paper explains that "if assistance is not provided these industries may be disadvantaged relative to their international competitors."

The Australian proposal deals with competitiveness and emissions leakage problems through aid to certain carbon-intensive industries. Because domestic aid is involved, an examination of the WTO legality of this provision requires consideration of the ASCM. Part III of the ASCM contains disciplines for actionable subsidies. For a measure to come within the scope of Part III, it must be a subsidy and it must be specific. As noted above, the question of whether an emissions allowance or a carbon pollution permit is a subsidy does not have a clear answer, and there has been no WTO jurisprudence on this point. If the free allocation of a pollution permit is a financial contribution, then it is a subsidy. If it is a subsidy, then the facts of the Australian program make it a specific subsidy because it is targeted to carbon-intensive industries. The analysis below assumes that the Australian measure is a specific subsidy.

Part III of the ASCM prohibits subsidies that cause adverse effects to the interests of other members (ASCM, Article 5). The most pertinent form of adverse effect is "serious prejudice," which may arise in a few ways. One is having the effect "to displace or impede the imports of a like product of another Member into the market of the subsidizing Member."[47] Here

---

46. We also note that, despite proposals to do so, no government over the past eight years has imposed border measures on the United States on the grounds that the US government had not adopted a climate program comparable to its own. Nor to our knowledge has any government released a legal analysis suggesting that such a border measure would comply with WTO rules. During the George W. Bush administration, US trade officials argued that such a measure would violate WTO rules. The European Commission considered such a proposal a few years ago for the European Union Emission Trading Scheme but did not adopt it (see box 3.2).

47. ASCM, Article 6.3(a). Another relevant provision is Article 6.3(c) regarding significant price undercutting because of the subsidy.

Box 3.2 European Union Emission Trading Scheme

In January 2005 the European Union launched its Emission Trading Scheme (ETS), a cap-and-trade system.[1] The EU ETS was originally designed to help member states meet their targets under the Kyoto Protocol. However, the EU ETS is an independent scheme, since it was enacted before the Kyoto Protocol became legally binding.

After its three-year trial period (Phase I, 2005–07), the EU ETS entered its second trading period (Phase II, 2008–12), which corresponds with the compliance period of the Kyoto Protocol. The EU ETS currently covers more than 10,000 installations in the energy and industrial sectors—which account for about half of the overall EU CO_2 emissions—across all 27 EU member states plus three other members of the European Economic Area: Norway, Iceland, and Liechtenstein.[2]

While the EU ETS is considered successful because it put a price on carbon and created a multinational climate regime,[3] the two trading periods revealed fundamental problems. For both the first and second phases, member states were required to draft their national allocation plans (NAPs), which determine their total levels of emissions and the EU allowances (EUAs) that each installation in their country would receive. NAPs then needed approval by the European Commission. This approach created huge differences in each member's allocation rules, giving rise to fears about unfair competition between members. Another issue is that the ETS has provided little incentive to develop new energy technology, as it gave away large numbers of free allowances during the two trading periods.

Keeping these concerns in mind, the European Commission proposed a far-reaching climate action and energy package in January 2008, and the European Parliament approved the package with revised terms on December 17, 2008. Under a so-called 20-20-20 proposal, the European Union sets a stringent reduction target of greenhouse gas emissions at least 20 percent below 1990 levels by 2020 (or a possible 30 percent reduction if a post-Kyoto regime were to agree), and a 20 percent target share for renewable energies in energy use by 2020.

While the European Union has extended the scope and coverage of the ETS by approving the climate package, some criticized the European Union for failing to ensure the original climate package. Citing heavy costs on certain industries and the prospect of a sharp recession, some members threatened to veto the EU climate package unless the package addressed their concerns. Consequently, a series of concessions were granted to selected industries and to poorer members in the final version. The EU climate package does not include trade restrictive measures, but there are growing concerns about the possible loss of competitiveness by domestic industries to non-EU suppliers. As a result, discussions continue within

Box 3.2   European Union Emission Trading Scheme *(continued)*

the European Union on the imposition of carbon taxes or kindred fees on imports from countries that do not have comparable domestic climate programs.[4]

While the package includes provisions for auctioning permits that will start in 2013 and gradually increase as a share of the total over Phase III, a significant number of permits are still planned to be given away free. For example, the package allows the European Community to allocate 100 percent of allowances free of charge to certain industries that are exposed to a significant risk of carbon "leakage" if they meet certain criteria.[5] The auctions for manufactured goods will start at 20 percent in 2013 and then rise to 70 percent in 2020. For most EU utilities, full auctioning will start in 2013, but for existing Eastern European power plants, permit auctions will start at 30 percent in 2013 and not rise to 100 percent until 2020.[6] As mentioned earlier, free allowances would be examined under the Agreement on Subsidies and Countervailing Measures, even though it is still unclear whether an emissions allowance amounts to a subsidy.

---

1. The EU ETS is based on Directive 2003/87/EC, which entered into force October 25, 2003. The directive can be found at http://eur-lex.europa.eu (accessed on January 12, 2009).

2. See Memo/08/35, available at http://europa.eu (accessed on January 12, 2009).

3. See appendix E for details about the EU ETS as a carbon market.

4. For example, the European Union considered the inclusion in its Phase III plan of a requirement that European importers of carbon-intensive products buy carbon allocations. However, this proposal was dropped at the last minute due to opposition from the United States. See *Inside US Trade* 26, no. 4, January 25, 2008. Also, the day before the parliament approved the package, French President Nicolas Sarkozy urged that the United States and other countries take similar action, matching the EU commitment. See Associated Press, "Sarkozy: Others Must Match EU Climate Change Cuts," December 16, 2008, http://news.yahoo.com (accessed on January 12, 2009).

5. The full text adopted by the European Parliament on December 17, 2008 is available at www.europarl.europa.eu (accessed on January 12, 2009).

6. See Jonathan Stearns, "EU Slashes Emission Caps on Utilities, Factories," Bloomberg News, December 17, 2008, www.bloomberg.com (accessed on January 12, 2009).

Australia would be the subsidizing member, and another WTO member challenging Australia's subsidy would have a cause of action if its potential exports to Australia from emissions-intensive industries are being displaced or impeded by Australia's domestic subsidy.

One cannot say in advance whether the proposed subsidy would be actionable, because under ASCM rules, that conclusion has to be demonstrated by evidence of a subsidy's effects. But a yellow flag must be raised regarding the Australian proposal because, by its own admission, its very purpose is to prevent trade disadvantage to emissions-intensive, trade-exposed domestic industries. Thus, if the program succeeds, it would surely be displacing imports from a country that could bring and win a WTO case.

4

Future Climate Policy and the World Trade Organization

At the climate change conference in Bali in December 2007, countries agreed to launch a two-year process of formal negotiations on a successor pact to the Kyoto Protocol. The post-Kyoto regime is scheduled to be finalized in Copenhagen in December 2009. While it is expected to include new ambitious targets for reducing greenhouse gas emissions and to commit both developing and developed countries to take action, it may well leave many controversial issues unsolved, such as the nonparty issue,[1] the extent and binding force of obligations undertaken by both developed and developing countries, and the permissible nature of measures that one country can take to induce compliance by other countries.

At the ministerial session of the UN General Assembly in February 2008, representatives from developing countries cautioned that a new treaty to tackle climate change might hamper their efforts to achieve sustainable development. In his statement, China's special representative Yu Qingtai emphasized that any framework for future arrangements must be firmly based on the principle of "common but differentiated responsibilities" as previously established by the United Nations Framework Convention on Climate Change (UNFCCC) and the Kyoto Protocol. He also stated that the effective participation of developing countries will depend

---

1. The main nonparty issue inherent in multilateral environmental agreements (MEAs) is the old free-rider question, which also raises a competitiveness concern. Nonparties to an MEA can enjoy the environmental benefits while making little or no contribution of their own. Under the Kyoto Protocol, a related issue was how to link a nonparty country's national emissions trading program with flexible trading mechanisms.

on financial and technological assistance from developed countries.[2]

On the other hand, developed countries such as the United States and those of the European Union have urged developing countries to be more cooperative. The clean development mechanism, one of the core mechanisms of the Kyoto Protocol, allows Annex I countries (developed countries) to meet their commitment by funding projects in non-Annex I countries (developing countries). Three key mechanisms under the Kyoto Protocol are summarized in box 4.1. Under the Kyoto Protocol, developing countries are not obligated to do more than facilitate these offset projects. However, at the carbon market conference in Copenhagen in March 2008, Yvon Slingenberg, the EU Commission's head of emissions trading, stated that the world will not reach appropriate emissions levels if developing countries play a role only as offset suppliers. He urged developing countries to gradually shift from offsetting to cap and trade. However, at the same conference, Yvo de Boer, executive secretary of the UNFCCC, pointed out that the developing world has repeatedly stated that it is not willing to adopt cap-and-trade systems.[3]

Given these huge differences—which reflect the basic disagreement between "per capita comparability" and "carbon price equivalency" discussed at the outset—the possibility of reaching clear-cut international standards and obligations seems remote for the Copenhagen conference in 2009. However, the scientific case for climate change will likely become even more persuasive over the next two years. Thus, compromise targets and time paths are likely to be agreed upon, while leaving ample room for national interpretation. Under these circumstances, we foresee that countries will enact their own unique mixes of domestic measures accompanied by import bans, border adjustments, and other mechanisms to address competitive concerns and to encourage action abroad. Already, the European Union, the United States, Canada, and Australia are well along in designing unique national systems with international measures to mitigate climate change. The next section examines how the World Trade Organization (WTO) should respond to the looming clash between climate change policies moving at different speeds.

Dispute Settlement Approach

The most obvious way to determine whether trade measures in support of greenhouse gas emissions controls are compatible with WTO agreements

---

2. The full statement is available at www.fmprc.gov.cn (accessed on January 12, 2009).

3. de Boer added that developing countries claim that carbon offsetting under the Kyoto clean development mechanism is the only serious money now on the table and that EU proposals would constrain the level of offset payments. For more details, see Gerard Wynn, "EU Wants Developing Nations to Do More on Climate," Reuters, March 11, 2008, www.reuters.com (accessed on January 12, 2009).

Box 4.1 Mechanisms under the Kyoto Protocol

The Kyoto Protocol adopted three major "flexibility mechanisms" for members to enlist the cooperation of other countries in applying cost-effective methods for reducing emissions or removing carbon from the atmosphere. All three mechanisms are based on the protocol's system of scoring success in meeting national targets. Under the system, Annex I countries should reduce their emissions over the five-year commitment period by the assigned amount units (AAUs—each unit equals one ton of CO_2e). Annex I countries should provide information to demonstrate that their use of the mechanisms is "supplemental to domestic action" to achieve their targets; this information is to be assessed by the Facilitative Branch of the Compliance Committee.

Clean development mechanism (CDM): This mechanism enables Annex I countries to implement projects that reduce emissions in non-Annex I countries (which do not have an obligation to reduce their greenhouse gas emissions), or to absorb carbon through afforestation or reforestation activities, in return for certified emissions reductions (CERs, tCERs, and lCERs), and to assist the host countries in achieving sustainable development and contributing to the ultimate objective of the convention. The CDM is supervised by the CDM Executive Board. The challenges and issues embedded in the CDM are discussed in appendix D.

Joint implementation: Under this mechanism, an Annex I country may implement an emissions-reducing project, or a project that enhances removals by sinks in the territory of another Annex I country, and count the resulting emission reduction units (ERUs) toward meeting its own Kyoto target.

Emissions trading: This provides for Annex I countries to acquire units from other Annex I countries. These units may be in the form of AAUs and various removal units, namely ERUs, CERs, tCERs and lCERs. Further, the protocol enables a group of several Annex I countries to join together to create a market-within-a-market. Under this provision, the European Union created the Emission Trading Scheme, and each EU allowance unit is equivalent to one Kyoto AAU. Short summaries of the major carbon markets (schemes) in operation in are provided in appendix E.

Source: United Nations Framework Convention on Climate Change, http://unfccc.int (accessed on January 12, 2009).

---

is to let the dispute settlement process run its course. Eventually, a record of decided cases will define the contours of WTO obligations. The Appellate Body's rulings in previous cases showed considerable sympathy with environmental concerns and increased the likelihood that trade measures that further greenhouse gas emissions controls will pass muster under WTO rules. Nevertheless, it is worth noting that the trade measures adjudicated in previous dispute cases did not have a major restrictive impact on commerce. By contrast, serious carbon emissions controls could heavily impact trade. Hence, trade disputes are likely to be more intense, and both panels and the Appellate Body may show greater concern with the ramifications of disputes for the trading system.

Moreover, in the absence of clear-cut and uniform international standards, the greenhouse gas control systems adopted by various countries will differ in major respects—both as to the severity of limitations and the details of operation. The combination of enormous costs, huge "quota rent" values, and systemic differences will generate tremendous lobbying pressure and give entrée to protectionist forces. Out of the political maelstrom, it seems certain that some countries will use domestic greenhouse gas controls, at least in part, as a rationale for curtailing imports and giving a boost to domestic firms. In 2009 economic stimulus in the United States and other countries may provide legislative vehicles for new subsidies in the name of clean energy or clean transport.

Under this scenario, many cases will be brought to the WTO, and decisions are unlikely to produce clear guidelines within a short time frame (a big WTO case can easily take at least three years to run the course of litigation through the Appellate Body and the Dispute Settlement Body). In other words, the case approach foretells a long period of uncertainty and trade frictions. As trade battles are fought, some countries may become more devoted to winning legal cases than to fighting the common enemy, climate change.

In general, we believe that relegating these matters to the WTO dispute system is not the best course. If the Appellate Body is too strict on trade-related climate measures, that could inspire greater criticism of the already-fragile WTO system. If the Appellate Body is too lenient on trade-related climate measures, by according users of unilateral measures excessive deference, that could open the door to widespread opportunistic protectionism and rent-seeking behavior. Even a middle ground is not optimal because the decisions at stake should not be made by international trade judges on the basis of the complex and ambiguous WTO jurisprudence spelled out earlier in this study. So even if the Appellate Body gets it just right under the existing framework of articles, codes, and prior decisions, and balances trade and environment in a way that we would consider reasonable, others with a different sense of balance will challenge the outcome as illegitimate. Moreover, bringing a dozen climate cases to the WTO would put great stress on its dispute settlement mechanism.

One never-used WTO institution that could usefully come into play is the Permanent Group of Experts (PGE) for questions about subsidies. The PGE consists of five independent experts selected by the WTO's Subsidies and Countervailing Measures Committee. Upon the request of a panel, the PGE can make an authoritative determination as to whether a measure is a prohibited export subsidy.[4] Upon the request of the committee, the PGE may be asked to issue an advisory opinion on the nature or existence of any subsidy.[5] Upon the request of a WTO member, the PGE will issue an advisory opinion on the nature of any subsidy that a member itself has or is proposing for introduction. This type of advisory opinion is supposed to remain confidential and may not be invoked in WTO dispute proceedings regarding actionable subsidies.[6]

Negotiation Approaches

Efforts have already been made to accommodate environmental controls by amending articles of the General Agreement on Tariffs and Trade (GATT) and other parts of the WTO legal text. The European Union has argued for modifications to GATT/WTO disciplines for environmental reasons, but its attempts have so far failed due to objections from many countries.[7] Within the WTO, legal text can only be amended by a consensus of members, which means that no member objects to the change. The continuing stalemate in Doha Round negotiations makes any WTO amendment for climate even less likely.

Apart from rewriting the WTO legal text, another approach would be to ask WTO members to approve a waiver to WTO obligations for a forthcoming climate agreement. A waiver, unlike a revision of the text, does not require a consensus among WTO members, but it does require approval from at least three-quarters of members.[8] Even a three-fourths requirement would make it difficult to get a waiver on a controversial subject. While waivers have been discussed for other MEAs (besides the Kyoto Protocol), none have been enacted.

The post-Kyoto regime agreed upon in Copenhagen in 2009 might propose such a waiver. For this to be likely, however, there would first need to have been broad agreement on appropriate trade measures within the post–Kyoto Protocol. In our view, reaching such agreement will be a bridge too far for the Copenhagen negotiations.

In the absence of a negotiated compact that defines WTO "green spaces" with respect to trade measures that foster greenhouse gas controls

---

4. Agreement on Subsidies and Countervailing Measures (ASCM) Article 4.5.

5. ASCM Article 24.3. Such a request by the committee would require consensus.

6. ASCM Article 24.4.

7. Among others who urge modification of existing WTO rules, the Public Citizen (2008) contends that the current rules do not allow enough space for domestic measures (such as cap-and-trade systems) that are designed to restrict greenhouse gas emissions.

8. In practice, waivers are approved by consensus, but voting is always possible.

worldwide, tit-for-tat retaliation and prolonged WTO litigation are likely. Faced with this prospect, countries could work together to reach agreement on trade measures that are acceptable and comply with core tenets of the WTO system (Pataki 2008, 59). The key for such a code to be practical is to enlist a critical mass of countries. By a WTO code, we mean a plurilateral agreement under Annex 4 of the WTO agreement.[9] In a plurilateral agreement, a subset of WTO members may commit to a set of rules that is binding among them and can be enforced in WTO dispute settlement. Such plurilateral agreements "do not create either obligations or rights for Members that have not accepted them."[10] Although such a code would require consensus of all WTO members to be formally added to the WTO agreement, such action could be politically possible because it would not necessarily require that all members agree to the text or substance of the code.[11]

Our proposal for a code is consistent with the policy direction given at the 2008 G-8 Summit in Hokkaido, Japan. The Declaration of Leaders Meeting of Major Economies on Energy Security and Climate Change states that the leaders will "[d]irect our trade officials responsible for WTO issues to advance with a sense of urgency their discussions on issues relevant to promoting our cooperation on climate change."[12] This statement was noteworthy in calling for normative action about climate in the WTO.

If negotiating a code as a WTO plurilateral agreement proves politically impossible, then a group of like-minded member governments could negotiate a code outside of the WTO. It might be called a Code of Good WTO Practice on Greenhouse Gas Emissions Controls. The advantage of acting outside the WTO is that nonparticipating countries could not block the negotiation of such a code. Of course, with an extra-WTO code, WTO dispute settlement would not be available for enforcement. But we do not see that as a serious disadvantage because other forms of dispute settlement could be used if needed.

Regardless of whether the code is negotiated inside the WTO as a plurilateral agreement or outside the WTO among like-minded countries, the code would not directly apply to countries that did not subscribe to it. So the purpose of such a code would be not to regulate the legal relation-

---

9. US law is ambiguous as to whether congressional approval is required for the United States to agree to such a plurilateral agreement in the WTO. The one precedent was the amendment to the Agreement on Trade-Related Aspects of Intellectual Property Rights that the Bush administration accepted for the United States without any explicit ex ante or ex post congressional approval.

10. WTO agreement, Article II:3.

11. If a particular WTO member objected to adding the code as a plurilateral agreement, that member might be induced to put aside its objections with side payments.

12. The declaration is available at www.mofa.go.jp (accessed on January 12, 2009).

ship between code members and nonmembers but rather for participating governments to agree in advance to a set of rules for trade-related climate measures in the interest of heading off disputes among those governments in the WTO. If such a code could prevent disputes coming to the WTO between the United States, European Union, Canada, Japan, and a few other countries from the Organization for Economic Cooperation and Development, that in itself would be an important accomplishment. If it could head off disputes involving China and India as well, that would be a great accomplishment.

Bringing Multilateral Environmental Norms into the World Trade Organization as Standards

In contrast to a code on trade and climate among like-minded governments, the climate regime itself could act multilaterally to create norms on trade and climate. If a forthcoming international protocol on climate contained provisions regarding trade measures, such a treaty would be considered by a WTO panel in interpreting the related WTO provisions. A key question would be whether the MEA had been agreed to by a WTO member invoking dispute settlement.[13] If the WTO member invoking dispute settlement is not a party to the MEA (e.g., the United States with respect to the Kyoto Protocol), then the WTO defendant country is probably not going to be able to use the MEA as a defense.

In recent speeches, WTO Director-General Pascal Lamy has suggested that norms agreed to in MEAs would be taken seriously at the WTO. For example, in a speech to a European Parliament Committee in May 2008, Lamy said "[a] multilateral agreement that includes all major emitters would be the best placed international instrument to guide other instruments, such as the WTO...."[14] In a speech to the Informal Trade Ministers' Dialogue on Climate Change in Bali in December 2007, Lamy said that a deal on climate change struck in the UNFCCC would "then send the WTO an appropriate signal on how its rules may best be put to the service of sustainable development; in other words, a signal on how this particular toolbox of rules [the WTO] should be employed in the fight against climate change."[15]

Building on Lamy's remarks, one can imagine that an international environmental forum could establish nonbinding principles for the use

---

13. Because Taiwan is not allowed to participate in MEAs, no MEA can be agreed to by all WTO members.

14. Pascal Lamy, "A Consensual International Accord on Climate Change Is Needed," Temporary Committee on Climate Change, European Parliament, May 29, 2008.

15. Pascal Lamy, "Doha Could Deliver Double-Win for Environment and Trade," Informal Trade Ministers' Dialogue on Climate Change, December 9, 2007.

of trade measures for climate change. Such principles could be used by a panel in applying Article XX. Indeed, the Appellate Body referred to extra-WTO norms in the *United States—Shrimp* case by considering the Rio Declaration on Environment and Development.[16] All else being equal, we think that a WTO panel is more likely to reject a purely unilateral measure under the Article XX chapeau than an approach stamped with some intergovernmental imprimatur of international best practices (Howse and Eliason 2008, 35). We could also imagine a multilateral climate agreement adopting binding rules regarding the use of trade measures, but this is unlikely because many countries would object to trying to write rules in an MEA that override the WTO agreement.

Given the December 2008 stalemate in WTO negotiations, it is possible that adding the issue of trade and climate could help stimulate the trade talks, with the aspiration of writing a WTO climate code. To encourage WTO negotiating efforts, US climate legislation and the legislation of other important emitting countries should contain a moratorium, to expire in January 2012, on the application of border measures or other extraterritorial controls to imported products.[17] While recognizing that negotiating a WTO code on climate will be a difficult venture, three years would seem time enough to determine whether a new WTO code can be forged that provides guidelines for countries on trade-related climate policies and heads off contentious disputes in the WTO. More details on the proposal for a WTO code are presented in chapter 5.

Reinvigorating the Doha Round

During 2008, WTO negotiators made several unsuccessful efforts to bring the Doha Round to a conclusion. The last attempt in December 2008 foundered, among other reasons, on the argument that negotiators should await the new administration of Barack Obama to see what its attitude toward the WTO and the Doha Round will be. Over the past year, some observers have suggested that 2009 offers an opportunity to breathe new life into the Doha negotiations by specifically adding climate to the negotiating agenda. No detailed proposals along these lines have surfaced, but the kernel of the idea is that synergies may be gained by linking climate negotiations to WTO negotiations. The political argument for issue linkage is somewhat elusive because major developing countries will be asked to do more than they currently want to in both arenas. However, if the Doha agenda is revised to include climate, then the negotiators would

---

16. Appellate Body Report, *United States—Import Prohibitions of Certain Shrimp and Shrimp Products*, WT/DS58/AB/R, adopted on November 6, 1998, paragraphs 154, 168.

17. For similar reasons, and to facilitate talks in Copenhagen, the EU Commission has deferred consideration of border measures (see box 3.2).

have an opportunity to discuss adoption of a code along the lines of that presented in chapter 5.

As a more ambitious approach, one could imagine a renegotiation of the entire harmonized tariff system to distinguish products as to whether they are climate-friendly.[18] The Doha negotiators are already considering tariff cuts for environmental goods,[19] and those negotiations could be fine-tuned if the definition of environmental goods were to be linked to an international climate agreement.[20] The real political purchase of a revised tariff schedule would not be just the expanded tariff classifications but, more importantly, an agreement in the WTO to allow higher tariffs (above current bound levels) on goods whose production is not being accounted for under national commitments to a multilateral accord. Negotiations would also be needed in the World Customs Organization. However, there is no reason to believe that countries like China and India would go along with the WTO consensus needed to allow a comprehensive retariffication.

Another possibility for the WTO is to initiate sectoral agreements on climate that would restrict international trade in a particular commodity (e.g., steel) to countries with qualifying greenhouse gas emission limits. The use of trade-restrictive sectoral agreements (e.g., textiles and apparel) has a long history in the trading system, and one of the achievements of the Uruguay Round was the phaseout of those agreements.[21] That said, it would be possible to reintroduce a commodity approach to controlling trade for climate reasons if all WTO members agreed. This could be done by an amendment to the WTO or perhaps a WTO agreement with the International Energy Agency. In addition, one should note that GATT Article XX contains a long-dormant exception for measures "undertaken in pursuance of obligations under any intergovernmental commodity agreement that conforms to the criteria submitted to the contracting

---

18. For example, any climate-sensitive tariff classification could be divided into a plain and starred (*) classification, with the latter for goods produced in a climate-friendly way.

19. To our knowledge, there is no WTO-approved definition of an environmental good or service. In the most recent paper (November 2005) on the topic available on the WTO website, the designation of a good as "environmental" seems to be based on its end use rather than its production process. WTO Committee on Trade and Environment Special Session, "Synthesis of Submissions on Environmental Goods. Informal Note by the Secretariat," TN/TE/W/63 (November 17, 2005). Four more recent papers are listed on the WTO portal on this topic but carry a "JOB" designation, which means that the document is classified and not available to the public. See TN/TE/INF/4.Rev.13 (April 30, 2008, 6).

20. An agreement to reduce tariffs on environmental goods could be modeled on the WTO Information Technology Agreement.

21. The Multi-Fiber Arrangement did not have social or environmental provisions, but other trade provisions have contained social provisions regarding labor conditions (notably the Generalized System of Preferences).

parties and not disapproved by them, or which is itself submitted and not so disapproved."[22] This might allow international climate sectoral agreements, open to all WTO members, to be countenanced by the GATT.

---

22. GATT Article XX(h) and Ad Article XX, paragraph (h) regarding the UN Economic and Social Council resolution. The meaning of the provision was discussed in a GATT panel decision, *EEC—Import Regime for Bananas*, DS38/R, adopted on February 11, 1994 [*Bananas II*], paragraphs 165–66.

5

Elements of a Trade and Climate Code

A Code of Good WTO Practice on Greenhouse Gas Emissions Controls should delineate a large "green space" for measures that are designed to limit greenhouse gas emissions both within the territory of the member country and globally. By a "green space," we mean a policy space for climate measures that are imposed in a manner broadly consistent with core World Trade Organization (WTO) principles even if a technical violation of WTO law could occur. Measures that conform to the green space rules would not be subject to challenge in WTO dispute settlement by governments subscribing to the code.[1] In other words, there would be a "peace clause" to head off disputes in the WTO between countries that subscribe to this code. If a government does not subscribe to the code, then the code would have no effect on that government's obligations and procedural rights in the WTO.

Within the green space, the greenhouse gas code should encourage, but not require, members to adopt greenhouse gas carbon taxes, or to auction emissions permits, as preferred greenhouse gas control measures. The reason is that to the extent the award of emissions permits becomes a commercial transaction, the room for subsidies is narrowed, and the basis of comparing emissions costs between activities and across countries is vastly improved. The greenhouse gas code could also explicitly prohibit

---

1. The question of whether the code has been followed could be litigated. If the code qualifies as a plurilateral WTO agreement, then WTO dispute settlement could be used by code members. If the code is outside the WTO, then a WTO panel could be asked to take it into account as an inter se agreement among the parties. Another approach is to provide for arbitration outside the WTO.

a few greenhouse gas–related measures that might be permitted under some interpretations of existing WTO articles and codes. The sections that follow outline some of the elements of our proposal for a greenhouse gas code.

A. Definitions Applicable to the "Green Space"

1. Trade-Related Greenhouse Gas Measures

Greenhouse gas controls that affect international trade in goods and services are defined to include the following measures, whether enacted by the member national government itself or by subsidiary political units within the member country (e.g., states or provinces):

a. taxes or charges on the volume of carbon equivalent emissions released in association with the production of imported or exported products (goods and services);

b. performance standards expressed in terms of maximum carbon equivalent emissions associated with the production of a designated quantity of the imported or exported product;

c. cap-and-trade systems that require the submission of emission permits in conjunction with imported products, or that distribute such permits in conjunction with exported products, whether the permits are distributed by government free of charge, sold at a fixed price, or auctioned;

d. comparability systems that evaluate the greenhouse gas controls of other WTO members and impose regulatory requirements on imports from, or exports to, another member country that fails to meet the prescribed standard;

e. any other greenhouse gas control measure that directly regulates or raises the landed cost of imported products, or that directly regulates or lowers the free-on-board cost of exported products; and

f. subsidies that finance research and development or physical infrastructure for the production of alternative energy sources with lower greenhouse gas emission characteristics than traditional energy sources; subsidies that finance the sequestration of greenhouse gas emissions; and subsidies for climate adaptation.

2. Like Products

For the purpose of ensuring comparability between imported and domestic products, like domestic products shall be defined as all goods belonging to the same four-digit harmonized tariff system (HTS) code or group of codes and, at the option of the member country that imposes greenhouse gas control measures, the ancillary goods used in making the final domestic products.

B. Exported Products

Because a significant percentage of world production is exported (about 25 percent in 2007),[2] a global system for greenhouse gas control ought to adopt some convention for how exports will be treated in national greenhouse gas accounting. The solution proposed here is to maintain producer responsibility for the climate externalities of exported production, but to allow importing nations to take additional measures, consistent with their national regimes, to address the externalities of consumption. Thus, the rule for exports would be that no greenhouse gas control measure shall accord more favorable treatment to exported products than to like products used or consumed domestically by the member country. In other words, rules akin to the "origin system" for border tax adjustments shall apply to exports of carbon-intensive products, so that trade-related greenhouse gas measures are not waived for exports. Under the "origin system," for example, assuming that the United States and Canada both impose equivalent greenhouse gas controls, steel plate exported from the United States to Canada would be subject to the climate-related controls of the exporting country ("origin"), which in this case is the United States, but normally exempted from the climate controls of the importing country ("destination"), which is Canada. Of course, if Canada imposes more stringent controls than the United States on the production of steel plate, then Canada could apply the incremental regulation to steel plate imports from the United States. By contrast with "destination system" rules,[3] this choice will accomplish two goals: (1) between two countries that both impose equivalent greenhouse gas controls on imported goods, origin system rules will simplify international accounting for emissions; and (2) the origin system will discourage countries from promoting carbon-intensive production for shipment to countries that do not impose greenhouse gas control measures on imported goods, or that impose lighter controls than the exporting country. Although we propose that climate-related taxes or permits on domestic production not be exempted or rebated on exports, it

---

2. Total world real GDP in 2007 (at market exchange rates) was $54,312 billion, and total world exports of goods were $13,729 billion (IMF 2008b).

3. Under the "destination system," traded goods are subject to the climate-related taxes of the importing ("destination") country and exempted from the climate-related taxes of the exporting ("origin") country. In the case that climate-related taxes are already paid to the exporting country, such taxes will be refunded upon export.

is noted that this rule would have competitive effects. Most important is that exporting firms may be disadvantaged by comparison with firms that produce in a country with weaker greenhouse gas controls.

C. Border Adjustments for Carbon Equivalent Taxes

A member may impose its own carbon equivalent taxes on imported products. The calculation of carbon equivalent taxes may include taxes imposed both directly and indirectly on like domestic products. In calculating the appropriate border adjustment, the member may average the taxes imposed directly and indirectly on like domestic products made by different domestic firms. In assessing its border adjustments, the member shall give tax credit for any carbon equivalent taxes imposed directly and indirectly (and not rebated) on like products by another member country on exports within the same four-digit HTS code or group of codes. The rationale for this approach is to encourage countries to impose their own carbon taxes on production whether for domestic use or export, not rebate the taxes on exports, and instead keep the revenue.

D. Performance Standards on Imported Products

A member shall not impose more burdensome performance standards on imported products than it imposes directly and indirectly on like products made domestically.[4] Prior to imposing performance standards on imported products, a member shall consult with its principal supplying nations. The member imposing performance standards shall periodically engage and pay for a recognized conformity assessor to assess greenhouse gas emissions levels for like products made within the member country itself and by individual exporting firms among its foreign suppliers. In the event that an exporting firm does not furnish adequate information, the conformity assessor may use the best information available to estimate the exporter's greenhouse gas emissions levels.

E. Cap-and-Trade System

1. Permits Distributed Free of Charge

A code member government may distribute a defined quantity of greenhouse gas emissions permits free of charge to firms of its choosing, and

---

4. By "performance standards" we mean regulations or standards set by a government, usually expressed in terms of maximum carbon equivalent emissions associated with the production of a designated quantity of the good. Under GATT Article III, such performance standards might not be a valid basis for differentiating like products.

such distributions shall not be regarded as a subsidy for purpose of the Agreement on Subsidies and Countervailing Measures (ASCM) unless a distribution is linked to exportation. The member that is distributing permits may designate the method of certification to ensure compliance with stated emissions levels. The permits so distributed may specify the type of greenhouse gas emission (CO_2, CH_4, etc.) and the industry of use. The member country may allow permits to be banked, and the permits may be nontransferable or transferable. However, if permits may be transferred, by sale or otherwise, to another party, no restriction shall be placed on the transfer to a qualifying firm based in another member country.

2. Permits Sold at a Fixed Price

A member may distribute a flexible quantity of greenhouse gas emissions permits by sale at a fixed price; however, the price may be changed from time to time. The permits so sold may specify the type of greenhouse gas emission (CO_2, CH_4, etc.) and the industry of use. No restriction shall be placed on permit or allowance purchases by a qualifying firm based in another member country.[5] The member that is selling permits may designate the method of certification to ensure compliance with stated emissions levels.

3. Permits Distributed by Auction

A member may distribute a defined quantity of greenhouse gas emission allowance permits by public auction. The permits so auctioned may specify the type of greenhouse gas emission (CO_2, CH_4, etc.) and the industry of use. No restriction shall be placed on permit or allowance purchases by a qualifying firm based in another member country. The member that is auctioning permits may designate the method of certification to ensure compliance with stated emissions levels.

---

5. Under some bills introduced in Congress in 2008, the United States would not allow foreign firms to buy US permits but instead would require them to buy US-issued foreign allowances. However, we expect the global carbon market to evolve toward more flexible and freer permit trading systems. Therefore, permits sold at a fixed price and those distributed at auction are included in an attempt to promote fairness and nondiscrimination in permit trading. In addition, we expect the post-Kyoto regime would allow countries more flexibility in trading various emissions units so countries can meet their emission reduction targets. As a matter of information, under the current Kyoto regime, emissions trading between countries (as set out in Article 17 of the Kyoto Protocol) allows countries that have extra emission units after achieving their commitment to sell those units to countries that are over their targets. Also, through joint implementation or clean development mechanisms of the Kyoto Protocol, the country can earn emissions reduction units to meet its own target.

F. Comparability Assessments of Foreign Climate Regulation

A member's comparability system that evaluates the greenhouse gas controls of other WTO members and assesses charges on imports from, or exports to, another member country that fails to meet the regulations of the originating member, shall observe the following principles:

1. Comparability shall be assessed by an international entity, for example, the compliance committees of the United Nations Framework Convention on Climate Change (UNFCCC). If delegation to an international entity is not possible under the constitution of the government, the assessment of comparability shall be done by an agency independent of the trade and environmental ministries.
2. Comparability shall be determined at the most specific level possible— for example, comparing domestic and foreign firms, industries, and sectors, in that order.
3. Border charges for noncomparability shall be expressed in terms of ad valorem charges per unit of imports or exports, provided that domestic firms, industries, or sectors that do not meet the same standard shall be assessed an equivalent charge.

G. Noncompliance Measures for Climate Commitments

Members of the code could agree to allow other code members to impose trade measures on them in response to noncompliance with international commitments. For example, country A could agree that countries B and C could impose additional tariffs if country A is adjudged by an independent international arbitral panel or a UNFCCC institution as not in compliance with A's own international legal climate commitment. The idea behind such a provision is that, if most of the major climate emitters sign on, they could jointly police each other's commitments and thereby give confidence that other countries will be taking reciprocal measures. The workability of such an approach assumes that the existence of this agreement would effectively stop country A from complaining to the WTO about B's and C's tariffs on A.

H. Preferences for Least-Developed Countries

In applying greenhouse gas control measures, member countries may choose to omit equal coverage for least-developed countries, and such preferences shall not be considered to violate the WTO agreement. Code members may also choose to exempt small developing countries that are de minimis exporters. With either approach, however, governments are not obligated to offer such a preference.

I. Climate Subsidies for Sequestration and Alternative Energy Sources

A "peace clause" should be in place among members to forestall WTO challenges to qualifying climate-related domestic subsidies. Qualifying subsidies would be for research and development[6] on alternative energy and sequestration, physical infrastructure[7] for sequestration, and the production and transport of alternative energy for domestic use or export.[8] This latitude for qualifying domestic subsidies would be subject to two bright-line exclusions: First, such subsidies shall not be contingent upon the use of domestic over imported goods; and second, such subsidies shall not be contingent upon exportation. If a subsidy is given to production of fuel or equipment that is exported, then the subsidizing member shall affirmatively establish that the subsidized export replaces a traditional energy source in the importing country that emits a greater quantity of greenhouse gas per unit of energy, taking into account the entire production process for both the alternative and traditional energy sources.[9] Subsidies reported to the WTO under ASCM Article 25.3 shall include a calculation of their anticipated greenhouse gas effects. All subsidies allowed under this peace clause and an evaluation of their results in terms of reducing greenhouse gas emissions shall be reported every two years to the WTO's Committee on Subsidies and Countervailing Measures.[10]

---

6. Article 8.2(a) of the ASCM made certain research subsidies nonactionable, but that provision has expired. Note also that research services are covered by the GATS.

7. As noted above, government grants for "general infrastructure" are excluded from the ASCM.

8. In other words, the proposed peace clause would provide more legal certainty that generally available climate subsidies would not be challenged in WTO dispute settlement. Our proposed subsidy peace clause provision does not cover subsidies that are specific under ASCM Article 2.

9. Our intention is not to encourage export subsidies. Rather, this sentence acknowledges that developing alternative energy sources is crucial to reduce greenhouse gas emissions and mitigate climate change. Hence, it is very important to promote alternative energy sources both domestically and globally. By "affirmatively establish," we mean that the exporting member country government shall make public a credible statement from the importing member country government.

10. Sadeq Z. Bigdeli (2008, 87–88) has offered a thoughtful suggestion that the WTO committee set up a subsidiary body to collect and analyze energy subsidy data. Authority to do so exists under ASCM Articles 24.2 and 24.5.

J. Climate Subsidies for Adaptation

The peace clause would also extend to environmental adaptation subsidies to firms taken in response to multilateral climate commitments. Under such a peace clause, qualifying subsidies could not be challenged in the WTO as a prohibited or actionable subsidy or countervailed. The now-expired carve-out for such subsidies in the ASCM could be incorporated by reference. That provision permits "...assistance to promote adaptation of existing facilities to new environmental requirements imposed by law and/or regulations which result in greater constraints and financial burden on firms, provided that the assistance:

(i)   is a one-time non-recurring measure; and

(ii)   is limited to 20 percent of the cost of adaptation; and

(iii)   does not cover the cost of replacing and operating the assisted investment, which must be fully borne by firms; and

(iv)   is directly linked to and proportionate to a firm's planned reduction of nuisances and pollution, and does not cover any manufacturing cost savings which may be achieved; and

(v)   is available to all firms which can adopt the new equipment and/or production processes."[11]

K. Climate-Unfriendly Subsidies

As part of the Doha Round agenda, governments have been negotiating to discipline fishery subsidies. The consensus to include this item in the round was remarkable. The principle in the Agreement on Agriculture of limiting domestic subsidies for trade and budget reasons was extended to fisheries for reasons of resource sustainability. The WTO negotiations on fishery subsidies provide a precedent for action to address other subsidies that adversely affect the environment. In the context of climate, for example, the Code might commit parties to cease (or curtail) government subsidies that promote deforestation.

---

11. ASCM Article 8.2(c).

APPENDICES

Appendix A
Four Big Uncertainties

This appendix summarizes four major uncertainties in the realm of climate change. The purpose is not to question calls to action but rather to recite these uncertainties in order to argue that "policy autopilot" would be a mistake. Climate change may prove more or less severe than contemporary estimates, damages could be inflicted in unexpected ways or on unsuspecting locations, and technology might or might not ride to the rescue.

Reaching agreement on a collective action plan and assigning targets to the principal emitting countries will be difficult. The corresponding temptation may be to engrave the agreed-upon plan in stone, making future amendments difficult. But scientific and economic uncertainties require a flexible approach and room for periodic revision—for example, requiring a consensus among the principal emitting nations to renew the original action plan every decade.

On the other hand, trading system rules with respect to climate change measures should be designed for the long haul. The key rules should accommodate a wide range of climate outcomes and mitigation measures while preserving the basic precepts of national treatment, most favored nation treatment, subsidy disciplines, and the legal stability of commercial relations.

Average Temperature Projections

Al Gore's movie *An Inconvenient Truth* in 2006 became an amazing box office hit, attracting enormous public attention to the dangers of climate change. Contributing to the movie's success were striking images that showed, for example, shrinking ice and snow on Mount Kilimanjaro and in Glacier National Park, and the famous "hockey stick" chart of Northern Hemisphere temperatures over the past thousand years.

In its Fourth Assessment Report (IPCC AR4), issued in 2007, the Intergovernmental Panel on Climate Change (IPCC) concluded that the average temperature of the Earth's surface has definitely warmed: The observed surface temperature has increased by about 0.74°C (Celsius) over the past hundred years, with most of the increase occurring over the last three decades. The IPCC stated that "most of the observed increase in global average temperatures since the mid-20th century is very likely due to the observed increase in anthropogenic greenhouse gas concentrations."[1] According to the IPCC AR4, global average sea level rose at an average rate of 1.9 millimeters per year over four decades between 1961 and 2003 and 3.1 millimeters per year over the decade between 1993 and 2003. Satellite data show a 2.7 percent decrease per decade in annual average Arctic Sea ice extent.

Under various emissions scenarios and different assumptions, future global warming is widely predicted. William Cline (1992) summarized climate change projections made by three teams of well-known modelers—Nordhaus-Yohe, Reily-Edmonds, and Manne-Richels[2]—and found that those models were surprisingly close. Subsequent estimates are often very similar as well. Virtually all studies point to global warming trends.

The IPCC (2007a) estimated that the Earth's average temperature would increase by 2°C to 6°C and that the sea level would rise by 0.18 meters to 0.60 meters by 2100, relative to 1980–90.[3] The IPCC also raised its estimated range of "climate sensitivity" to 2°C to 4.5°C, with a best estimate of about 3°C.[4] The previous range of climate sensitivity, reported in the 1990 IPCC report, was the range of 1.5°C to 4.5°C, with a best estimate of 2.5°C.

Other recent studies have predicted similar changes in global tem-

---

1. Using expert judgment, the following terms have been used in the IPCC AR4 to indicate the assessed likelihood of an outcome or a result: virtually certain >99 percent probability of occurrence; extremely likely >95 percent; very likely >90 percent; likely >66 percent; more likely than not >50 percent; unlikely <33 percent; very unlikely <10 percent; and extremely unlikely <5 percent. For more details, see IPCC (2007a).

2. Data of those three models are specified at sensitivity 2.5, which was a best estimate of the IPCC report at the time.

3. The IPCC has devised scenarios that are called the "Emission Scenarios of the IPCC Special Report on Emission Scenarios." Each scenario starts with a different future emissions range, depending on demographic, technological, and economic developments.

4. "Climate sensitivity" is an important concept in climate change modeling: It measures how the climate system responds to sustained radiative forcing, defined as the equilibrium global average surface warming following a doubling of CO_2 concentrations.

perature.[5] CO_2 abundances rose to about 380 parts per million (ppm) in 2005 compared with about 280 ppm in preindustrial periods (around 1750). The predictions commonly assume that, in the absence of action, the level of greenhouse gas concentrations will reach 550 ppm by 2050, almost double preindustrial levels. In turn, the models predict that this will commit the Earth's average temperature to a rise in the range of 2°C to 5°C. Dr. James Hansen, director of the NASA Goddard Institute for Space Studies, claimed that the goal of keeping global warming less than 2°C, which is often adopted by other studies, is "a recipe for global disaster," not "salvation," and that our planet is near a "tipping point" at which greenhouse gases reach a level where major climate changes can proceed mostly under their own momentum, without adding more greenhouse gas emissions. The safe level of atmospheric CO_2, according to Hansen, is no more than 350 ppm, a figure slightly below the 2005 level.[6]

Despite the reigning consensus and Hansen's more alarming views, it would be a mistake to think that the scientific debate has been settled. To illustrate how scientific opinion can change, it is worth recalling the views of a few decades ago, when respected scientists were forecasting an episode of global cooling. In reviewing the earlier literature on climate change, Thomas C. Peterson, William M. Connolley, and John Fleck (2008) note that in the 1970s there was widespread concern about global cooling (escalating to fears of another ice age), prompted by a temperature drop in the 1950s and 1960s in the Northern Hemisphere. One of the articles they reviewed is a 1971 paper by S. Ichtiaque Rasool and Stephen H. Schneider that suggested that the increase by a factor of four in global aerosol concentrations could be enough to trigger an ice age and that the cooling effect by the dirty air could outweigh the warming effect of carbon dioxide.[7]

A *Newsweek* article in 1975 brought the global cooling debate to public attention, citing the work of respected climatologists and meteorologists. The article conveyed a similar tone to contemporary popular articles on global warming, quoting scientists who warned that global cooling could lead to major climatic changes and cause local weather extremes that could

---

5. Stern (2006) summarized some studies on temperature projections at different stabilization levels (parts per million). Ranges of temperature increase at the stabilization level of 550 ppm CO_2e are 1.5°C to 4.4°C, 2.4°C to 5.3°C, and 1.2°C to 9.1°C (some 11 studies).

6. See Dr. James Hansen, "Global Warming Twenty Years Later: Tipping Points Near," briefing before the US House of Representatives Select Committee on Energy Independence and Global Warming, June 2008, available at www.columbia.edu.

7. Peterson, Connolley, and Fleck (2008) note that Rasool and Schneider's paper received a lot of criticism at the time for overestimating cooling while underestimating greenhouse warming and that Rasool and Schneider acknowledged flaws in subsequent papers. For more details, see Peterson, Connolley, and Fleck (2008), who also listed other cooling papers by McCormick and Ludwig in 1967, Barrett in 1971, Hamilton and Seliga in 1972, Chýlek and Coakley in 1974, Bryson and Dittberner in 1976, and Twomey in 1977.

severely diminish food supplies, which in turn would force economic and social adjustments on a global scale. *Newsweek* added that scientists were very pessimistic that the government would take appropriate action.[8]

In light of current scientific knowledge, the global cooling forecasts can be faulted for inadequate evidence and primitive models. Peterson, Connolley, and Fleck (2008) described the "myth" propounded by the 1970s studies on global cooling by saying that "…when climate researcher Reid Bryson stood before the members of the American Association for the Advancement of Science in December 1972, his description of the state of scientists' understanding of climate change sounded very much like the old story about the group of blind men trying to describe an elephant."

But if climate is an elephant and scientists in the 1970s were blind men, how can we be so sure that today's scientists will not be faulted by their successors? Writing in the *Washington Post* in 2003, James Schlesinger, former US secretary of defense, secretary of energy, and director of the CIA, pointed out that only slow progress has been made in understanding the underlying science, even though many scientists feel pretty certain about the causes, effects, and extent of climate change.[9]

The reason the debate continues is that climate change entails very complex calculations, covering many factors that are hard to measure, hard to forecast, and often interact with one another. For example, some observers argue that there has not been much increase in temperature since 1998, when the El Niño warmed the globe. Some scientists found that natural climate variability can mask the global warming effect of greenhouse gases and that a simulation that looks into a short period—one or two decades into the future—forecasts short-term cooling effects in some regions in the next decade. Such effects may override the long-term contribution of rising greenhouse gases. For example, temperatures may rise or fall due to variation in the Gulf Stream, even in the absence of human interference (Kerr 2008, 595).

The brief review indicates that climate change skepticism has not disappeared, even though some of the debate has moved underground.[10] In

---

8. The article also acknowledged uncertainties arising from gaps in the scientific evidence. See "The Cooling World," *Newsweek*, April 28, 1975, www.washingtontimes.com (accessed on January 12, 2009).

9. See James Schlesinger, "Climate Change: The Science Isn't Settled," *Washington Post*, July 3, 2003, A17, www.washingtonpost.com (accessed on January 12, 2009).

10. An example is the Petition Project run by the Oregon Institute of Science and Medicine, which released a signatory list of knowledgeable persons who reject the assertion that global warming has reached a crisis stage or that it is caused by human activity. The current list includes 31,072 Americans with college degrees in science, including 9,021 with PhD degrees in various scientific fields. For more details, visit the Petition Project website at www.petitionproject.org (accessed on January 12, 2009).

our view, an upward trajectory of average temperatures on account of rising greenhouse gas concentrations is the most certain of our "four uncertainties." That said, we do not subscribe to the view that the debate has been settled or that mitigation targets agreed to at the Copenhagen conference in 2009 will necessarily seem appropriate in 2019.

Projections of Extreme Events

Extremes are characteristic of the climate system. Two recent extreme weather events raised popular awareness of this basic fact. In 2003 Europe was hit by a wave of unusually hot days that caused about 20,000 deaths.[11] In August 2005 Hurricane Katrina devastated areas along the north-central coast of the Gulf of Mexico, causing a reported $125 billion in economic losses, more than 1,300 deaths, and temporary displacement of millions of people.[12] These two events symbolize the scary climate change scenarios emphasized in reputable studies, including the Stern Review (Stern 2006) and the IPCC AR4: that extreme events are likely to be more intense, more frequent, and longer lasting. In turn, this is the peg for advocating bold if costly action against greenhouse gas emissions as a "global insurance payment." In the absence of concerted greenhouse gas control measures, it is said, extreme weather events, triggered by the rise in average temperatures, may inflict enormous damage. If the risk of these events and the associated damage can be mitigated at the cost of a few percent of GDP, the reasoning goes, then it makes eminent sense to spend that money, just like insuring against more common hazards such as fire.[13]

Again, despite the prevailing consensus, it remains a major uncertainty whether rising average temperatures will increase the frequency and intensity of extreme events. To be sure, there is strong evidence of a causal connection. According to a recent study of US weather by the US Climate Change Science Program (2008), conducted under the auspices of the National Oceanic and Atmospheric Administration, extreme precipitation, defined as the heaviest 1 percent of daily precipitation totals, increased by 20 percent over the past century while total precipitation increased by only 7 percent. The study also found a strong connection over the past 50 years between tropical Atlantic Sea surface temperatures and Atlantic hurricane activity. Extrapolating from these observations, extreme episodes such as hot days, heavy precipitation, droughts, and storms may become more frequent and intense as average temperature rises.

---

11. For more details, see Munich Re (2004).

12. For more details, see Munich Re (2006).

13. As a matter of comparison, in the United States, net written premiums for property and casualty insurance were about $430 billion, about 3.5 percent of GDP in 2005. For more details, see US Census Bureau (2007).

In the same spirit, the IPCC (2007b) analyzed more than 29,000 observational data series from 75 studies covering physical phenomena (snow, ice, frozen ground, hydrology, and coastal processes) and biological systems (territorial, marine, and freshwater biological systems). The IPCC found that about 90 percent of data series are consistent with the direction of change expected as a response to average warming. Moreover, based on a range of models, the IPCC AR4 projected that it is very likely that hot extremes, heat waves, and heavy precipitation events will continue to become more frequent and that it is likely that future tropical cyclones will become more intense, with larger peak wind speeds and heavier precipitation associated with ongoing increases of tropical sea surface temperatures (IPCC 2007a).

Even so, many scientists are reluctant to bet on extreme weather events. Using a new method of computer modeling in a recent study, well-known hurricane scientists Kerry Emanuel, Ragoth Sundararajan, and John Williams (2008) found that hurricane frequency and intensity may not substantially rise during the next two centuries even with a dramatic increase in the global average temperature. Emanuel and his colleagues argued that while global warming may raise the intensity of hurricanes, other factors are likely to moderate the impact. The new results were striking not only to other scientists but also to Emanuel himself, who had previously argued the link between global warming and stronger hurricanes. Moreover, the new results contrast with earlier studies conducted by his MIT team, which were popularly cited by Al Gore. As Emanuel noted on his website, reliable records of wind speeds in hurricanes over the open ocean go back only to around 1950, and the lack of reliable data, among other unknowns, amplifies the uncertainty of projecting future weather events.[14] Even Stern (2006) and IPCC (2007a), which both project more frequent and intense extreme weather events as a general tendency, note that some regions may experience fewer tropical cyclones due to the increased stability of the tropical troposphere in a warmer climate.

In our view, extreme weather events amount to a reasonable forecast, but one characterized by large error bars. The insurance argument warrants concerted collective action; however, given the current level of uncertainty, we question whether the argument can be pushed to the point of justifying extreme measures. To be specific, while costs of 1 or 2 percent of world GDP may well be justified as an insurance premium (around $540 billion to $1.1 trillion annually),[15] we do not think that the world trading system should be sacrificed as part of the payment.

---

14. See Kerry Emanuel's website at http://wind.mit.edu/~emanuel/anthro2.htm.

15. Based on total global GDP in 2007 (IMF 2008b).

Mitigation Costs

If extreme weather events do visit planet Earth with greater frequency, the consequences of climate change could be catastrophic, sparking mass population movements, huge levels of mortality, and large economic costs. The "catastrophic tail" of climate change outcomes has in turn prompted calls for immediate collective action. Many argue that early action at relatively small costs is like a public insurance premium against the risk of enormous future losses. As already said, we can only agree with this proposition. But how large is the insurance premium? This is our third uncertainty.[16]

After examining several leading models available in the late 1980s and early 1990s, Cline (1992) estimated that a carbon reduction of 50 percent from his baseline in 2050 would require a cost of about 2 percent of GNP in that year.[17] As a mid-range estimate, Cline's figure has stood up remarkably well. The IPCC (2007c) estimated that, to stabilize greenhouse gas concentrations between 710 ppm and 445 ppm CO_2e by 2050, the annual cost in 2050 would fall in the range of a net gain of 1 percent to a cost of 5.5 percent of global GDP. Stern (2006) placed the annual cost of stabilizing greenhouse gas concentrations at 550 ppm CO_2e by 2050 in the range of a net gain of 1 percent to a cost of 3.5 percent of global GDP, with a central estimated cost of around 1 percent in 2050. Recently, Stern increased his central average estimate from a cost of about 1 percent to a cost of about 2 percent of global GDP annually.[18] Obviously, if the goal is to stabilize CO_2 concentrations at the current level of around 350 ppm, as urged by Hansen in his briefing before the House, the costs would be much higher, but we cannot cite a responsible estimate.[19]

---

16. For the understanding of readers, it is worth noting that targets for reducing emissions are usually set relative to a base year (commonly relative to 1990 or 2005), referred to as the baseline. Estimates of mitigation costs are often shown as a percentage of the target year's projected GDP, unless another year is specified. For example, suppose it is asserted that, in 2030, the world should reduce its emissions by 30 percent from the baseline and that this will cost about 1 percent of global GDP. The 1 percent figure usually means 1 percent of global projected GDP in 2030.

17. Cline estimated a baseline of global carbon emissions rising from 5.6 GtC (billion tons of carbon) in 1990 to a range of 15 GtC to 27 GtC in 2100. There are two models broadly used to examine the cost of abatement: top-down and bottom-up. Top-down models use macroeconomic theory and econometric techniques to calculate economic costs. The 2 percent of GNP figure is based on a top-down model. Bottom-up models examine the characteristics of specific activities and processes, considering technological, engineering, and cost details. Based on a bottom-up model, a carbon reduction of 50 percent from his baseline in 2050 would require a cost of about 1.6 percent of GNP in that year.

18. Remarks by Lord Nicholas Stern at the Third Richard H. Sabot Lecture, Center for Global Development, June 26, 2008. See http://blogs.cgdev.org/globaldevelopment (accessed on January 12, 2009).

19. See footnote 6.

Differences in assumed technology pathways are a major reason for the wide range in cost estimates for stabilizing CO_2e at a level around 550 ppm. As mentioned, some estimates even contemplate net gains from liming greenhouse gas emissions. The technologies considered are either known or around the corner[20]—both are considered in the next section along with "over-the-horizon" technologies.

McKinsey & Company (2008) introduced the concept of "carbon-productivity" in a study that stressed that any action on climate change should pursue two objectives: stabilizing greenhouse gases and sustaining economic growth. To help evaluate success in achieving both goals, carbon productivity measures the amount of GDP produced per unit of CO_2e emitted. According to McKinsey, this factor should increase tenfold by 2050—from about \$740 GDP per ton of CO_2e today to \$7,300 GDP per ton of CO_2e (in constant dollars). McKinsey argues that the annual macroeconomic costs for this degree of enhancement in carbon productivity are likely to be manageable, on the order of 0.6 to 1.4 percent of global GDP by 2030.[21]

Other studies, which strongly emphasize new technologies in the spirit of McKinsey, go so far as to suggest that significant emissions reductions can be achieved for free. They argue that, by investing in low-carbon and efficient means of producing energy, countries can generate huge "negative costs" to offset positive abatement costs. If large enough, the negative costs can, theoretically, produce the sort of net gains referenced at the outset of this section. Negative costs reflect the proposition that certain investments in energy efficiency could have positive returns regardless of the carbon impact. They are calculated by reference to alternative ways of producing or consuming a given amount of energy. For example, they assume that if companies redirect their investment from building coal power plants to building nuclear power plants, which are both cleaner and more energy efficient, then the companies will enjoy positive returns on their investment. This switch results in negative costs that offset positive abatement costs. In an earlier study by McKinsey (2007), for example, the United States is projected to achieve 40 percent of its abatement at "negative" marginal costs.

These are alluring estimates, but some scholars have questioned the

---

20. In a 2008 article in the *Wall Street Journal*, Bjorn Lomborg, a director of Copenhagen Consensus and also the author of the best-selling and controversial book *The Skeptical Environmentalists*, argued that many of the technologies currently discussed do not exist and that existing technologies are very expensive. According to Lomborg, policy focusing solely on mitigating emissions can only yield a small benefit at a high expense. Investing in clean energy would yield better results. See Bjorn Lomborg, "How to Get the Biggest Bang for 10 Billion Bucks," *Wall Street Journal*, July 28, 2008, A15, http://s.wsj.net (accessed on January 12, 2009).

21. The annual cost is expressed as a percentage of each year's projected global GDP.

concept of negative costs. Lawrence J. Makovich (2008) argued that such estimates reflect a seriously flawed hypothesis and, as a result, the projected costs are much too low. He argued that the logic of negative costs does not hold up in the context of an efficient market for allocating capital. Negative cost studies assume positive returns for the cleaner and more efficient energy investment. However, not all the investments with positive returns get done, owing to the scarcity of capital. An investment that might reduce greenhouse gas emissions and has a positive financial return, but does not make the cut in the marketplace and can only be undertaken with public assistance, has a net positive cost in opportunity cost terms (Makovich 2008).

In our view, an emphasis on negative costs conveys the wrong impression that greenhouse gas abatement can be done on the cheap. In turn, we think both proponents and opponents are misled. Proponents of bold action tend to say, "this won't cost much, so let's get started." Opponents say, "wait a minute, let's invest in technology for the next decade." In our view, both conclusions are wrong. Forceful action will be costly; it will hurt. But postponing action will likely delay the search for "carbon productivity" technologies because the price signals will not be strong enough.

We draw three conclusions from this survey. First, the range between the low cost and the high cost for the "consensus" CO_2e target—namely, stabilized at 550 ppm in 2050—is at least a factor of two. At today's world GDP, each 1 percent of GDP amounts to about $540 billion, so the difference between a 1 percent "global insurance premium" and a 2 percent "premium" amounts to at least $540 billion annually.[22] This is no small amount. Just for perspective, the net amount of bilateral and multilateral official development assistance to developing countries was about $100 billion in 2006.[23] Second, since the requisite CO_2e stabilization target is still a matter of debate, the cost range is substantially larger than a factor of two. Third, carbon productivity technologies are vital, just to keep costs bearable, but we are very skeptical that a free lunch will be found in emissions controls.

Technological Fixes

Will technology deliver a silver bullet to defeat climate change? Perhaps. But the International Energy Agency (IEA 2008a) observes that public- and private-sector spending on energy research, development, and deployment (RD&D) has decreased since the 1980s and now remains at a relatively low level. Even so, optimism as regards technology holds great appeal, since it promises huge reductions both in greenhouse gas emissions and costs.

---

22. Total world GDP in 2007 was about $54,312 billion (IMF 2008b).

23. For more details, see UNCTAD (2008).

However, the cost studies already cited typically take into account technology options that either exist today or seem to be around the corner. In other words, only a wild optimist can envisage stabilizing greenhouse gas concentration at low or zero cost. Technology options popularly discussed include carbon (or carbon dioxide) capture and storage (CCS), nuclear power, hydrogen for heat and transport fuels, electric and hybrid cars, biofuels, and wind, solar, and tidal energy. Some of these options have a great potential to reduce carbon emissions. In some cases, the main question is whether public resistance can be overcome; in most cases, the question is whether economic incentives will be sufficient to put new technologies to work.

CCS has gained the most attention, given booming demand for coal-fired power stations.[24] In a special report, the IPCC (2005) estimated that a power plant with CCS could reduce CO_2 emissions by up to 90 percent. In most scenarios for stabilizing greenhouse gases at levels between 450 ppm and 750 ppm CO_2, the contribution of CCS accounts for 15 to 55 percent of the cumulative global mitigation effort, at least until 2100. Stern (2006) estimated that, without CCS, marginal abatement costs would rise from $25 to $43 per ton in Europe, and from $25 to $40 per ton in China, while global emissions would be 10 to 14 percent higher.

Uncertainty over Future Carbon Prices

Since private firms only invest in hopes of a return, and since the benefits of new technology are seldom captured in their entirety by the original investor, various policy measures are contemplated to furnish economic incentives for creating and implementing new technology. Popular measures point to a combination of subsidies for alternative energy sources and permits or taxes to boost the cost of carbon emissions. To be sure, rising oil prices also help, but they are not directly correlated with CO_2 emissions. A higher price for oil reduces energy consumption and encourages cleaner substitutes, but it also encourages the use of coal, which emits considerably more CO_2 per megawatt of power.

A favorite answer to the coal emission problem is CCS, either mandated, subsidized, or inspired by CO_2 limits. The IPCC (2005) has estimated the costs of CCS in a wide range from zero to around $270 per ton of CO_2, depending on the fuel, location, and type of power plant. The IPCC has also suggested that CCS systems will begin to be widely deployed when

---

24. CCS refers to carbon dioxide as well as carbon capture and storage (or sequestration) because the capture schemes generally apply to CO_2, not pure carbon. CCS entails the separation of CO_2 from energy sources, transporting the CO_2, and storing it in a fashion that does not leak into the atmosphere. CCS has gained considerable attention for two reasons: first, because the component technologies to carry it out now exist; and second, because the use of coal, which is abundant and relatively cheap, will likely increase to meet world energy demands.

CO_2 emission prices reach about \$25 to \$30 per ton (either through taxes or tradable permits). A team from the Massachusetts Institute of Technology (2007) offers a similar estimate.[25] As the CCS story illustrates, the speed at which technology to reduce greenhouse gas emissions is adopted will be significantly determined by the level of CO_2 emission prices or by the public provision of subsidies.

The deployment of new technology often requires major long-term investment in infrastructure. For example, an integrated CCS system requires pipelines for transporting and facilities for storing CO_2. In the case of wind and solar power, while the technologies are already in use, little progress has been made in improving the US grid for transmitting wind and solar energy (Kopp 2008). Testifying before the Senate Homeland Security and Government Affairs Committee on July 22, 2008, Texas oil mogul T. Boone Pickens claimed that installing wind farms and solar power facilities in the midwest could produce about 20 percent of electricity consumed domestically.[26] He asked Congress to at least clear the path for the private sector to invest money to build a grid.

Some technology options involve safety issues. In the case of CCS, high pressure transport and safe storage of CO_2 are the main concerns. Safety issues are more acute for nuclear power. The International Energy Agency (IEA 2008a) suggested that 30 percent of global energy demand needs to be met from nuclear sources. However, a large swath of the public opposes nuclear power for a variety of reasons, and bureaucratic obstacles to building new plants, both at a federal and local level, are correspondingly severe.

Biofuels are a good example. Biofuels have gained attention both as an alternative energy source and as a means of cutting carbon emissions. Many countries have jumped on the biofuel bandwagon—notably Brazil (the pioneer), the United States, and the European Union. However, studies now find that the increase in biofuel production contributes to rising food prices, while the net reduction in CO_2 emissions may be modest. The biggest proponents of biofuels are no longer climate change experts but rather agricultural land owners. Appendix B examines issues in the biofuels debate.

"Over the Horizon" Technology and Side Effects

"Geoengineering" ideas have been advanced as one means of preventing global warming. In the context of climate change, geoengineering

---

25. Both the IPCC and the MIT acknowledge that their estimates of CCS costs are uncertain.

26. See Suzannes Gamboa, "Texas Oilman: Clear Path for Wind Power," Associated Press, July 22, 2008, www.foxnews.com. For more information about the "Pickens Plan," see www.pickensplan.com (by subscription only).

encompasses techniques to reduce atmospheric absorption of incoming solar radiation by various schemes: injecting particles of sulfur into the stratosphere; blasting clouds with chemicals; spreading iron fillings on the ocean surface to nurture plankton and sequester carbon dioxide; and installing orbital mirrors in space to reflect solar radiation. An attraction of geoengineering is its relatively cheap cost, compared with conventional means of reducing greenhouse gas emissions.[27] But many scientists warn that attempts to engineer the planet may cause unforeseen negative impacts both on the environment and on human health. For example, large-scale iron seeding in the ocean, or injecting particles in the atmosphere, may alter complex biological and geological processes, contribute to ozone depletion, and worsen ultraviolet levels on the Earth's surface.[28]

Based on this survey, it appears that technology will deliver higher carbon productivity, but the pace of improvement will critically depend on the path of carbon prices, the size of government subsidies, and the severity of public mandates. To a modest extent, therefore, higher mitigation costs will self-correct by inspiring faster creation and implementation of new technology. However, we are very skeptical that new technology will deliver anything resembling a free lunch for greenhouse gas mitigation. Indeed, since most of the cost mitigation studies already assume brisk improvement of carbon productivity, we believe that the current cost estimates for mitigation in the more distant future (e.g., 2 percent of world GDP in 2030) are probably on the low side. However, we do not dismiss the prospect of geoengineering solutions, especially if extreme weather frequently visits the planet.

Conclusion

What do we conclude from these four uncertainties?

- The likelihood of a persistent rise in global average temperatures seems very high.
- Large error bands need to be placed around contemporary forecasts of extreme weather events, the calculations of future mitigation costs, and speculation about new technology "around the corner" or "over the horizon."

---

27. There was considerable interest in these ideas in 2006, when atmospheric scientist Paul Crutzen, the 1995 Nobel Laureate in Chemistry, raised the possibility that releasing sulfurous debris into the atmosphere may create some cooling effects. See Bryan Walsh, "Geoengineering," *Time*, March 12, 2008, www.time.com (accessed on January 12, 2009).

28. See Pat Mooney, "Global Warming: The Quick Fix Is In," *Foreign Policy in Focus*, February 21, 2007, www.fpif.org (accessed on January 12, 2009).

- A plan for concerted collective action that assigns targets to the principal emitting countries should be reached at the Copenhagen conference in 2009. However, the Copenhagen action plan should build in ample room for future amendments, depending on the evolution of the Earth's climate, and on the successes, failures, and costs of meeting agreed-upon targets.

- Finally, new trading system rules should be designed both to accommodate climate mitigation measures that will be shaped and reshaped over the next several decades and to preserve the basic values of the trading system.

Appendix B
Will Biofuels Save Energy and Reduce CO_2 Emissions?

Biofuels clearly have a downside. Studies reported that soaring food prices in 2007 and early 2008 were strongly connected with the expansion of biofuel production. The International Monetary Fund (IMF 2008a) calculated that biofuel production had diverted 20 to 50 percent of feedstocks from food to biofuels, with a substantial impact on food prices. Citing a confidential World Bank report, the *Guardian* reported that biofuels have forced global food prices up by 75 percent.[1] In April 2008 UN special rapporteur Jean Ziegler strongly condemned the United States and the European Union for taking a "criminal path" by contributing to an explosive rise in global food prices through the use of food crops to produce biofuels.[2]

According to the Organization for Economic Cooperation and Development (OECD 2008), global production of biofuels amounts to about 62 billion liters, which equals about 2 percent of total global transport fuel consumption in energy terms. The world's largest producers of biofuels are the United States, Brazil, and the European Union, but new players such as Canada, China, India, and Indonesia are jumping into the game. The United States and Brazil accounted for about 51 and 37 percent, respectively, of world ethanol production in 2007, while the European Union accounted for about 60 percent of world biodiesel production. Propelled by climate change concerns and the rising price of oil and gas (through mid-2008), the OECD projected that production of biofuels would double in the next decade.

---

1. See Aditya Chakrabortty, "Secret Report: Biofuel Caused Food Crisis," *Guardian*, July 4, 2008.

2. See "Biofuel Production is 'Criminal Path' Leading to Global Food Crisis—UN Expert," UN News Center website, April 28, 2008, www.un.org (accessed on January 12, 2009).

A controversial issue in the biofuel debate is government support. The United States and the European Union have provided the greatest amount of public support to agricultural producers, accounting for 60 percent of total OECD agricultural producer support (Elliott 2006).[3] The United States, the European Union, and Canada, among others, have offered public support in various forms, including subsidies, tax incentives, and consumption mandates.[4] Making matters worse, the United States and the European Union have high import tariffs on ethanol. The World Bank (2007) warns that the current biofuels programs are not economically viable and depend excessively on government support. In the United States, more than 200 support measures (costing approximately $5.5 billion to $7.3 billion a year) are provided to biofuel producers.[5]

Today, the strongest proponents of these programs are not climate or energy experts but rather lobbyists who represent agricultural interests that directly benefit.[6] In an article posted on the Center for Global Development's website, Kimberly Ann Elliott argued that the biofuels industry and corn state legislators are contesting the charge that their favorite policies are an important cause of rising food prices. Whatever the impact on food prices, it can be questioned whether the leading biofuel—ethanol—meets the two principal goals invoked by its supporters—energy security and climate change—to justify government support.[7]

---

3. The percentage figure is an average for the period of 2002 to 2004, based on the dollar amount of subsidies.

4. The United States passed the Energy Independence and Security Act of 2007 (originally named the Clean Energy Act of 2007), with provisions that increase taxpayer funding for the production of biofuels and increase the amount of biofuels that must be added to gasoline from 4.7 billion gallons in 2007 to 36 billion gallons by 2022. The United States signed a biofuel agreement with Brazil in March 2007 and has recently concluded a similar agreement with Colombia. Both agreements contemplate technology exchanges.

5. Such measures amount to 38 to 49 cents per liter of petroleum equivalent for ethanol and 45 to 57 cents for biodiesels. See World Bank (2007).

6. The biofuel lobby has become quite active, and the National Biodiesel Board has lobbied on a range of measures intended to expand use of biofuels. See "Biodiesel Board Spent $384,000 to Lobby in 1Q," Associated Press, July 14, 2008, http://bioenergy.checkbiotech. org/news (accessed on January 12, 2009). In July 2008 a new lobby group, the Alliance for Abundant Food and Energy, was formed by Archer Daniels Midland Company, DuPont, Deere & Company, Monsanto, and the Renewable Fuels Association. Among other legislators, Senator Charles Grassley (R-Iowa) is a big supporter of biodiesel and extending the biodiesel tax incentive. See "Sen. Grassley Tells NBB He Will Continue to Champion Biodiesel Tax Incentive," National Biodiesel Board press release, June 18, 2008, www.biodiesel.org (accessed on January 12, 2009).

7. See Kimberly Ann Elliott, "Another Volley in the Battle over Biofuels," Center for Global Development, July 10, 2008, http://blogs.cgdev.org/globaldevelopment (accessed on January 12, 2009).

Saving Fossil Fuel Energy?

Producing ethanol involves several steps: growing, harvesting, milling, and transporting feedstock; then processing, refining, and transporting biofuels. Each step requires energy in various forms. David Pimentel and Tad Patzek (2007) estimated the energy inputs in ethanol production from sugar cane and found that approximately one kilocalorie (kcal) of fossil fuel energy is expended to produce each 1.12 kcal of ethanol energy in the United States, or 1.38 kcal of ethanol energy in Brazil. According to Pimentel and Patzek, other studies have overlooked energy inputs required for ethanol production, resulting in unrealistically low fossil fuel energy costs for each kcal of ethanol energy.

Saving Greenhouse Gas Emissions?

According to OECD (2008), ethanol based on sugarcane—the main feedstock of Brazilian production—generally reduces greenhouse gas emissions by 80 percent or more over the whole production and use cycle, relative to emissions from fossil fuels. By contrast, ethanol based on corn—the main feedstock of US production—reduces greenhouse gas emissions by less than 30 percent relative to emissions from fossil fuels.

However, neither calculation takes account of land clearing that might result from increased production of sugarcane or corn. When land is cleared, substantial amounts of CO_2 are released. In fact, some studies have found that, when land use changes are taken into account, many biofuels are worse from a climate perspective than the fossil fuels that they replace. Joseph Fargione et al. (2008) found that converting rain forests, peat lands, savannas, or grasslands to produce food-based biofuels would outweigh the carbon savings made from biofuels and create a "carbon debt" of 17 to 420 times more CO_2. This amount could take centuries to "pay back" through the growth of new vegetation. In an article in *Science*, Timothy Searchinger et al. (2008) expressed the same view, calculating that, owing to land use changes, corn-based ethanol almost doubles greenhouse gas emissions over a 30-year horizon in comparison with equivalent energy from fossil fuels. The increase in greenhouse gas concentrations, they maintained, might persist for 167 years until new vegetation absorbs the additional load of CO_2.

Appendix C
Summaries of Selected
Environmental Dispute Cases

Brazil—Tyres, 2007 (DS 332): Measures Affecting Imports of Retreaded Tyres

The European Communities (EC) brought this case against Brazil's import ban on retreaded tyres. Brazil claimed that the measure had a public health and environmental purpose, namely, to prevent the accumulation of waste tyres as a breeding ground for mosquito-borne illnesses. The World Trade Organization (WTO) found that the measure violates the General Agreement on Tariffs and Trade (GATT) Article XI: 1 and is not justified by Article XX (b) because the measure did not qualify under the Article XX chapeau. It was noteworthy, however, that the Appellate Body agreed with Brazil that the import ban met the balancing test for necessity under Article XX (b). The failure of Brazil's import ban to meet the chapeau requirement stemmed in part from the fact that Brazil was importing retreaded tyres from Southern Common Market (Mercosur) countries. Because this discrimination went against the environmental purpose of the legislation, the Appellate Body concluded that Brazil was engaging in arbitrary and unjustifiable discrimination between countries and a disguised restriction on international trade. In addition, the chapeau was also being violated because of Brazilian court injunctions that permitted the importation of used tyres by domestic retread firms.

Case summaries in this appendix are arranged in descending chronological order. Further information on Panel and Appellate Body reports is available at http://worldtradelaw.net (accessed on September 8, 2008).

European Communities—Asbestos, 2001 (DS 135): Measures Affecting Asbestos and Asbestos-Containing Products

Canada brought this case against the European Communities with respect to a French ban on the manufacture, processing, sale, and import of asbestos and products containing asbestos, enacted pursuant to Decree No. 96-1133. While Canada argued that these measures violated the Agreement on Technical Barriers to Trade (TBT), GATT Article III: 4 and certain other articles, the EC defended the ban on the grounds that its purpose was to protect human health, pursuant to Article XX (b). The Appellate Body reversed the panel's finding against the EC and found that the TBT agreement applied to the measure viewed as an "integrated whole." However, the Appellate Body did not determine whether the measure conformed to the terms of the TBT agreement. Examining the panel's findings related to Article III:4 (the obligation not to discriminate against "like" imported products), the Appellate Body noted that the panel had excluded the health risks associated with asbestos when it determined "likeness" and that Canada failed to satisfy its burden of proving that imports and domestic goods were like products. Consequently, the Appellate Body reversed the panel's conclusion that the measure was inconsistent with Article III: 4. In determining whether the measure was justified under Article XX (b), both the panel and the Appellate Body emphasized the objective of a French ban and noted that the purpose of the measure was "both vital and important" in the "highest degree" and that no reasonable alternatives were available to achieve the same objective as the measure at issue. Therefore, the measure was "necessary" to protect human life or health, pursuant to Article XX (b). It is noteworthy that this was the first case in which the WTO accepted the respondent's defense under Article XX (b).

United States—Shrimp, 1998 (DS58) and 2001 (DS58/Article 21.5): Import Prohibition of Certain Shrimp and Shrimp Products[1]

India, Malaysia, Pakistan, and Thailand brought this case to challenge the US import restrictions on shrimp and shrimp products harvested in a manner that causes incidental killings of endangered sea turtles. The United States defended its measure as justified under Article XX (g). The WTO found that the measure violates GATT Article XI: 1 and was not justified by Article XX. With respect to Article XX, the WTO found that, while the US import ban fell within the scope of Article XX (g), it could not be justi-

---

1. Also known as the "shrimp-turtle" case.

fied because it failed to meet the nondiscrimination test in the chapeau of Article XX. In reaching this conclusion, the Appellate Body reasoned, in part, that the measure had a coercive effect on the policy decisions made by other member countries, without taking into consideration the different conditions prevailing in those countries. Moreover, the operating details of the measure were shaped in a unilateral way without consultation with other member countries. Later, in a compliance review case brought by Malaysia that was referred to the original panel pursuant to Article 21.5 of the Dispute Settlement Understanding mechanism, the Appellate Body rejected Malaysia's contention and found that the revised US guidelines met the conditions of the chapeau of Article XX. Under the revised guidelines, US restrictions were no longer applied in a manner that constituted arbitrary discrimination.

United States—Reformulated Gasoline, 1996 (DS2): Standards for Reformulated and Conventional Gasoline

Brazil and Venezuela brought this case against the US "gasoline rule" under its Clean Air Act, which required oil companies to reformulate the gasoline sold in the United States. The WTO agreed with Brazil and Venezuela that by applying different air pollution emissions standards, US rules treated products from foreign oil refineries less favorably than "like products" from domestic oil refineries and therefore violated Article III: 4 on national treatment. With respect to the US defense under Article XX (g), it is noteworthy that the Appellate Body determined that the measure was "related to" the conservation of exhaustible natural resources and also "made effective" in conjunction with restrictions on domestic production or consumption because the measure was imposed with respect to both imported and domestic products and therefore fell within the scope of Article XX (g). However, the Appellate Body concluded that the measure was not justified by Article XX because it constituted arbitrary and unjustifiable discrimination between countries and a disguised restriction on international trade.

United States—Taxes on Automobiles, 1994 (GATT DS31/R): Taxes on Automobiles[2]

This case was brought by the European Communities against the United States. The EC alleged that three US measures on automobiles—the corporate average fuel economy (CAFE) regulations, the gas guzzler tax, and the

---

2. The Panel Report was circulated in 1994 (during the GATT-1947 era) but not adopted. The conclusion of the Uruguay Round and the establishment of the WTO in 1995 rendered prior GATT panel reports moot. The European Union did not renew the case under the auspices of the WTO Dispute Settlement Mechanism.

luxury tax—all discriminated against EC auto exports. The panel found that the luxury tax and the gas guzzler tax were consistent with Article III: 2. With respect to CAFE regulations, the panel found that they were inconsistent with Article III: 4 because they discriminated against imported products by applying a separate fleet accounting system on imported cars in a way that differentiated between imported and domestic cars on the basis of factors unrelated to product characteristics (namely, the control or ownership of foreign producers or importers). Replying to the US defense of CAFE regulations under Article XX, the panel found that the measure was not justified under Article XX (g) because the separate fleet accounting method was not "primarily aimed at" the conservation of exhaustible natural resources.

United States—Tuna/Dolphin I, 1991 (GATT DS21/R) and United States—Tuna/Dolphin II, 1994 (GATT DS29/R): Restrictions on Imports of Tuna[3]

Mexico brought this case against the US import ban on tuna and tuna products from Mexico and intermediary countries handling the tuna en route from Mexico to the United States, enacted pursuant to the US Maritime Mammal Protection Act. The United States claimed that its measure had an environmental purpose, namely to protect dolphins from incidental mortality caused by methods used to capture tuna. However, the panel rejected the US assertion that its measure could be justified under Article XX (b) or (g), as it failed to meet the necessity test and could not be regarded as being "primarily" aimed at conservation of dolphins. It is important that the panel held that Article XX (b) could not justify a measure which is intended to protect something outside the territorial jurisdiction of the nation that adopted a measure. The same reasoning was applied to Article XX (g). Also, the panel found that the import prohibitions under the direct and intermediary embargoes did not constitute internal regulations within the meaning of Article III.

The second *United States—Tuna/Dolphin* case involved the same US measures as the first case but was brought by different countries, namely the European Economic Community (EEC) and the Netherlands. As in the first *United States—Tuna/Dolphin* case, the panel found that US measures were inconsistent with Article XI and not justified under Article XX. However, one important difference should be noted. In contrast to the panel's finding in the first *United States—Tuna/Dolphin* case, the second panel held that no valid reason existed for the conclusion that the provisions of Article XX (g) would apply only to policies related to the conservation of exhaustible

---

3. Neither of the two panel reports was adopted.

natural resources located within the territory of the country that adopted the measure. Therefore, US measures that applied outside the United States would fall within the range of policies protected by Article XX (g). However, the panel found that US measures were not "primarily" aimed at conservation of dolphins and did not render effective restrictions on domestic production and consumption. The panel's rationale was that Article XX did not permit governments to take trade measures so as to force other contracting parties to change their policies within their jurisdiction. Therefore, US measures were not justified under Article XX.

Thailand—Cigarettes, 1990 (GATT DS10/R): Restrictions on Importation of and Internal Taxes on Cigarettes

The United States brought this case against Thailand's import restrictions on cigarettes. Thailand claimed that import restrictions had a public health purpose since they aimed at reducing the general consumption of cigarettes and protecting the public from harmful ingredients specifically found in imported cigarettes, and thus could be justified under Article XX (b). However, the panel found that the import restrictions violated Article XI: 1 and were not justified under Article XX (b). In determining whether the measure could fall within the exceptions of Article XX, the panel found that the measure failed to satisfy the "necessary" requirements under Article XX (b) because Thailand allowed the sale of domestic cigarettes and also because Thailand could adopt alternative measures to achieve the same objectives.

Canada—Unprocessed Herring and Salmon, 1988 (BISD 35S/98): Measures Affecting Exports of Unprocessed Herring and Salmon

The United States brought this case against Canadian export restrictions on certain unprocessed herring and salmon, pursuant to the 1976 Canadian Fisheries Act. Canada argued that these export restrictions were part of a system of fishery resource management aimed at preserving fish stocks, and therefore were justified under Article XX (g). Canada also argued that its measures fell under the Article XI: 2(b) exception that permits export prohibitions for the purposes of ensuring quality or regulations relating to the international marketing of a good. However, the panel found that export prohibitions were not justified under Article XX (g) because they were not primarily aimed at conserving salmon and herring stocks or rendering effective the restrictions on the harvesting of salmon and herring. Also, the panel found that export prohibitions could not be justified under Article X1: 2(b) because unprocessed fish was not the target of marketing or promotion.

United States—Tuna and Tuna Products, 1982 (BISD 29S/91): Prohibition of Imports of Tuna and Tuna Products from Canada

Canada brought this case against the US import ban on tuna and tuna products, enacted pursuant to the 1975 Fishery Conservation and Management Act.[4] The panel found that the US measure was inconsistent with Article XI. And, while the United States claimed that its measure was related to the conservation of tuna, the panel found that the measure failed to satisfy the requirements of Article XX (g) because it applied to all kinds of tuna, including ones not in danger of depletion, and because the United States did not impose equivalent restrictions on domestic production.

---

4. In fact, the US import ban was imposed in retaliation for Canada's seizure of 19 US fishing vessels and arrest of US fishermen fishing without authorization from the Canadian government in waters considered by Canada to be under its jurisdiction.

Appendix D
Clean Development Mechanism: A Big Challenge for the Post-Kyoto Regime

Among three major "flexibility mechanisms" adopted in the Kyoto Protocol to help countries meet their emission targets (see box 4.1), the clean development mechanism (CDM) has been most widely used. One reason for its popularity is that the CDM gives emitting countries greater flexibility in achieving their targets at lower costs by financing emissions reduction in developing countries. Another reason is that substantial funds are transferred to developing countries.

Of the more than 3,000 projects in the CDM pipeline as of September 2008, about 1,160 projects had been registered by the CDM Executive Board under the mechanism, estimated to cover some 1.3 billion certified emissions reductions (CERs) in total over their lifetime.[1] By the end of 2012, when the Kyoto Protocol expires, all the projects in the CDM pipeline are expected to generate some 2.7 billion CERs over the project lifetimes, which would be worth up to about €57 billion at current market rates.[2]

According to the United Nations Framework Convention on Climate Change (UNFCCC), among 1,162 currently registered CDM projects, India is the largest host country with 358 projects, and China is second with 267 projects. In terms of expected average annual CERs from registered projects by host country, China is in the lead, accounting for more than 50 per-

---

1. Each CER is equivalent to one metric ton of CO_2 or its equivalent and corresponds to a reduction of one metric ton of CO_2e.

2. According to *Carbon Positive*, on December 9, 2008 the benchmark CER contract for December 2008 delivery closed at about €13 on the European Climate Exchange. See "CERs Find New Lows as Oil Plunges," *Carbon Positive*, December 9, 2008, www.carbonpositive.net (accessed on January 12, 2009).

cent of the total expected annual average 220 million CERs from registered projects, followed by India (14 percent) and Brazil (9 percent).[3] By region, the Asia Pacific is the largest host, covering 65 percent of total registered projects by number, followed by Latin America and the Caribbean (32 percent) and Africa (2 percent). By scope, the energy industry (both renewable and nonrenewable sources) accounts for more than 55 percent of total registered projects by number; waste handling and disposal, 20 percent; fugitive emissions from fuel production, 8 percent; agriculture, 6 percent; and manufacturing industries, 5 percent.[4]

As the CDM has flourished, its criticism has mounted. Procedural inefficiencies and regulatory bottlenecks have caused delays in registration of CDM projects and issuance of CERs. A key issue is the "additionality" test under the CDM. To avoid abuses of the CDM, industrial countries that wish to purchase credits from CDM projects must meet several requirements. An industrial country must secure the consent of a host developing country, and the project must qualify under the UN registration and issuance process. This process is meant to ensure "additionality," as defined in the Kyoto Protocol. Under Article 12, which defines the purpose and requirements of the CDM, Article 12.5(c) states that "emission reductions resulting from each project activity shall be certified…on the basis of…(c) reductions in emissions that are additional to any that would occur in the absence of the certified project activity."[5]

Critics argue that the concept of "additionality" on a project basis is both vague and disturbing. At the Carbon Expo trade fair in Germany in May 2008, Ken Newcombe, the former director of the World Bank Carbon Finance Unit and managing director of US Carbon Emissions Trading for Goldman Sachs, claimed that "additionality" is an impossible concept and that the associated requirements increase transaction costs, raise the burden of proof, and augment risk for the private sector—all with the result of discouraging investment.[6] Citing an unpublished report by the United Nations, the *Guardian* claimed that "the CDM has been contaminated by gross incompetence, rule-breaking and possible fraud by companies in the

---

3. For comparison, the world total of CO_2e emissions in 2000 was 36 billion metric tons, while the world total of just CO_2 emissions in 2006 was 28 billion metric tons (see tables 1.1 and 1.2). In other words, the CDM as presently managed makes a very small contribution to reducing CO_2e, far less than 1 percent of annual emissions.

4. For more details, see the UNFCCC CDM website at http://cdm.unfccc.int (accessed on January 12, 2009).

5. Another important requirement is stated under Article 6.1(d) of the Kyoto protocol: "The acquisition of emission reduction units shall be supplemental to domestic actions for the purposes of meeting commitments under Article 3." See the Kyoto Protocol text at http://unfccc.int (accessed on January 12, 2009).

6. See "Time to Rethink CDM Additionality," *Carbon Finance*, May 7, 2008, www.carbonfinanceonline.com (accessed on January 12, 2009).

developing world." The *Guardian* also cited findings by Axel Michaelowa, a member of the CDM board of expert advisers, to the effect that, among 52 CDM projects hosted in India that were registered up to May 2006, one-third actually failed to meet the additionality test.[7]

Critics have also questioned the effectiveness of the CDM. From an environmental standpoint, the mechanism may not contribute to an over-all reduction in emissions because it allows an industrialized country to emit an additional ton of CO_2e by buying one CER from developing countries. The World Bank has criticized the CDM as "most expensive and time consuming."[8]

Controversial questions have also been asked about one specific greenhouse gas, namely hydrofluorocarbons (HFCs). According to *Scientific American*, about a third of CDM credits come from projects that focus on preventing the emission of HFC-23 (also known as trifluoromethane), a potent greenhouse gas that is a byproduct of the manufacture of refrigerant gases. HFC-23 has about 11,700 times the global warming potential (GWP) of CO_2, but it can be destroyed using relatively cheap technology.[9] However, the CDM payment mechanism is scaled to the reduction of GWP, so the payoff from reducing a ton of HFC-23 is very high—almost 12,000 times the payoff from reducing a ton of CO_2. It is important to prevent detrimental greenhouse gases like HFC-23 from entering the atmosphere. However, it is arguable whether the CDM should pay for removing gases like HFC-23 at their GWP rate, when they can be removed at very low costs. As a perverse result of the present system, manufacturing firms in developing countries delay the installation of devices that destroy HFC-23 so that they can raise their baseline values in order to claim very large CDM credits.

Another example illustrates the flaws in the current CDM rules. Rhodia SA, the French chemical maker, is expecting to receive a billion dollar windfall by implementing CDM projects that remove nitrous oxide (laughing gas) from its own factories in South Korea and Brazil.[10] Under the Kyoto Protocol, certain highly industrialized countries such as South Korea are categorized as non-Annex I countries and thus have no obliga-

7. See Nick Davies, "Abuse and Incompetence in Fight Against Global Warming," *Guardian*, June 2, 2007, www.guardian.co.uk (accessed on January 12, 2009). According to the article, Michaelowa found evidence that some projects provided false information that was then approved without checking. The *Guardian* also cited one senior figure who suggested there may be faults with up to 20 percent of the CERs already sold.

8. See Mathew Carr, "UN Carbon Trade Expensive and Slow, World Bank Says," Bloomberg News, August 26, 2008, www.bloomberg.com (accessed on January 12, 2009).

9. See David G. Victor and Danny Cullenward, "Making Carbon Markets Work," *Scientific American*, September 24, 2007, www.sciam.com (accessed on January 12, 2009).

10. See Charles Forelle, "French Firm Cashes in Under UN Warming Program," *Wall Street Journal*, July 23, 2008, http://online.wsj.com (accessed on January 12, 2009).

tion to reduce emissions. These countries have hosted many CDM projects. This conflicts with a central purpose of the CDM, which is to stimulate investment and technology transfer to poor countries. As revealed by the statistics already mentioned, CDM projects have been concentrated in certain countries—notably China, India, and Brazil. The Asia-Pacific region has hosted about 65 percent of total CDM projects, while Africa has hosted only 2 percent. The Rhodia example also raises other questions, such as whether the additionality test is appropriately conducted and whether it is justifiable that a company can earn a profit by reducing CO_2e in its own facilities located in developing countries.

In response to the many criticisms, it seems that the United Nations regulators who administer the CDM have become more cautious when approving projects. In 2007 the CDM Executive Board reportedly rejected about 9 percent of proposed projects, in contrast to previous years (2004 and 2005), when virtually all projects were approved.[11] However, major reforms to the CDM system seem inevitable during the course of the Copenhagen negotiations. Success of the post-Kyoto CDM regime will depend on whether it can be redesigned to cure its faults in a systemic manner. The Kyoto Protocol expires in 2012; the clock is ticking for a new and better clean development mechanism.

---

11. See Jeffrey Ball, "UN Effort to Curtail Emissions in Turmoil," *Wall Street Journal*, April 12, 2008, http://online.wsj.com (accessed on January 12, 2009).

Appendix E
Rise of Global Carbon Markets

Carbon trading markets have seen huge growth in recent years, both in value and volume. Global carbon markets were worth about $64 billion in 2007, more than double the $31 billion level in 2006. By trading volume, global carbon markets grew from 1.7 billion tons of CO_2e in 2006 to about 3 billion tons of CO_2e in 2007 (table E.1).[1] Growth is expected to remain strong in 2008 and beyond, since 2008 is the first year of the compliance period (2008–12) under the Kyoto Protocol and also the first year of Phase II (2008–12) of the European Union Emission Trading Scheme (EU ETS).[2] Over the next few years, more countries are likely to adopt their own national cap and trade schemes, which will further boost the value and volume of carbon trading.

Two distinct carbon markets are now in operation: allowance markets and credit (project-based) markets. In allowance markets, such as the EU ETS, allocated greenhouse gas emissions rights are traded, while in credit markets, notably the clean development mechanism (CDM) and the joint implementation system, "offsets" are traded that were awarded for specific projects related to greenhouse gas reductions. Each carbon market has its own operating rules and profiles, and no uniform CO_2 price yet exists, but discussions are under way to link carbon markets. This appendix provides short summaries of the major carbon markets (or schemes) now in operation.

---

1. The figures include both allowance and credit (project-based) markets.

2. Annex I countries that signed and ratified the Kyoto Protocol have to meet their own targets listed in Annex B.

Table E.1   Carbon markets: Volumes and values of transactions, 2006 and 2007

Market	2006 Volume (MtCO$_2$e)	2006 Value (millions of US dollars)	2007 Volume (MtCO$_2$e)	2007 Value (millions of US dollars)
Allowance-based markets				
European Union Emission Trading Scheme	1,104	24,436	2,061	50,097
New South Wales	20	225	25	224
Chicago Climate Exchange	10	38	23	72
Subtotal	1,134	24,699	2,109	50,393
Project-based markets				
Primary clean development mechanism (CDM)	537	5,804	551	7,426
Secondary CDM	25	445	240	5,451
Joint implementation	16	141	41	499
Other compliance and voluntary transactions	33	146	42	265
Subtotal	611	6,536	874	13,641
Total	1,745	31,235	2,983	64,034

MtCO$_2$e = million tons of carbon dioxide equivalent

Source: World Bank (2008a, table 1).

European Union: Emission Trading Scheme

By far, the EU ETS is the largest carbon trading scheme. In 2007 it covered 69 percent of the total global carbon market in volume terms and 78 percent in value terms (table E.1). The major marketplaces for EU emissions allowances (EUAs) are the European Climate Exchange, covering more than 80 percent of exchange-traded transaction volume, and the London Energy Brokers Association, covering more than 50 percent of over-the-counter activity (World Bank 2008a).

Based on Directive 2003/87/EC, which entered into force in October 2003, the EU ETS came into operation on January 1, 2005. The main objective during Phase I (a three-year trial period lasting from 2005 to 2007) was to acquire experience and build the infrastructure for success in Phase II and beyond. During Phase I, the price of EUAs fluctuated in a wide band: The price of a future contract, for delivery in December 2007, soared to more than €30 per metric ton of CO_2e in April 2006, and then dropped nearly to zero one year later, following release of the actual 2005 emissions data that showed that emissions were below the targeted level.[3] Since May 2007, the EUA price for use during the Phase II period has become less volatile. For example, the EUA contract for December 2008 delivery has moved in a price band of €20 to €25 per metric ton of CO_2e.

In light of the experience with Phases I and II, the European Commission proposed a reform package in January 2008 and the European Parliament approved the package with revised terms on December 17, 2008. Under the package, the European Union announced a more stringent overall emissions target (at least 20 percent below 1990 levels by 2020) and held open a possible 30 percent emissions reduction target if a post-Kyoto regime is agreed upon. The package includes other provisions such as permit auctions, broader coverage of energy-intensive industries, and a target of 20 percent for the share of renewable energy use. The package restricts the use of certified emissions reductions (CERs) and emissions reductions units (ERUs) in Phase III by making them contingent on the post-Kyoto regime.[4] For a time, this restriction may undermine project-based carbon markets.

The EU ETS is valued as a successful market scheme in two respects. First, it has utilized the price mechanism for mitigating carbon emissions. EU price signals not only provide a benchmark but also motivate project developers. Second, it has furthered a multinational climate regime, embracing countries with diverse historic, economic, and political backgrounds. The number of countries participating in the ETS has increased from 15 in Phase I to 30 Phase II (including all EU-27 members and three non-EU members, Norway, Iceland, and Liechtenstein).

Citing projections made elsewhere, the World Bank (2008a) suggested that the price of the EUA would reach around €30 to €35 per ton of CO_2e by the end of Phase II and €40 at the start of Phase III. *Point Carbon* forecasts that the European carbon price will average €37 per ton of CO_2e between 2009 and 2012.[5]

---

3. The EU ETS did not allow banking between Phase I and Phase II, but it did allow banking within a phase. Ellerman and Joskow (2008) argue that, if there had been no trade restriction between the two phases, the EUA price for use during Phase I period would not have dropped to zero.

4. CERs are issued under the CDM, while ERUs are issued under the joint implementation system.

5. See "Carbon Market Analyst Raises 2009–2012 EU Allowance Price Forecast," *Power Engineering International*, September 19, 2008, http://pepei.pennnet.com (accessed on January 12, 2009).

Clean Development Mechanism

Even though it has been plagued with loopholes (see appendix D), the CDM has attracted considerable attention. In 2007 CDM permits accounted for about 94 percent of project-based transactions in value term (table E.1).[6] Of note is the fast growth of secondary markets for the CDM. Facing procedural delays and the growing risk of regulatory hiccups in the issuance of individual CER permits, CER markets have shifted toward secondary markets that are largely based on a portfolio of guaranteed CER (gCER) contracts. In 2007 the secondary market for gCERs grew by more than 10 times in value terms compared with 2006 (table E.1). The primary buyers of CDM and joint implementation system permits were European firms (and governments), accounting for almost about 90 percent of the overall volume, followed by Japanese firms (11 percent) (World Bank 2008a).

Australia: New South Wales Greenhouse Gas Abatement Scheme

New South Wales launched an emissions trading scheme in 2003 that requires electricity retailers to obtain and submit a certain numbers of emissions reduction credits, so-called New South Wales greenhouse abatement certificates. Each certificate is worth one metric ton of CO_2e. Under the New South Wales scheme, electricity retailers and other participants are required to reduce their annual emissions to 7.27 tons of CO_2e per capita by 2012.[7]

While the New South Wales market increased by 25 percent in traded volume in 2007, its value fell slightly from $225 million in 2006 to $224 million in 2007, since the greenhouse abatement certificates price dropped from AU$10 to AU$5 in 2007.[8]

United States: Chicago Climate Exchange (CCX)

The Chicago Climate Exchange (CCX), launched in 2003, is the world's first voluntary but legally binding carbon trading system. Under this scheme, members make a voluntary but legally binding commitment to reduce their aggregate greenhouse gas emissions by 6 percent below a

---

6. The figures include both primary and secondary CDM markets.

7. An initial target was 8.65 tons of CO_2e per capita in 2003, and it was dropped to 7.27 tons of CO_2e per capita in 2007. For more details, see the New South Wales greenhouse gas abatement scheme website at www.greenhousegas.nsw.gov.au (accessed on January 12, 2009).

8. The price collapse resulted mainly from an oversupply of credits. See World Bank (2008a).

baseline period (1998 to 2001) by 2010. Members can sell or bank surplus allowances or they can meet their targets by purchasing CCX carbon financial instrument (CFI) contracts. Each CFI contract represents 100 metric tons of CO_2e. On January 14, 2009, the closing prices for all vantages of CCX CFI contracts were in the vicinity of $1.90 per metric ton of CO_2e.[9] CCX transactions have doubled in both volume and value terms in 2007 (table E.1). The CCX has expanded its coverage to other contracts as well. For example, the CCX started listing futures on CER contracts in August 2007; futures on EUA contracts in September 2007; and CER options in December 2007 (World Bank 2008a).

United States: Regional Greenhouse Gas Initiative

The Regional Greenhouse Gas Initiative, a program initiated by nine Northeast and mid-Atlantic states, currently has 10 participating states: Connecticut, Delaware, Maine, Maryland, Massachusetts, New Hampshire, New Jersey, New York, Rhode Island, and Vermont. Under the program, these 10 states will stabilize their total CO_2 emissions at a cap of 188.1 million short tons through 2014.[10] Six states—Connecticut, Maine, Maryland, Massachusetts, Rhode Island, and Vermont—took part in the first US auction for CO_2 allowances held on September 25, 2008. This auction offered about 12.5 million CO_2 allowances with a reserve price of $1.86 per CO_2 allowance (equal to one short ton of CO_2), and all allowances were cleared at a price of $3.07 per metric ton of CO_2. Any CO_2 allowances purchased at the auction can be used by a regulated facility for compliance in any of the 10 participating states.[11]

---

9. For more details, see the CCX website at www.chicagoclimatex.com (accessed on January 12, 2009).

10. See Carbon Market North America Newsletter, *Point Carbon* 3, no. 15, July 30, 2008.

11. For more details, see the Regional Greenhouse Gas Initiative website at www.rggi.org (accessed on January 12, 2009).

Bibliography

Arimura, Toshi H., Dallas Burtraw, Alan Krupnick, and Karen Palmer. 2007. *US Climate Policy Developments*. Discussion Paper 07-45. Washington: Resources for the Future.

Auld, Douglas. 2008. *The Ethanol Trap: Why Policies to Promote Ethanol as Fuel Need Rethinking*. C. D. Howe Institute Commentary no. 268 (July). Toronto.

Australian Government. 2008. *Carbon Pollution Reduction Scheme Green Paper Summary* (July). Available on the Australian Department of Climate Change website, www.climatechange.gov.au (accessed on January 12, 2009).

Barrett, Earl. W. 1971. Depletion of Short-Wave Irradiance at the Ground by Particles Suspended in the Atmosphere. *Solar Energy* 13: 323–37.

Bernasconi-Osterwalder, Nathalie, Daniel Magraw, Maria Julia Oliva, Marcos Orellana, and Elisabeth Tuerk. 2005. *Environment and Trade: A Guide to WTO Jurisprudence*. London: Earthscan.

Bhagwati, Jagdish, and Petros C. Mavroidis. 2007. Is Action Against US Exports for Failure to Sign Kyoto Protocol WTO Legal? *World Trade Review* 6, no. 2: 299–310.

Biermann, Frank, and Rainer Brohm. 2005. Implementing the Kyoto Protocol without the USA: The Strategic Role of Energy Tax Adjustments at the Border. *Climate Policy* 4, no. 3: 289–302.

Bigdeli, Sadeq Z. 2008. Will the "Friends of Climate" Emerge in the WTO? The Prospects of Applying the "Fisheries Subsidies" Model to Energy Subsidies. *Carbon and Climate Law Review*, no. 1: 78–88.

Bonsi, Richard, A. L. Hammett, and Bob Smith. 2008. Eco-Labels and International Trade: Problems and Solutions. *Journal of World Trade* 42, no. 3: 407–432.

Bordoff, Jason E. 2008. International Trade Law and the Economics of Climate Policy: Evaluating the Legality and Effectiveness of Proposals to Address Competitiveness and Leakage Concerns. Paper presented at a conference on "Climate Change, Trade and Competitiveness: Is a Collision Inevitable?" Brookings Institution, Washington, June 9.

Brack, Duncan (with Michael Grubb and Craig Windram). 2000. *International Trade and Climate Change Policies*. London: Earthscan.

Breehey, Abraham. 2008. Support the IBEW-Boilermakers-UMWA-AEP International Provision in Climate Change Legislation. Memorandum to the Obama-Biden Transition Team. Available on Obama-Biden Transition website http://change.gov.

Broome, Stephen A. 2006. Conflicting Obligations for Oil Exporting Nations? Satisfying Membership Requirements of Both OPEC and the WTO. *George Washington International Law Review* 38, no. 2: 409–436.

Bryson, Reid A., and Gerald J. Dittberner. 1976. A Non-Equilibrium Model of Hemispheric Mean Surface Temperature. *Journal of the Atmospheric Sciences* 33, no.11: 2094–106.

Button, Jillian 2008. Carbon: Commodity or Currency? The Case for an International Carbon Market Based on the Currency Model. *Harvard Environmental Law Review* 32, no. 2: 571–96.

Cameron, James, and Karen Campbell. 2002. A Reluctant Global Policymaker. In *The Greening of Trade Law*, ed. Richard H. Steinberg. Lanham: Rowman & Littlefield.

Carmody, Geoff. 2008. *It's No Contest—We Need an ETS Based on Consumption*. Available on Onlineopinion (Australia) at www.onlineopinion.com.au (accessed on January 28, 2009).

Chambers, W. Bradnee. 2001. *Inter-linkages: The Kyoto Protocol and the International Trade and Investment Regimes*. Tokyo: United Nations University Press.

Charnovitz, Steve. 2003. Trade and Climate: Potential Conflicts and Synergies. In *Beyond Kyoto: Advancing the International Effort Against Climate Change*. Washington: Pew Center on Global Climate Change.

Charnovitz, Steve, Jane Earley, and Robert Howse. 2008. *An Examination of Social Standards in Biofuels Sustainability Criteria*. IPC Discussion Paper (December). Available on the International Food & Agricultural Trade Policy Council website at www.agritrade.org (accessed on January 28, 2009).

Chylek, Petr, and James A. Coakley, Jr. 1974. Aerosols and Climate. *Science* 183: 75–77.

Cline, William R. 1992. *The Economics of Global Warming*. Washington: Institute for International Economics.

Cline, William R. 2004. Meeting the Challenge of Global Warming. Copenhagen Consensus Challenge. Paper prepared for the Copenhagen Consensus Program of the National Environmental Assessment Institute, Copenhagen, Denmark, March, available at www.copenhagenconsensus.com (accessed on January 12, 2009).

Congressional Research Service. 2008. *Greenhouse Gas Reduction: Cap-and Trade Bills in the 110th Congress*. CRS Report for Congress (updated June 27). Washington.

Cosbey, Aaron. 2007. Unpacking the Wonder Tool: Border Charges in Support of Climate Change. *Bridges* 11 (November/December): 15–16.

Cosbey, Aaron. 2008a. *Border Carbon Adjustment*. Winnipeg: International Institute for Sustainable Development.

Cosbey, Aaron, ed. 2008b. *Trade and Climate Change: Issues in Perspective*. Winnipeg: International Institute for Sustainable Development.

de Cendra, Javier. 2006. Can Emissions Trading Schemes be Coupled with Border Tax Adjustments? *Review of European Community & International Environmental Law* 15, no. 2: 131–45.

Demaret, Paul, and Raoul Stewardson. 1994. Border Tax Adjustments under GATT and EC Law and General Implications for Environmental Taxes. *Journal of World Trade* 28: 5–65.

Dröge, Susanne, Harald Trabold, Frank Biermann, Frédéric Böhm, and Rainer Brohm. 2004. National Climate Change Policies and WTO Law: A Case Study of Germany's New Policies. *World Trade Review* 3, no. 2: 161–87.

Elizalde Carranza, Miguel A. 2007. MEAs with Trade Measures and the WTO: Aiming Toward Sustainable Development? *Buffalo Environmental Law Journal* 15: 43–96.

Ellerman, A. Denny, and Paul L. Joskow. 2008. *The European Union's Emissions Trading System in Perspective*. Washington: Pew Center on Global Climate Change.

Elliott, Kimberly Ann. 2006. *Delivering on Doha: Farm Trade and the Poor*. Washington: Center for Global Development and Institute for International Economics.

Emanuel Kerry, Ragoth Sundararajan, and John Williams. 2008. Hurricanes and Global Warming: Results from Downscaling IPCC AR4 Simulations. *Bulletin of American Meteorological Society* 89: 347–67.

Esty, Daniel C. 1994. *Greening the GATT: Trade, Environment, and the Future.* Washington: Institute for International Economics.

Esty, Daniel C., and Andrew S. Winston. 2006. *Green to Gold.* New Haven, CT: Yale University Press.

Fargione, Joseph, Jason Hill, David Tilman, Stephen Polasky, and Peter Hawthorne. 2008. Land Clearing and the Biofuel Carbon Debt. *Science* 319 (February 29): 1235–238.

Fauchald, Ole Kristian. 1998. *Environmental Taxes and Trade Discrimination.* The Hague: Kluwer Law International.

Frankel, Jeffrey A. 2008. Options for Addressing the Leakage/Competitiveness Issue in Climate Change Policy Proposals. Paper presented at a conference on "Climate Change, Trade and Investment: Is a Collision Inevitable?" Brookings Institution, Washington, June 9.

Galeotti, Marzio, and Claudia Kemfert. 2004. Interactions between Climate and Trade Policies: A Survey. *Journal of World Trade* 38, no. 4: 701–24.

Garnaut, Ross. 2008. *The Garnaut Climate Change Review: Final Report.* Melbourne: Cambridge University Press. Available at www.garnautreview.org.au (accessed on January 12, 2009).

Goh, Gavin. 2004. The World Trade Organization, Kyoto and Energy Tax Adjustments at the Border. *Journal of World Trade* 38, no. 3: 395–423.

Green, Andrew. 2005. Climate Change, Regulatory Policy and the WTO. How Constraining Are Trade Rules? *Journal of International Economic Law* 8, no. 1: 143–89.

Green, Andrew. 2006. Trade Rules and Climate Change Subsidies. *World Trade Review* 5, no. 3: 377–414.

Halvorssen, Anita M. 2008. UNFCCC, the Kyoto Protocol, and the WTO—Brewing Conflicts or Are They Mutually Supportive? *Denver Journal of International Law and Policy* 36 (Summer/Fall): 369–78.

Hamilton, Wayne L., and Thomas A. Seliga. 1972. Atmospheric Turbidity and Surface Temperature on the Polar Ice Streets. *Nature* 235: 320–22.

Hawkins, Slayde. 2008. Skirting Protectionism: A GHG-Based Trade Restriction Under the WTO. *Georgetown International Environmental Law Review* 20, no. 3 (Spring): 427–50.

Horn, Henrik, and Petros C. Mavroidis. 2008. The Permissible Reach of Environmental Policies. *Journal of World Trade* 42, no. 6: 1107–78.

Houser, Trevor, Rob Bradley, Britt Childs, Jacob Werksman, and Robert Heilmayr. 2008. *Leveling the Carbon Playing Field: International Competition and US Climate Policy Design.* Washington: Peterson Institute for International Economics and World Resources Institute.

Howse, Robert. 2006. A New Device for Creating International Legal Normativity: The WTO Technical Barriers to Trade Agreement and "International Standards." In *Constitutionalism, Multilevel Trade Governance and Social Regulation*, ed. Christian Joerges and Ernst-Ulrich Petersman. Oxford, UK: Hart Publishing.

Howse, Robert, and Antonia Eliason. 2008. Domestic and International Strategies to Address Climate Change: An Overview of the WTO Legal Issues. In *International Trade Regulation and the Mitigation of Climate Change*, ed. Thomas Cottier, Sadeq Bigdeli, and Olga Nartova. Cambridge, UK: Cambridge University Press.

Hufbauer, Gary Clyde. 1996. *Fundamental Tax Reform and Border Tax Adjustments.* Washington: Institute for International Economics.

IPCC (Intergovernmental Panel on Climate Change). 2005. *IPCC Special Report on Carbon Dioxide Capture and Storage.* Contribution of Working Group III of the Intergovernmental Panel on Climate Change. Cambridge and New York: Cambridge University Press.

IPCC (Intergovernmental Panel on Climate Change). 2007a. *Climate Change 2007: The Physical Science Basis.* Contribution of Working Group I to the Fourth Assessment Report of the Intergovernmental Panel on Climate Change. Cambridge and New York: Cambridge University Press.

IPCC (Intergovernmental Panel on Climate Change). 2007b. *Climate Change 2007: Impacts, Adaptation and Vulnerability*. Contribution of Working Group II to the Fourth Assessment Report of the Intergovernmental Panel on Climate Change. Cambridge and New York: Cambridge University Press.

IPCC (Intergovernmental Panel on Climate Change). 2007c. *Climate Change 2007: Mitigation*. Contribution of Working Group III to the Fourth Assessment Report of the Intergovernmental Panel on Climate Change. Cambridge and New York: Cambridge University Press.

ICTSD (International Centre for Trade and Sustainable Development). 2008. *Climate Change and Trade on the Road to Copenhagen*. Information Note no. 6 (May). Available at http://ictsd.net (accessed on January 12, 2009).

IEA (International Energy Agency). 2008a. *Energy Technology Perspective 2008*. Paris: Organization for Economic Cooperation and Development and International Energy Agency.

IEA (International Energy Agency). 2008b. *Issues Behind Competitiveness and Carbon Leakage: Focus on Heavy Industry*. Paris: Organization for Economic Cooperation and Development and International Energy Agency.

IEA (International Energy Agency). 2008c. CO_2 *Emissions from Fuel Combustion, 2008 Edition*. Paris: Organization for Economic Cooperation and Development and International Energy Agency.

IMF (International Monetary Fund). 2008a. Riding a Wave. *Finance and Development* 45, no. 1. Washington.

IMF (International Monetary Fund). 2008b. *World Economic Outlook, April 2008*. Washington.

Jackson, John H. 1992. World Trade Rules and Environmental Policies: Congruence or Conflict? Reprinted in John H. Jackson, *The Jurisprudence of GATT & the WTO*. Cambridge: Cambridge University Press, 2000.

Janzen, Bernd G. 2008. International Trade Law and the "Carbon Leakage" Problem: Are Unilateral U.S. Import Restrictions the Solution? *Sustainable Development Law and Policy* 8, no. 2 (Winter): 22–26.

Kejun, Jiang, Aaron Cosbey, and Deborah Murphy. 2008. Embodied Carbon in Traded Goods. Paper presented at the Trade and Climate Change Seminar, Copenhagen, June 18–20. Available at www.iisd.org (accessed on January 12, 2009).

Kerr, Richard A. 2008. Mother Nature Cools the Greenhouse, But Hotter Times Still Lie Ahead. *Science* 320, no. 5876 (May 2): 595.

Kopp, Raymond J. 2008. The Public Policy Response. Presentation prepared for the Senate Energy and Natural Resources Committee Hearing, Washington, June 25, 2008.

Leggett, Jane A., Jeffrey Logan, and Anna Mackey. 2008. *China's Greenhouse Gas Emissions and Mitigation Policies*. CRS Report for Congress (September 10). Washington: Congressional Research Service.

Lieberman, Ben, and William W. Beach. 2007. *Global Climate-Change Bills Before Congress*. Backgrounder no. 2075. Washington: Heritage Foundation.

Lodefalk, Magnus, and Mark Storey. 2005. Climate Measures and WTO Rules on Subsidies. *Journal of World Trade* 39, no. 1: 23–44.

Machado-Filho, Haroldo. 2008. Climate Change and the International Trade of Biofuels. *Carbon & Climate Law Review* 1: 67–77.

Makovich, Lawrence J. 2008. *The Cost of Energy Efficiency Investments: The Leading Edge of Carbon Abatement*. Cambridge Energy Research Associates Special Report (May 28). Cambridge, MA: Cambridge Energy Research Associates.

Matthews, H. Damon, and Ken Caldeira. 2008. Stabilizing Climate Requires Near-Zero Emissions. *Geophysical Research Letters* 35: L04705. American Geophysical Union.

McBroom, Marty. 2008. How the IBEW–AFL-CIO–AEP International Proposal Operates within Climate Legislation. Presentation at the Understanding Climate Change Law Seminar Series, Environmental Law Institute, Washington, May 16. Available at www.eli.org (accessed on January 12, 2009).

McCormick, Robert A., and John H. Ludwig. 1967. Climate Modification by Atmospheric Aerosols. *Science* 156, no. 3780: 1358–59.

McKenzie, Michael. 2008. Climate Change and the Generalized System of Preferences. *Journal of International Economic Law* 11, no. 3: 679–95.

McKinsey & Company. 2007. *Reducing US Greenhouse Gas Emissions: How Much at What Cost?* Executive Report of the U.S. Greenhouse Gas Abatement Mapping Initiative. Available at www.mckinsey.com (accessed on January 12, 2009).

McKinsey & Company. 2008. *The Carbon Productivity Challenge: Curbing Climate Change and Sustaining Economic Growth.* Report of the McKinsey Climate Change Special Initiative (June). Available at www.fypower.org (accessed on January 12, 2009).

Michaels, Patrick J. 2006. *Is the Sky Really Falling? A Review of Recent Global Warming Scare Stories.* Cato Institute Policy Analysis no. 576. Washington: Cato Institute. Available at www.cato.org (accessed on January 12, 2009).

MIT (Massachusetts Institute of Technology). 2007. *The Future of Coal: Options for a Carbon-Constrained World.* Boston.

Munich Re Group. 2004. *Annual Review: Natural Catastrophes 2003.* Munich.

Munich Re Group. 2006. *Annual Review: Natural Catastrophes 2005.* Munich.

Murase, Shinya. 2008. Trade and the Environment: With Particular Reference to Climate Change Issues. In *Agreeing and Implementing the Doha Round of the WTO*, ed. Harald Hohmann. Cambridge: Cambridge University Press.

National Board of Trade of the Government of Sweden. 2004. *Climate and Trade Rules—Harmony or Conflict?* Available at www.kommers.se.

Nordhaus, William. 2007. *The Challenge of Global Warming: Economic Models and Environmental Policy.* New Haven, CT: Yale University.

OECD/FAO (Organization for Economic Cooperation and Development and the United Nations Food and Agriculture Organization). 2007. *Agriculture Outlook 2007–2016.* Paris.

OECD (Organization for Economic Cooperation and Development). 2008. *Biofuel Support Policies: An Economic Assessment.* Paris.

Parry, Ian W.H., and William A. Pizer. 2007. Combating Global Warming. *Regulation* 30, no. 3 (Fall): 18–22.

Pataki, George E., Thomas J. Vilsack, Michael D. Levi, and David G. Victor. 2008. *Confronting Climate Change: A Strategy for U.S. Foreign Policy.* Council on Foreign Relations Independent Task Force Report no. 61 (June).

Pauwelyn, Joost. 2003. WTO Compassion or Superiority Complex? What to Make of the WTO Waiver for 'Conflict Diamonds.' *Michigan Journal of International Law* 24: 1177–221.

Pauwelyn, Joost. 2007. *US Federal Climate Policy and Competitiveness Concern: The Limits and Options of International Trade Law.* Nicholas Institute Working Paper 07-02. Nicholas Institute for Environmental Policy Solutions, Duke University.

Peterson, Thomas C., William M. Connolley, and John Fleck. 2008. The Myth of the 1970s Global Cooling Scientific Consensus. *Bulletin of the American Meteorological Society* 89, no. 9 (September): 1325–337.

Pimentel, David, and Tad Patzek. 2007. Ethanol Production: Energy and Economic Issues Related to U.S. and Brazilian Sugarcane. *Natural Resources Research* 16, no.3 (September): 235.

Pizer, William A. 2007. *A US Perspective on Future Climate Regimes.* Washington: Resources for the Future.

Ponnambalam, Arjun. 2008. US Climate Change Legislation and the Use of GATT Article XX To Justify A "Competitiveness Provision" in the Wake of *Brazil—Tyres. Georgetown Journal of International Law* (Fall): 261–89.

Potts, Jason. 2008. *The Legality of PPMs under the GATT.* Winnipeg: International Institute for Sustainable Development.

Price, Alan H. 2008. Output-Based Rebates: A Proposal to Address the Impact of Federal Climate Policy on Energy-Intensive Industries Exposed to International Competition. Paper presented at a seminar on International Competition and Climate Change Legislation, Environmental Law Institute, Washington, May 16. Available at www.eli. org (accessed on January 12, 2009).

Public Citizen. 2008. Presidential Candidates' Key Proposals on Health Care and Climate Will Require WTO Modifications. Washington.

Quick, Reinhard. 2008. "Border Tax Adjustment" in the Context of Emission Trading: Climate Protection or "Naked" Protectionism." *Global Trade and Customs Journal* 3, no. 5: 163–75.

Rasool, S. Ichtiaque, and Stephen H. Schneider. 1971. Atmospheric Carbon Dioxide and Aerosols: Effects of Large Increases on Global Climate. *Science* 173: 138–41.

Runnalls, David. 2007. Trade Policy Tools and Instruments Addressing Climate Change and Sustainable Development. Paper presented to the Trade Ministers' Dialogue on Climate Change Issues, Bali, December.

Sampson, Gary. 2005. Effective Multilateral Environment Agreements and Why the WTO Needs Them. In *The WTO, Trade and the Environment*, ed. Gary Sampson and John Whalley. Cheltenham, UK: Edward Elgar Publishing Limited.

Searchinger, Timothy, Ralph Heimlich, R. A. Houghton, Fengxia Dong, Amani Elobeid, Jacinto Fabiosa, Simla Tokgoz, Dermot Hayes, and Tun-Hsiang Yu. 2008. Use of US Croplands for Biofuels Increases Greenhouse Gases Through Emissions from Land-Use Change. *Science* 319, no. 5867: 1238–40.

Sindico, Francesco. 2008. The EU and Carbon Leakage: How to Reconcile Border Adjustments with the WTO? *European Energy and Environmental Law Review* 17, no. 6: 328–40.

Speth, James Gustave. 2004. *Red Sky at Morning: America and the Crisis of the Global Environment*. New Haven, CT: Yale University Press.

Stern, Nicholas. 2006. *The Stern Review on the Economics of Climate Change*. Cambridge, UK: Cambridge University Press. Available at www.hm-treasury.gov.uk (accessed on January 12, 2009).

Syunkova, Alina. 2007. *WTO—Compatibility of Four Categories of U.S. Climate Change Policy*. Washington: National Foreign Trade Council. Available at www.nftc.org (accessed on January 12, 2009).

Taira, Satoru. 2008. Live With a Quiet but Uneasy Status Quo? An Evolutionary Role the Appellate Body Can Play in Resolution of "Trade and Environment" Disputes. In *Agreeing and Implementing the Doha Round of the WTO*, ed. Harald Hohmann. Cambridge: Cambridge University Press.

Twomey, Sean A. 1977. The Influence of Pollution on the Shortwave Albedo of Clouds. *Journal of the Atmospheric Sciences* 34, no. 7: 1149–52.

UNCTAD (United Nations Conference on Trade and Development). 2008. *UNCTAD Handbook of Statistics 2008*. Paris.

UNDP (United Nations Development Programme). 2007. Climate Change and Forced Migration: Observation, Projections and Implications. Oil Brown. In *Human Development Report 2007/2008: Fighting Climate Change: Human Solidarity in a Divided World*. New York.

US Census Bureau. 2007. *Statistical Abstract of the United States: 2008. The National Data Book 127th Edition*. Washington: US Government Printing Office.

CCSP (US Climate Change Science Program). 2008. *Weather and Climate Extremes in a Changing Climate. Regions of Focus: North America, Hawaii, Caribbean, and US Pacific Islands*. Final Report, Synthesis and Assessment Product 3.3, by the US Climate Change Science Program and the Subcommittee on Global Change Research. Washington: US Government Printing Office.

US Energy Information Administration. 2008. *Annual Energy Outlook 2008*. Washington: US Government Printing Office.

US House of Representatives Energy and Commerce Committee. 2008. Climate Change Design Legislation White Paper on Competitiveness Concerns/Engaging Developing Countries (January). Washington. Available at www.pewclimate.org.

Van Asselt, Harro, Francesco Sindico, and Michael A. Mehling. 2008. Global Climate Change and the Fragmentation of International Law. *Law & Policy* 30, no. 4: 423–49.

Verrill, Charles Owen, Jr. 2008. Maximum Carbon Intensity Limitation and the Agreement on Technical Barriers to Trade. *Carbon & Climate Review* 1, no. 1: 43–53.

Victor, David G. 2004. *Climate Change: Debating America's Policy Options.* New York: Council on Foreign Relations.

Voigt, Christina. 2008. WTO Law and International Emissions Trading: Is There Potential for Conflict? *Carbon and Climate Law Review* 1, no. 2: 54–66.

Westin, Richard A. 1997. *Environmental Tax Initiatives and Multilateral Trade Agreements.* The Hague: Kluwer Law International.

Wiers, Jochem. 2008. French Ideas on Climate and Trade Policies. *Carbon & Climate Review* 2, no. 1: 18–32.

Wolfrum, Rüdiger, and Nele Matz. 2003. *Conflicts in International Environmental Law.* Heidelberg: Springer.

World Bank. 2007. *World Development Report 2008: Agriculture for Development.* Washington.

World Bank. 2008a. *State and Trends of the Carbon Market 2008.* Washington.

World Bank. 2008b. *International Trade and Climate Change.* Washington.

World Resources Institute. 2008. Climate Analysis Indicators Tool (CAIT) Version 5.0. Washington.

World Trade Organization Committee on Trade and Environment. 1995. Negotiating History of Footnote 61 of the Agreement on Subsidies and Countervailing Measures. Note by the Secretariat WT/CTE/W/16 (December 1). Geneva.

World Trade Organization Committee on Trade and Environment. 1997. Taxes and Charges for Environmental Purposes—Border Tax Adjustment. Note by the Secretariat WT/CTE/W/47 (May 2). Geneva.

World Trade Organization Committee on Trade and Environment. 2005. Synthesis of Submissions on Environmental Goods. Note by the Secretariat, TN/TE/W/63 (November 17). Geneva.

WTO (World Trade Organization). 2008. *The Multilateral Trading System and Climate Change.* Geneva. Available at www.wto.org (accessed on January 28, 2009).

Zhang, Zhong Xiang, and Lucas Assunção. 2004. Domestic Climate Policies and the WTO. *The World Economy* 27, no. 3: 359–86.

Index

arbitrary discrimination, 52–60, 84–87
Archer-Daniels-Midland Company, 78, 128n
Argentina—Hides and Leather case, 35n,
    35–36, 57
asbestos case. See European Communities—
    Asbestos case
ASCM. See Agreement on Subsidies and
    Countervailing Measures
Asia Pacific region. See also specific country
    CDM projects in, 138, 139, 140
assigned amount units (AAUs), 95b
auction on consignment, of emission
    allowances, 87–88, 91b, 107
Australia
    carbon pollution reduction scheme, 89,
        91–92
    Garnaut Climate Change Review, 11
    New South Wales emissions trading
        scheme, 142t, 144, 144n
automobile industry
    government assistance for, 78
    taxes case (See United States—Taxes on
        Automobiles case)
autonomy, in environmental policy, 65
average temperature projections, 113–17,
    124

Bali conference (2007), 1–2, 2n, 12, 93, 99
banking, under EU ETS, 143n
Basel Convention, 76b
Bingaman, Jeff, 25t
biofuels, 123, 127–29
    under Agreement on Agriculture, 64n
    import tariffs on, 128
    lobby for, 128, 128n
    production of
        food prices and, 127
        fossil fuel energy used in, 129
        statistics on, 127
    research spending on, 122
    standards for, 71
    subsidies for, 4b, 78, 123, 128
border tax adjustments (BTAs), 39–46
    definition, 39–40, 40n, 66
    eligibility for, 40–41
    on exports, 41, 42b–43b, 44–46, 69–70
    GATT rules on, 66–69, 73
    in hybrid systems, 78
    on imports, 39, 41
    as leverage, 70–71
    on services, 73
    within WTO green space, 106
bottom-up models, 119n
Boucher, Richard, 19, 27t, 80n

Boxer, Barbara, 19, 22t, 25t, 78
Brazil
    biofuel agreement with US, 128n
    biofuel production, 123, 127, 129
    CDM projects in, 138, 140
    gasoline case (See United States—Gasoline
        case)
    greenhouse gas emissions, 5t, 6
        by carbon taxes, 7t–8t
        projected, 10t
Brazil—Tyres case, 47, 51, 54
    discrimination and, 57–60, 84n, 85–86
    summary of, 131
bright-line exclusions, 109
BTAs. See border tax adjustments
Bush (George W.) administration
    border measures against US and, 89
    EPA regulation case, 20b
    fuel economy standards, 4b
    Kyoto Protocol rejected by, 2
    TRIPS amendment, 98n
Byrd-Hagel Resolution, 2, 2n

CAFE (corporate rate average fuel
    economy) regulations, 134
California, climate policy, 2–3, 4b
Canada
    asbestos case (See European
        Communities—Asbestos case)
    tuna case (See United States—Tuna and
        Tuna Products case)
Canada—Autos case, 46
Canada—Periodicals case, 38
Canada—Unprocessed Herring and Salmon
    case, 135
Canadian Fisheries Act, 135
cap-and-trade systems
    Australian proposal for, 89, 91–92
    resisted by developing countries, 94
    shift from offsetting to, 94
    US climate bills including, 13–16, 19, 21,
        22t–28t, 78
    within WTO green space, 104, 106–107
carbon capture and storage (CCS), 122n,
    122–23
carbon debt, of biofuel production, 129
carbon dioxide (CO_2), 6
    atmospheric concentration of, 6n
    from fuel combustion, 3, 5t, 6
    global warming potential of, 139
    carbon emissions. See greenhouse gas
        emissions
carbon equivalent taxes, within WTO green
    space, 106

Carbon Expo trade fair (Germany 2008), 138
carbon financial instrument (CFI) contracts, 145
carbon footprint
    border tax adjustments for, 66, 68
    certificates stating, 68n, 68–69
    regulation of, GATT rules on, 48
    standards, 13, 71–73, 78
carbon free riding, 70, 93n
carbon intensity standards. *See* performance standards
carbon-intensive imports
    US, 13, 14t–15t
    within WTO green space, 105
carbon laundering, 65–66
carbon leakage, 65–66, 84n, 89
carbon market conference (Copenhagen 2008), 94
carbon offsetting, 94, 94n, 141
carbon passports, 68n, 68–69
    new climate protocol establishing, 74–75
carbon permits
    allocation of, 75
        under Australian system, 89
        under EU scheme, 90b–91b
        under US climate bills, 107n
        within WTO green space, 106–107
    auction on consignment, 87–88, 91b, 107
    under Climate Security Act, 79, 81
    cost *versus* value, 9–10
    fixed prices for, 107
    free, 106–107
        as subsidies, 61–64, 87–88, 89, 91b
    price volatility of, 19
    rebates for, 69–70, 75, 77, 84
        as subsidies, 88
    within WTO green space, 103
carbon price(s)
    European, 143
    future, uncertainty over, 122–23
carbon price equivalency
    emission permits and, 9–10
    limit setting by, 3, 7t
    versus per capita comparability, 3, 3n, 94
carbon productivity, concept of, 120–21
carbon tax(es)
    cost *versus* value, 9–10
    destination principle for, 69
    on exports, rebate of, 68–70
    greenhouse gas emissions by, 3, 7t–8t
    as indirect taxes, 44–45
    price impact of, 16, 16n, 17t–18t
    process-related, 66, 66n, 68
    US climate bills including, 13–16, 29t

within WTO green space, 103, 104
carbon tax comparability, 79
carbon trading markets, 141–45. *See also* *specific market*
Caribbean, CDM projects in, 138
CCS (carbon capture and storage), 122n, 122–23
CCX (Chicago Climate Exchange), 142t, 144–45
CDM. *See* clean development mechanism
certified emission reductions (CERs), 95b, 137n, 137–38, 143
CFI (carbon financial instrument) contracts, 145
chapeau discrimination, 52–60, 84–87
Chicago Climate Exchange (CCX), 142t, 144–45
Chile—Price Band System case, 39
China
    carbon price equivalency and, 10
    CDM projects in, 137–38, 140
    climate policy, 4n, 12n
    greenhouse gas emissions, 5t, 6, 9
        by carbon taxes, 7t–8t
        projected, 10t
China—Auto Parts case, 36
cigarettes case. *See* *Thailand—Cigarettes* case
Clean Air Act, 20b
clean development mechanism (CDM), 94, 94n, 95b
    in carbon markets, 141, 142t, 144
    in post-Kyoto regime, 137–40
Clean Energy Act, 128n
climate bills (US), 13–21, 22t–29t. *See also* *specific bill*
    cap-and-trade systems, 13–16, 19, 21, 22t–28t, 78
    carbon permit allocation rules, 107n
    carbon tax systems, 13–16, 29t
    with competitive provisions, 4, 12–13, 25t–29t
    without competitiveness provisions, 22t–24t
climate change
    consequences of, 119
    modeling, 114, 114n, 118, 119n
    scientific evidence for, 1, 6, 6n, 113–17
    skepticism about, 3n, 116n, 116–17
    uncertainties, 113–25
Climate Matters Act, 27t–28t
climate measures. *See also* *specific measure*
    Australian proposal for, 89, 91–92
    China, 4n, 12n
    collective action on, obstacles to, 3

Doha Round, 97, 100–102, 110
dolphin cases. *See United States—Tuna/*
Dolphin cases
domestic consumption, production for,
climate effects of, 75
domestic producers, definition, 38*n*
domestic regulations
Agreement on Technical Barriers to Trade
and, 48–49
national treatment on (*See* national
treatment (GATT Article III))
trade measures effective in conjunction
with, 52
domestic subsidy exclusion, in Article III,
38, 46
Dominican Republic—Import and Sales of
Cigarettes case, 37–38
Drug Arrangements, 57–58
dumping, qualification for, 35
DuPont, 128*n*

economic adjustment ratio, 81, 81*n*, 85
electric cars, 122
electricity
as good *versus* service, 63*n*
under New South Wales emissions
trading scheme, 144
Electric Utility Cap and Trade Act, 22*t*–23*t*
El Niño, 116
embedded energy. *See* carbon footprint
emerging technology. *See* technological fixes
emissions allowances. *See* carbon permits
emissions reduction units (ERUs), 95*b*, 143
emissions trading
carbon markets for, 141–45 (*See also*
specific market)
under Kyoto Protocol, 95*b*, 107*n*
under US climate bills, 107*n*
within WTO green space, 107
Emission Trading Scheme. *See* European
Union Emission Trading Scheme
energy footprint. *See* carbon footprint
Energy Independence and Security Act,
128*n*
energy investment, cost studies of, 120–21
energy standards, US, 4*b*
energy taxes. *See* carbon tax(es)
environmental adaptation subsidies, 64, 110
environmental dispute cases, 131–36. *See*
also specific case
environmental goods, tariff cuts for, 101,
101*n*
Environmental Protection Agency (EPA)
administration of Climate Security Act
by, 79, 81

climate change and, 19, 20*b*–21*b*
ERUs (emission reduction units), 95*b*, 143
ethanol. *See* biofuels
ETS. *See* European Union Emission Trading
Scheme
EUA (European Union allowance unit), 9*n*,
90*b*, 142
Europe, heatwave in, 117
European Communities—Asbestos case
discrimination and, 60, 84*n*
national treatment and, 36–37
performance standards and, 71
summary of, 132
TBT Agreement and, 48
European Communities—Bananas case, 46,
102*n*
European Communities—Commercial Vessels
case, 38
European Communities—Tariff Preferences
case, 47, 57–58
European Union
automobile taxes case (*See United States—*
Taxes on Automobiles case)
biofuel production, 123, 127–28
biofuel standards, 71
border tax adjustment case, 41
carbon price equivalency and, 10
dispute with Brazil (*See Brazil—Tyres*
case)
emission permits, 9–10
GATT/WTO modifications sought by, 97
greenhouse gas emissions, 5*t*, 6, 9
by carbon taxes, 7*t*–8*t*
projected, 10*t*
tuna/dolphin case (*See United States—*
Tuna/Dolphin cases)
European Union allowance unit (EUA), 9*n*,
90*b*, 142
European Union Emission Trading Scheme
(EU ETS), 90*b*–91*b*, 95*b*
effect on trade flows, 13
leverage proposal, 89*n*
overview of, 141–43, 142*t*
excess, definition, 36
exclusions
under Climate Security Act, 80–81
within WTO green space, 108–109
exports
border tax adjustments on, 41, 42*b*–43*b*,
44–46, 69–70
emission allowances on, rebate of, 84
energy taxes on, rebate of, 68–70
within WTO green space, 105–106
ex post system, 77

Kimberley Certification Scheme, 68n
Korea—Beef case, 37, 47
Kyoto Protocol, 2
    adoption of, 2n
    development mechanisms, 94, 95b, 137,
        141, 144
    emissions trading under, 95b, 107n
    nonparty issue, 73–74, 93, 93n
    successor pact to, 93
    US rejection of, 2, 74n

labor conditions, social provisions
        regarding, 101n
Lamy, Pascal, 99
land clearing, for biofuel production, 129
Latin America. See also specific country
    CDM projects in, 138
legislative proposals. See climate bills (US);
        specific bill
level playing field concern, 66, 83, 83n,
        86–87
leverage
    in Climate Security Act, 79, 84n
    trade measures used as, 66, 70–71, 73–74
Lieberman, Joe, 19, 22t, 78. See also Climate
        Security Act
likeness test
    Article III cases on, 35–37, 85–86
    carbon passport and, 68n
    Climate Security Act and, 82n, 82–83,
        85–86
    European Communities—Asbestos case, 132
    United States—Gasoline case, 133
    within WTO green space, 104–105
London Energy Brokers Association, 142
Low Carbon Economy Act, 25t–26t

Malaysia, shrimp case. See United States—
        Shrimp case
mandatory measures, definition, 48
Mandelson, Peter, 71
Manne-Richels model, 114
manufacturing process, energy taxes based
        on, 66, 66n, 68
Massachusetts Institute of Technology
        (MIT), 118, 123
Massachusetts v. EPA, 20b
McCain, John, 22t
McKinsey & Company, 11, 11n, 120
MEAs. See multilateral environmental
        agreements
Mercosur (Southern Common Market), 58,
        131
methane (CH_4), 6

Mexico, tuna/dolphin cases. See United
        States—Tuna/Dolphin cases
Midwestern Greenhouse Gas Reduction
        Accord, 4b
MIT (Massachusetts Institute of
        Technology), 118, 123
mitigation programs
    Article XX exception for, 50–51
    baseline targets, 119n, 121
    costs of, 119–21
    trading system rules and, 125
Monsanto, 128n
Montreal Protocol on Substances that
        Deplete the Ozone Layer, 76b
most favored nation treatment (GATT
        Article I), 32t, 46–47
    carbon performance standards, 72
    carbon permit allocation, 75
    Climate Security Act and, 82–83
    food mile charges, 73
    hybrid systems, 78
    status of US climate policy under, 67f
    unilateral sanctions and, 70
    violation of, 55
Multi-Fiber Arrangement, 101n
multilateral environmental agreements
        (MEAs). See also specific agreement
    dispute settlement approach, 99–100, 103,
        103n
    as leverage against trade measures, 66,
        73–74
    nonparty issue, 73–74, 93, 93n
    with trade provisions, 74–75, 76b, 99–102
        (See also Code of Good WTO Practice
        on Greenhouse Gas Emission
        Controls)
    WTO rules and, 75, 76b, 99–100
multilateral environmental norms, as WTO
        standards, 99–102
multilateral trade sanctions, WTO
        implications of, 71

NAFTA (North American Free Trade
        Agreement), 81
NASA Goddard Institute for Space Studies,
        115
national allocation plans (NAPs), 90b
National Biodiesel Board, 128n
national champions, 78
National Oceanic and Atmospheric
        Administration (NOAA), 6n, 117
national treatment (GATT Article III),
        32t–33t, 35–38
    border tax adjustment rules, 41, 47b

Other Publications from the Peterson Institute

WORKING PAPERS

BOOKS

Financial Services Liberalization in the WTO
Wendy Dobson and Pierre Jacquet
June 1998 ISBN 0-88132-254-7

Restoring Japan's Economic Growth
Adam S. Posen
September 1998 ISBN 0-88132-262-8

Measuring the Costs of Protection in China
Zhang Shuguang, Zhang Yansheng,
and Wan Zhongxin
November 1998 ISBN 0-88132-247-4

Foreign Direct Investment and Development:
The New Policy Agenda for Developing
Countries and Economies in Transition
Theodore H. Moran
December 1998 ISBN 0-88132-258-X

Behind the Open Door: Foreign Enterprises
in the Chinese Marketplace Daniel H. Rosen
January 1999 ISBN 0-88132-263-6

Toward A New International Financial
Architecture: A Practical Post-Asia Agenda
Barry Eichengreen
February 1999 ISBN 0-88132-270-9

Is the U.S. Trade Deficit Sustainable?
Catherine L. Mann
September 1999 ISBN 0-88132-265-2

Safeguarding Prosperity in a Global Financial
System: The Future International Financial
Architecture, Independent Task Force Report
Sponsored by the Council on Foreign Relations
Morris Goldstein, Project Director
October 1999 ISBN 0-88132-287-3

Avoiding the Apocalypse: The Future
of the Two Koreas Marcus Noland
June 2000 ISBN 0-88132-278-4

Assessing Financial Vulnerability:
An Early Warning System for Emerging
Markets Morris Goldstein,
Graciela Kaminsky, and Carmen Reinhart
June 2000 ISBN 0-88132-237-7

Global Electronic Commerce: A Policy Primer
Catherine L. Mann, Sue E. Eckert, and Sarah
Cleeland Knight
July 2000 ISBN 0-88132-274-1

The WTO after Seattle Jeffrey J. Schott, ed.
July 2000 ISBN 0-88132-290-3

Intellectual Property Rights in the Global
Economy Keith E. Maskus
August 2000 ISBN 0-88132-282-2

The Political Economy of the Asian Financial
Crisis Stephan Haggard
August 2000 ISBN 0-88132-283-0

Transforming Foreign Aid: United States
Assistance in the 21st Century Carol Lancaster
August 2000 ISBN 0-88132-291-1

Fighting the Wrong Enemy: Antiglobal
Activists and Multinational Enterprises
Edward M. Graham
September 2000 ISBN 0-88132-272-5

Globalization and the Perceptions of American
Workers Kenneth Scheve/Matthew J. Slaughter
March 2001 ISBN 0-88132-295-4

World Capital Markets: Challenge to the G-10
Wendy Dobson and Gary Clyde Hufbauer,
assisted by Hyun Koo Cho
May 2001 ISBN 0-88132-301-2

Prospects for Free Trade in the Americas
Jeffrey J. Schott
August 2001 ISBN 0-88132-275-X

Toward a North American Community:
Lessons from the Old World for the New
Robert A. Pastor
August 2001 ISBN 0-88132-328-4

Measuring the Costs of Protection in Europe:
European Commercial Policy in the 2000s
Patrick A. Messerlin
September 2001 ISBN 0-88132-273-3

Job Loss from Imports: Measuring the Costs
Lori G. Kletzer
September 2001 ISBN 0-88132-296-2

No More Bashing: Building a New
Japan–United States Economic Relationship
C. Fred Bergsten, Takatoshi Ito, and
Marcus Noland
October 2001 ISBN 0-88132-286-5

Why Global Commitment Really Matters!
Howard Lewis III and J. David Richardson
October 2001 ISBN 0-88132-298-9

Leadership Selection in the Major
Multilaterals Miles Kahler
November 2001 ISBN 0-88132-335-7

The International Financial Architecture:
What's New? What's Missing? Peter Kenen
November 2001 ISBN 0-88132-297-0

Delivering on Debt Relief: From IMF Gold
to a New Aid Architecture
John Williamson and Nancy Birdsall,
with Brian Deese
April 2002 ISBN 0-88132-331-4

Imagine There's No Country: Poverty,
Inequality, and Growth in the Era
of Globalization Surjit S. Bhalla
September 2002 ISBN 0-88132-348-9

Reforming Korea's Industrial Conglomerates
Edward M. Graham
January 2003 ISBN 0-88132-337-3

Industrial Policy in an Era of Globalization:
Lessons from Asia Marcus Noland
and Howard Pack
March 2003 ISBN 0-88132-350-0

Reintegrating India with the World Economy
T. N. Srinivasan and Suresh D. Tendulkar
March 2003 ISBN 0-88132-280-6

After the Washington Consensus:
Restarting Growth and Reform
in Latin America Pedro-Pablo Kuczynski
and John Williamson, editors
March 2003 ISBN 0-88132-347-0

The Decline of US Labor Unions and the Role
of Trade Robert E. Baldwin
June 2003 ISBN 0-88132-341-1

DISTRIBUTORS OUTSIDE THE UNITED STATES

**Australia, New Zealand,
and Papua New Guinea**
D. A. Information Services
648 Whitehorse Road
Mitcham, Victoria 3132, Australia
Tel: 61-3-9210-7777
Fax: 61-3-9210-7788
Email: service@dadirect.com.au
www.dadirect.com.au

India, Bangladesh, Nepal, and Sri Lanka
Viva Books Private Limited
Mr. Vinod Vasishtha
4737/23 Ansari Road
Daryaganj, New Delhi 110002
India
Tel: 91-11-4224-2200
Fax: 91-11-4224-2240
Email: viva@vivagroupindia.net
www.vivagroupindia.com

**Mexico, Central America, South America,
and Puerto Rico**
US PubRep, Inc.
311 Dean Drive
Rockville, MD 20851
Tel: 301-838-9276
Fax: 301-838-9278
Email: c.falk@ieee.org

**Asia (*Brunei, Burma, Cambodia, China,
Hong Kong, Indonesia, Korea, Laos, Malaysia,
Philippines, Singapore, Taiwan, Thailand,
and Vietnam*)**
East-West Export Books (EWEB)
University of Hawaii Press
2840 Kolowalu Street
Honolulu, Hawaii 96822-1888
Tel: 808-956-8830
Fax: 808-988-6052
Email: eweb@hawaii.edu

Canada
Renouf Bookstore
5369 Canotek Road, Unit 1
Ottawa, Ontario KlJ 9J3, Canada
Tel: 613-745-2665
Fax: 613-745-7660
www.renoufbooks.com

Japan
United Publishers Services Ltd.
1-32-5, Higashi-shinagawa
Shinagawa-ku, Tokyo 140-0002
Japan
Tel: 81-3-5479-7251
Fax: 81-3-5479-7307
Email: purchasing@ups.co.jp
*For trade accounts only. Individuals will find
Institute books in leading Tokyo bookstores.*

Middle East
MERIC
2 Bahgat Ali Street, El Masry Towers
Tower D, Apt. 24
Zamalek, Cairo
Egypt
Tel. 20-2-7633824
Fax: 20-2-7369355
Email: mahmoud_fouda@mericonline.com
www.mericonline.com

**United Kingdom, Europe
(*including Russia and Turkey*), Africa,
and Israel**
The Eurospan Group
c/o Turpin Distribution
Pegasus Drive
Stratton Business Park
Biggleswade, Bedfordshire
SG18 8TQ
United Kingdom
Tel: 44 (0) 1767-604972
Fax: 44 (0) 1767-601640
Email: eurospan@turpin-distribution.com
www.eurospangroup.com/bookstore

**Visit our website at:
www.petersoninstitute.org
E-mail orders to:
petersonmail@presswarehouse.com**